TALES I NEVER TOLD!

This book is dedicated to
Geraldine Lynton-Edwards
my adorable, ever young ex-fiancée.
Wisest thing I ever did was when I managed
to bring her back into my life
after many years of being apart.
My powers of persuasion surprised even me...
... but they worked!
Whoopee!

Then things got even better.
On 19 September 2011 we got married!

MICHAEL WINNER

TALES I NEVER TOLD!

The Robson Press

First published in Great Britain in 2011 by
The Robson Press (an imprint of Biteback Publishing Ltd)
Westminster Tower
3 Albert Embankment
London SE1 7SP
Copyright © Michael Winner 2011

This paperback edition published in 2012

Michael Winner has asserted his right under the Copyright, Designs
and Patents Act 1988 to be identified as the author of this work.

Cover designed by Michael Winner. Cover photographs by Geraldine
Lynton-Edwards. All photos © Michael Winner Ltd. Cartoons by the author.

ISBN 978-1-84954-393-4

10 9 8 7 6 5 4 3 2 1

A CIP catalogue record for this book is available from the British Library.

Set in Chronicle Text G1 by Namkwan Cho
Printed and bound in Great Britain by CPI Group (UK) Ltd,
Croydon, CR0 4YY

CONTENTS

FOREWORD

Tales I Never Told! is a rather frightening title! It means that I have to be absolutely certain that every story I've put in this book has never been told anywhere, not in the sewers, not in skyscrapers, not on aeroplanes, not in any known or unknown society that exists on any planet. I could not put my hand on my heart and swear that was true because my memory as to what I've said where is not totally infallible. I have checked through other books I have written, particularly my autobiography and my last book, *Unbelievable!,* and as far as I can see, all these stories are absolutely freshly put before the public. If you find one that isn't, or even two that are not, please keep it to yourself. Do not tell anybody. Do not reveal such an embarrassing matter that could place me in public ridicule; a position I've been in for so long it wouldn't make much difference anyway!

The wonderful thing about stories is that we all tell them every day of our lives. We tell about what Mrs Smith the neighbour did, or what Harry Bloggs our uncle did or what some other idiot did. We relish the details, often rather obscenely, if they are details that show particular distress. There's always a certain delight in other people's misfortunes. It can be called "gossip". It can be called "passing information". It can be called commenting on life around us.

Life around me has largely been both eventful and full of very famous people. Some people, and I object to them strongly, say that I am a name-dropper. We all drop names. You drop names of the people you know or who your acquaintances know because they are people in your daily life. If I talk about people in my daily life, many of whom happen to be legendary or at least famous, that's because they're in my daily life. What am I supposed to do? Not talk about them? Go down the road to find someone I don't know at all and say, "What is your name?", have a long conversation and come back and gossip about it? That would be too much to bear – for me and the person that I was talking to.

There are many stories that I have not told, or at least only ever told to a very limited audience of friends, and many of these friends appear in this book. There are also a great many stories I have not told at all and still cannot tell because they are too revelatory about famous people I greatly like and who are alive.

So in a way, this is a book of gossip. Gossip is sometimes used as a word indicating shallowness or an inability to talk about higher and more intellectual matters. This is ridiculous! We all chat about our daily lives. If we wish, we talk about art, life and other intellectual matters. I am going to relieve you from the tedium of hearing me talk about art, life and intellectual matters – although, believe me, I am capable of it. This book is meant as a bit of fun to while away hours that otherwise might be less cheerful.

The second part of the book is a catch-up for you on the last year or so of reviews in the Winner's Dinners column of the *Sunday Times*. There are people who say I'm a food critic. That is far too grand a title for what I do. I consider myself a humour writer (that could depend on your sense of humour!) who writes stories about his time in restaurants and other places. I am certainly not a food expert. But having had the good fortune to be born to reasonably well off parents, I ate in the finest restaurants from around the age of five. Eventually, unless you're a total moron (which I am on occasions), you learn by continual tasting what is good and what is not. I write as an ordinary punter. I go to restaurants. I pay for every meal. If they refuse to give me a bill, I argue and go on a bit and if they still decline, then I give a large tip which I believe to be the equivalent of what I would have paid for the meal. That tip goes in to what is called a *tronc*, which is divided among all the waiting staff, and possibly cloakroom staff, and others in the restaurant. So I do my bit for humanity!

We also have in this book the Winner's Dinners Awards for 2011/12. These are unique in the history of awards. They attract the most marvellous people to present them. Last year it was Sir Michael Caine, Lord Andrew Lloyd Webber and Barbara Windsor. The only trouble was I left the awards at home so they couldn't actually present anything! They just told people what they'd got and later one of my staff rushed back to the house and got the awards and handed them out to those who were there. We got through some twelve awards in fourteen minutes. Probably (in fact definitely), an all-time record for the handing out of awards which is normally done by some boring head of a company at a dinner that goes on forever. The Winner's Dinners Awards are handed out at a champagne reception at the Belvedere restaurant and some very meaningful people are in the audience; last year we had Sir Tim Rice and Chris Rea, to mention but two.

I have never taken food writing too seriously. I've never taken life with total seriousness because it is so ridiculous, what's the point? But I have enjoyed it, as I hope you will enjoy this book, which reveals episodes in my life.

PART I
TALES I NEVER TOLD!

ARNOLD CRUST

One of my greatest creations, rather like she who rustled up Frankenstein's monster, is Arnold Crust. When I was working on a column called "In London Last Night" for the *Evening Standard* in the mid-1950s, we needed someone to make humorous remarks about the hundreds of debutantes, most of whom were not exactly bright. So Jeremy Campbell, the editor, and I invented a girl debutante called Venetia Crust. I also invented a father for her called Arnold. Arnold first appeared in the press at a restaurant owned by Tommy Yeardye who later married Diana Dors. Tommy was an irrepressible businessman, had previously been a stuntman, later became rich as a property dealer and had a considerable stake in the Vidal Sassoon brand. He also put money into the business of Hackney-based Malaysian shoe designer, Jimmy Choo. Tommy's daughter ran the business and it became an enormous success.

In those days Tommy was grovelling about. He opened a basement restaurant called The Paint Box. The idea was that people would eat and at the same time have an easel and oils and paint naked girls who were littered around the room. I guess I would have been asked to the opening, or some time later. It was there that Arnold Crust was born. He was seriously stated in the *Evening Standard* (written by me!) to have been present and painted a picture called "Trauma" with a stirrup pump. The 1950s were a very fun time!

I was so thrilled at having invented Arnold Crust that I used him again and again. I edited nearly all my own movies myself, sitting at the machine which in those days ran celluloid through something called a Movieola. I marked the film with a white wax crayon, cut the film myself and stuck it together with Sellotape. That's how editing was done before digital machines came in. Since I was already credited on most of my movies as producer, director and, frequently, as writer as well, I thought that to also have a single screen credit as editor was a bridge too far. So on most of my movies it says Editor, Arnold Crust. Arnold has had some very good reviews, often better than the film in general. It was many years before *Variety*, the trade newspaper, wrote that "Edited by Arnold Crust" meant "Edited by Michael Winner". Later, Arnold Crust blossomed again as a photographer. When I took a picture for my *Sunday Times* column, the photo credit at the top read "Arnold Crust". He's a wonderful fellow, Arnold. I don't know what happened to his daughter Venetia, but he has stayed in the public eye for years. I'm sure I will find other activities for him to pursue. A man of his talents cannot be kept down.

IN THE OFFICE

My father was a very big collector of paintings, furniture and jade. As you know, none of this came to me because my mother nicked it all and sold it to pay her debts to the Cannes casino. During my father's foraging through the salesrooms and shops of Mayfair and St James's he did something which was absolutely brilliant. I was only told about it well after he had died, by an old Jewish bronze dealer in Jermyn Street. He said to me, "You know, your father was famous in this area, St James's, where all the dealers are. He was famous for the words 'in the office'." I said, "What does that mean?"

In those days the dealers would come round to my father's house with paintings and jade, particularly paintings. They would leave the paintings in his house on approval, the price having been agreed, to see if he liked them. This was quite clever of the dealer because by putting a painting up in a man's house, the prospective buyer eventually got a proprietary feel for it, and most likely would want to keep it.

They reckoned without my dad! Apparently he would phone the dealer and say, "You know, I'm very fond of that oil painting you left here. I really like it but unfortunately my wife Helen hates it. She won't have it in the house. So all I can do is put it in the office. And if it goes in the office I can't pay as much for it as I would if it went in the house." Thus my father would renegotiate the price for the painting. I'm sure the paintings didn't all go in his office because it wasn't very large. If all those paintings had gone in his office he wouldn't have been able to get in! I think it's a wonderful gag to pull. The dealers sold the painting, they still made a profit, and dad had a bit left to indulge me. Or buy some more stuff for himself.

CHARLES BRONSON

Charles Bronson contracted Alzheimer's some six years before he died and was basically out of it. But before that, and after the death of his second wife Jill Ireland, he rang me and said, "I think at last, Michael, I've met someone who I want to spend my life with which I never thought I'd do after Jill died." The person involved was a lady called Kim Weeks who used to be secretary to an agent called Michael Viner. Charlie met her because of me. Michael Viner met Jill when she was visiting on my film *The Sentinel* in which Viner's wife Deborah Raffin was playing a leading role. Jill took him on as her book agent and thus Charlie met both him and his secretary Kim Weeks. I think Kim Weeks set her sights on getting Bronson from day one. It was rumoured that she was having an affair with Michael Viner but, either way, she and Charlie started to become an item. I remember Charlie saying to me one New Year when I asked him where he was going on New Year's Eve, "I shall be Connecticut and I'm having dinner with Kim Weeks. I really feel for her, Michael." I rang him a few days later and asked, "Have you fixed your New Year venue yet Charlie?" He replied, "No I shall be at home alone." I said, "I thought you were having dinner with Kim Weeks and some other people?" Charlie said, "No, she deceived me. I didn't know she was coming out here until a few days before New Year and then I discovered that she had come out a week earlier and was staying with Michael Viner." So Charlie stopped seeing her. I know he was genuinely very hurt. Later they got together and married, and were together for a considerable time, although I think Kim was not in favour of

Charlie being in too close contact with his previous friends or with his children. The children certainly didn't approve of her and there was some conflict over his will, where she thought she hadn't been left enough and the children thought she'd been left too much!

The *Daily Mail* asked me to write an obituary for Jill Ireland before she'd actually died. I said, "I can't deliver this while she's alive, it will be too painful." Jill was an ex-girlfriend of mine who I was madly in love with in the mid-1950s, well before she met Charlie. When she was very ill with cancer, towards the end Jill had a friend with her who was a journalist from Los Angeles. He spent a lot of time in the house. When the *Daily Mail* rang me and said, "Jill Ireland has just died. Your obituary will miss the first edition but can you get it in speedily?" I had written it but not given it to them. So I sent it in. Then I thought I'd better commiserate with Charlie. So I rang him at his home in Malibu and said, "Charlie, I'm so sorry." He responded, "What are you sorry about?" I said, "Well, Jill." He said, "What about Jill?" I explained, "I understand she's just died, Charlie." There was an intake of breath and Charlie said, "Jeez how did you know that?" Of course, the journalist had put it on the wire services and Charlie wasn't aware of how speedily news travelled at that time. When he said, "What about Jill?" I was terrified. I thought maybe she hadn't died and I was calling him up on a piece of untrue information. But sadly it was true.

THE MECHANIC

Charlie Bronson always believed that people were slighting him or cheating him. From an accusation that my assistant, Stephen, was watering down his Yuban instant coffee to endless querying of hotel bills and arguing whether or not he made a phone call on that particular night, he always thought he was being cheated. We were filming *The Mechanic* on the coast road between Amalfi and Positano. There was a tunnel through the road which we'd had closed. Charlie came out of the tunnel, sat next to me and said, "I'm going to kill that bastard." I said, "Who are you going to kill Charlie and why?" He said, "That arsehole Italian electrician keeps bumping into me." So saying, he got up to go back into the tunnel and sort him out. I'm sure the electrician was not bumping into him deliberately. I said, "Charlie, come back. Let's not have a fight. We're surrounded by an Italian crew of sixty people. I think they outnumber us. So it's best to keep quiet." The next thing I knew there were screams and shouts coming from the tunnel. For some reason, the Italian crew were having a bar room brawl. They were hitting each other, smashing each other about. The Italian assistant director went in and becalmed them. When I next saw the Italians, they were coming out of the tunnel, some of them bleeding, and were slapping each other on the back and shaking hands like they were blood brothers. Well they were but it was real blood.

On the same movie, we had major car chases along the coast road. One Saturday, the head of United Artists, David Picker, came down to see me with his wife. So we used the day, which was normally a day off, for the second unit to do shots with cars screeching round corners, and stick the camera out the window and photograph the wheels of the car as it drove at speed; all that sort of thing. Picker and I were in a car going along the Amalfi road to lunch at the San Pietro Hotel right on the top of a rock overlooking the Mediterranean. As we drove along we saw a car crunched to pieces which had hit the wall of the coast road. Rather forlorn-looking technicians were standing around it scratching their heads. David Picker said to me, "I hope that's not one of ours." I said, "Yes, David, it is. I'll deal with it after lunch." We had four identical cars in the same state. On that afternoon the second unit crashed two of them. So we desperately had to find another Fiat that looked the same. But it wasn't quite the same. The interior leather was a different colour and even the car itself was a slightly different colour. Nobody noticed it on the screen. It's just the sort of thing that happens on action movies. Bit of a giggle really.

◇◇◇

BURT LANCASTER

After his death Burt Lancaster was often written about as being someone who swung both ways. That is, with both men and women. In the leading biography of him after he died the writer claimed that he had been at a party with 167 US marines and Rock Hudson. I could imagine Burt phoning me and saying, "Did you see what that cocksucker wrote? She said there were 167 US marines at the party. There were 171."

◇◇◇

DINING STARS

The first TV series that bore my name was called *Michael Winner's True Crimes*. It appeared between 1991 and 1994 on London Weekend Television. It was a phenomenal success. Running at 10–10.30 p.m., it attracted viewing figures that ranged between twelve million and seven million. Admittedly those were different days but the figures, even in those times, were phenomenal. *True Crimes* told the story of how the police go out on a major investigation and end up catching the criminal. The sentence and the trial were also part of it. The series was directed by one of the most successful producers in television today, a lovely man called Jeff Pope. It was produced by Simon Shaps, who went on to become Director of Programmes for ITV. It was taken off air because my so-called friend, Michael Grade (who'd do anything to get into the newspapers) gave a speech at the end of the Edinburgh Television Festival in which he suddenly turned on me and said, "*Michael Winner's True Crimes* was just the sort of exploitative television which should not be on the air." There was nothing remotely exploitative about the show. Maybe it was because his channel, Channel 4, didn't have anything like it. In those days, the programmes were chosen by a cabal of people, meeting in a room, who decided what would go where. They were all terrified of Michael Grade. Therefore, not wishing to cross him, they ditched my programme. Considering Michael Grade and I used to lunch regularly and were supposedly friends, this seemed to me an act of treachery, which is not untypical of Michael Grade's behaviour.

It was not until early 2010 that I was given a new series called *Michael Winner's Dining Stars*. This came about because one of the great television executives of our day, Jimmy Mulville, approached me and said they had this show where I would go round to people's houses and comment on their cooking. A pilot programme was made by a partnership of Jimmy and another company called 12 Yard. The show was to be transmitted in the afternoon.

When the pilot was seen by Peter Fincham, Director of Television for the ITV network, things took a turn! Mr Fincham was so delighted with the pilot he decided to give it a peak time evening slot. This was to be 9–10 p.m. on Tuesdays. Four programmes were made as a kind of test run. Everyone at ITV was marvellous. In fact, they were so marvellous and so enthusiastic they probably killed the show with kindness!

I remember sitting in my cinema with Peter Fincham and ITV's Head of Factual Programming, Alison Sharman. I said, "What we need on this show is a producer. At the moment, it's like those games we used to play when we were kids, where someone comes over with a tray with a number of objects on it and we kind of linked them together and made a story." To which Peter Fincham said, "You've got Jimmy Mulville who is one of the greatest producers of all time!" I replied, "That's quite true Peter, Jimmy *is* one of the greatest producers of all time. But we never see him. He never phones, he never writes. We've got some man who produced a programme about people on a bus and while he is a very nice human being, I really don't think he's up to it." But nobody took any notice of me – we went ahead and made the programmes.

The critics were somewhat divided. The popular press wasn't crazy about it but others were. Charlie Brooker in *The Guardian* said: "It's the sort of programme that simultaneously makes you feel glad and aghast to be alive. Winner himself plays to the cameras with more knowing skill than anyone in any of his own films has ever managed. It's all put on for the cameras of course but somehow this in itself it fascinating. In the end, I simply admitted defeat and started laughing at him and with him. The show elevates from mere schedule-filler to amusing cultural artefact." Boyd Hilton, the TV Critic of *Heat* magazine, said: "I couldn't tear myself away from it, it was brilliant TV. It's fantastic. Michael Winner can be on every night as far as I'm concerned." Matthew Norman in *The Independent* said: "It's cracking television. A riot of more mirth and buoyancy." I could go on. But you might think I was being conceited!

Before we got to these reviews the show had to be made. Somewhere along the line, the word had filtered down from Peter Fincham that I had to be very menacing. The reason my column in the *Sunday Times* has run for over sixteen years and is so popular is that I take the piss out of myself. I realised very early on that menacing was not altogether sympathetic. But I went along with it. Many of the critics noticed I was playing the pantomime villain. Some did not. Perhaps the public took me more seriously than I should have been taken.

There were also some rather strange happenings. Quite early on, I made some silly comments about the north of England. I said I loved the people, I loved the scenery but that the food was dreadful and that the ladies didn't know how to dress. It was later that I learned that ITV's main audience is northern women. I ask myself now, why didn't someone say to me, "You can't really say that Michael, because our audience is northern women." We were not making *Hamlet*. I would have been happy to redo that bit. The comments were made in my house and since they were shooting in my house nearly every week it would have been very easy to change. It's so easy to look back in retrospect at what could and should have happened. Doesn't help really!

It was a wonderful romp going round people houses; I liked them greatly. Although some of the press suggested

I was a great bully, I stayed friends with all of the contestants. They were all invited to my house to dinner and I still speak to them regularly.

I'd been working with, and employing, technicians in film and television for well over fifty years before the advent of *Dining Stars*. What happened on this programme was beyond human belief. I have never seen anything like it! We had a youngish director, Nic Guttridge, and an executive producer, Matt Walton, who thought he was God's gift to the world. They were amusing and I liked them. Very near the beginning of the series I realised the trouble I was in. I was going on a private jet (which I was paying for) to Italy. The crew would meet me there later to do some shooting at a hotel on Lake Garda. First of all, I checked the weather. The day they were due to film in Lake Garda, which was four days after they shot me getting on the plane, the forecast showed total and continuous rain. Neither the executive producer nor the director had bothered to check, which is something every professional should do if they are shooting outdoors. I said to them, "Have you checked the weather forecast?" They replied, "No." I said, "Well I suggest you come tomorrow when the forecast is good. There's only three of you coming anyway. Why wait until it's raining and misty and you can't even see the other side of the lake or much else." So they did come earlier. If they'd come on the day they'd chosen it would have rained nonstop. I was there and saw nonstop rain and low cloud.

What was particularly bizarre was that I came in my Rolls-Royce Phantom to the plane for the journey and I said, "My fiancée Geraldine and I will get out and walk to the plane," whereupon the director replied, "No, Geraldine can't walk onto the plane. We only want you. We don't want Geraldine." I said, "Just a minute she's coming on holiday with me. You're going to be showing her in these luxurious places with me. How do you suggest she got there? Did she hitch hike? Did she swim and then take a train? Of course, she should walk onto the plane with me. If you want to interview me afterwards about what is going to happen that can be done without her." This blew into a major incident. Finally I said, "Look I'm paying for the plane, which ITV could not afford and would not wish to, and I don't blame them. If I'm paying for the plane, I've got news for you: Geraldine and I are going to walk from the car to the plane." This is what happened. Whereupon the executive producer, Matt Walton, sent me an email in which he threatened to quit unless he had total control and that did not include me saying who walks from car to the aeroplane. When we got to Lake Garda the director said, "Can I see you?" We went out on to the balcony of my suite and he asked, "Who's running this show?" I said, "Well it's quite clear you are, Nic. We've been filming all day and I've done absolutely everything you told me to. The business with the aeroplane was just ridiculous. So shut up and let's get on with life." Then the executive producer came out and announced he wanted to have a private conversation with me. I said, "No, I don't wish to talk about this. It's all over." Thus we continued.

I could list some quite extraordinary ineptitude in the organisation of the show but that doesn't help matters. It did produce for me the most extraordinary day I've ever had in the fifty-five years I've been in show business. Normally, the director leaves a TV series the second shooting is over. But thinking he would be helpful, I insisted that Nic Guttridge stayed on through the editing. This cost the show quite a bit of extra money. ITV was very kind and helpful and agreed to it. The editing period is normally supervised by the executive producer and the associate producer only. I was shown the intended cut of each episode and asked to make my comments. The third episode was, I thought, appallingly edited. It was slack. It left out incidents that were very funny. It was generally a mess. So I sought permission from ITV to go in myself and re-edit it. I had, after all, edited over thirty major feature pictures myself. I had not delegated that to an editor. I ran the celluloid through my hands on the Movieola, made the marks, cut it and pasted it together and thus made a movie. Today, of course, it's not done that way. It is done on the computer. I am not a world expert on computers. In fact, if there is anyone more stupid on computers than me, I'm yet to meet him. So I brought the editor of my commercials with me. We arranged to go into the cutting room and re-edit episode three!

The first thing was that none of the editors would give my editor any help at all. Probably instructed by the executive producer and director. They were totally belligerent. So we had dozens of tracks with things going on and none of the editors even showed up. They declined to be of any use at all. That is a disgrace. Regardless, we soldiered on and I re-edited episode three with my TV commercial editor and was very happy with it. At this point the director, Nic, said, "Well I've done a re-edit of episode three. I'd like you to see it." I replied, "I don't want to see it. I've done one already, I'm very happy with it and it will now be shown to ITV. If they like it, as far as I'm concerned that's the end of the matter. If ITV want to see your version, that's up to them."

There was then the most extraordinary meeting I have ever encountered in my life in show business. Into the cutting room came Alison Sharman, the excellent boss of Factual Programming at ITV; Jimmy Mulville, one of the most serious and respected producers in the history of television; and Alison Sharman's assistant, Jo Clinton-Davis, an extremely intelligent woman. They looked at my episode three and decided that was it. They far preferred it to the one that had been made originally by the editor and director. ITV put, as it were, the *Good Housekeeping* seal on my version. At this point, the director and executive producer started to argue. They said, "But you've got to see our version." The ITV people replied, "No, we don't want to. We've accepted Michael's. That's it."

As far as I'm concerned, if senior representatives of the

company that is paying everybody's salary and is putting up the money for the programme says, "That's it" then that is it! It is not a subject for debate. But these two, Nic and Matt, went on and on and on. It was quite the most pathetic performance I've ever seen. Finally I said, "Look, the top brass at ITV plus one of the greatest producers in the world of television is here and they've all said they would like to use my episode three. That is the end of the matter. These are not people you have to debate with. They've got their positions through having great skill and integrity. They are your boss and mine and they've spoken." At which point, when one of the ITV executives said, "Michael Winner is right, we're taking his version". The director, Nic, stood up, glared at everybody, went to the door, opened it, walked out and slammed the door with an enormous bang. Now if that is not unprofessional behaviour, then I do not know what is. If I'd behaved like that on my feature movies I'd have been fired from every one of them, and rightly so.

At that point, you might think the matter was over. But the minute the top brass left, I was literally waylaid in the corridor by Guttridge and Walton, insisting that I went and saw their version of episode three, assuring me that I had to see it and that they were not happy. Which did not interest me at all. The moaning and groaning went on for a very long time but ITV stood firm. Anyway, these people were employees. Anybody on a show who is not the owner or the boss is an employee. Even when I was directing the most important movies with major international stars I was an employee. If the head of the studio said he wanted this or that, you could have a brief discussion and then you'd better jolly well do it. Except the movie executives I worked for were highly intelligent and I never really had any trouble with them at all.

The show duly went out. By now everyone at ITV was so enthusiastic about it they not only moved it from the afternoon to 9 p.m. on a Tuesday, they decided they would put it on at the same time on a Friday to try and break the BBC's grip on Friday night and start the weekend early. I was doing the Piers Morgan show and was chatting with Piers about this. Piers said, "You're in trouble, Michael, 9–10 p.m. on Friday is the graveyard shift." Boy was he right!

Another thing about television is that it's not just how good you are but what are you up against on the other channels. If you're up against something really strong that has scooped up a lot of viewers, who might otherwise be floating about, you're not going to do as well.

Our first episode came out against the climax of a highly popular BBC series called *Five*. This was a thriller series and the final show of the series was going to be the denouement, telling who did what, and what it was all about. So while we got a respectable figure of around 2.5 million viewers, it was not enough. The second episode went out competing against the Wales v England rugby match. As fate would have it, England did very well and that got an enormous audience on BBC1. The third episode went out against the Eurovision song contest heats, which also got an impressive audience. Our fourth episode was screened at the same time as Sports Aid, which simply wiped everything out. So although our figures were more or less the same as other programmes achieved for a very long time in that slot, until Paul O'Grady took over, they were not enough for the series to be recommissioned. A large number of viewers were watching these big show rivals and there were not enough floating about as it were, some of whom would have settled on us to boost our ratings.

Unfortunately, and I quite understand their position and am sympathetic to it, ITV does not nurture shows. As one of their top executives said to me, "If this had been on Channel 4 or BBC2 they would have stuck with it and you'd have built up a big audience." I also believe, if it had been aired on Tuesday from 9 p.m. until 10 p.m., which is a much quieter time, it would probably have done very well. In the afternoon it would have been a sensation! None of that matters. I could be right, I could be wrong. This is showbiz. You have highs and lows, joys and disappointments. This was not so disappointing that I threw myself from the basement window. I left with great respect and liking for the people at ITV.

The whole thing reminded me of the time in my movie career when I made a film called *The Nightcomers* with Marlon Brando. It was a period film. Marlon was by no means at his peak, to put it mildly. In fact, he'd been in eleven flops in a row. The film was bought by the legendary US movie executive, Joseph E. Levine. *The Godfather* was due to come out six months later. I said, "Joe don't put my film out now. It's a Victorian film; it won't date. *The Godfather* will be a smash and you'll have one of the biggest stars in the world in your film instead of having someone who is not, although a great actor, in a good period." But Joe Levine was so crazy about the film and thought it was so wonderful, he took the view we could break through and do well anyway. The result is *The Nightcomers* did make a profit, and I still get profit cheques from it, but it was a very small profit! If we'd gone out after *The Godfather* it would have been an enormous profit.

That, as the saying goes, is life. I've had great successes. Some things have not always gone exactly as I would have liked them to. I bet that's the same in your life. Not perfect every day, is it?

◇◇◇

A CAINE JOKE

Here's a Michael Caine joke, one that he tells. He does it very well because he gets the accents so perfectly. This is the joke anyway: An American, visiting Ireland where he was born, meets up with an Irish farmer. The American says, "How much land have you got?" The farmer says, "Well you see that distant tree on the left there? That's

the end of my land there. Then you go to the right, you see
that hill? That's where my land ends. And then it comes
back towards the house by that river. It's a lot of land." The
American says, "That's nothing. I've got so much land in
Texas it takes me five hours to drive around it." "I had a car
like that once," says the Irishman.

◇◇

FAYE DUNAWAY

Faye Dunaway gave me one of my most embarrassing moments ever. She invited me to dinner with a number of people at the Cipriani restaurant in London. Before I went I asked her not to put me next to a certain lady. When we came to the table I was sitting on Faye's left and some Arab prince was on her right. The lady I did not wish to be sat next to was way down the table. As the meal progressed, Faye looked up and said to this lady, "You know Michael Winner particularly asked not to be sat next to you because he said you were boring." The lady went ash white, as one might expect. Somehow or other the meal carried on. The next day Faye rang me to ask me how the dinner had gone. "I don't know how it went for you, Faye," I said, "but for me it was a bloody nightmare. I asked not to be sat next to so-and-so but I didn't expect you to announce to them personally, in front of everyone else, that I didn't want to sit next to them because they were a bore." "Oh," said Faye, "I never thought of that. I do hope it didn't worry you." I said, "Worry me? Faye, I nearly threw myself out the basement window when I got home."

Although Faye was absolutely no trouble with me, in spite of my having been warned she was absolutely impossible, she was trouble to our brilliant lighting and cameraman Jack Cardiff. Jack, who has had all sorts of major awards, was going through a thin time. He was working on films in those days for something called the Children's Film Foundation which made films for children to be shown in the afternoon. So when I brought him on to *The Wicked Lady* it was a comeback for him in big feature movies. Unfortunately, Faye had a different idea of lighting to Jack. She would say to Dougie, the chief electrician: "Dougie take that 2-K light and move it there, point it right into my eyes." She'd proceed to relight the entire scene which Jack had so carefully laid out brilliantly. There's nothing you can do when something like that happens, because the star is the star and they're going to do what they want. Furthermore, I didn't really think, in spite of changing the texture of the scene to a degree, that it was doing any great harm. Jack Cardiff, of course, was absolutely furious. He said to me, "Michael, this is impossible, if Faye Dunaway keeps talking to my chief electrician and changing the lighting I'm going to quit." I said, "Jack, if you're going to quit I can't stop you. You can quit. But we're working close to London. Another cameraman will be here in half an hour. You've been cameraman on films for the Children's Film Foundation. This is not exactly a glorious end to your career. I'm bringing you back in to feature movies. I suggest you bite the bullet, shut up and get on with it." Which is exactly what Jack did. When *Time* magazine reviewed the film they said something to the effect that Faye's eyes were so lit and gleaming that she looked like Darth Vader. But it was still a beautifully lit film. Jack got much praise for it and deservedly so.

◇◇◇

SIDEWATER SAID

I'm always amused by one-liners that people come out with. The very famous Italian, turned American, film producer Dino De Laurentiis for whom I made *Death Wish*, and other movies, married the assistant accountant on his movie *Amityville II: The Possession* after his famous film actress wife Silvana Mangano died. He used to go around saying, "Who would have thought I'd marry a girl from Ohio." His ex-assistant, Fred Sidewater, who had a barbed wit said, "From Ohio via Bulgari."

◇◇◇

GLYNIS BARBER

Glynis Barber was a young actress who I chose to play the second lead in *The Wicked Lady* with Faye Dunaway, Alan Bates and John Gielgud. She had just done a series called *Jane* on television where she played a pin-up cartoon character that used to be in the *Daily Mirror*, mostly in high heels, sexy underwear and little else. She was a good-looking girl and I thought I would make her a star. She came to see me with her agent and I said, "Glynis, in between everything else I'm doing, I've decided I'm going to make you a big star. We'll get you a lot of publicity." Glynis replied, "I don't want anybody to know my age." I said, "Everybody knows your age, Glynis, it was just in the paper for you having been in *Jane*." She said, "Yes but you're not to tell anyone my age. You're absolutely not." I thought, "What am I bothering with this for?" I said, "OK Glynis, I withdraw the offer to make you a star. I'll have a cup of tea instead." People say to me stars are known to be difficult but Glynis Barber was impossible. If ever there was a costume and wig change where she and Faye Dunaway left the set and had to return with a new outfit and a new wig, Faye was always back considerably earlier than Glynis. So the whole unit waited for Glynis Barber. John Gielgud waited. Alan Bates waited. Faye Dunaway waited. I waited. Absolutely bloody ridiculous! She's one of the very few really difficult actresses I've ever come across.

There was nudity in *The Wicked Lady* too, which Glynis Barber absolutely refused to do. But she signed permission for us to get a body double. So we got a body double who was so good and the scenes were cut so well that everyone thought Glynis had these sizeable bosoms even though in real life she's a bit lacking there. She was naked in a sex scene with Oliver Tobias. Glynis was concerned when the film came out that people thought it wasn't her in the nude. So she employed a publicist to try and get this information about. Considering that Vanessa Redgrave, Glenda Jackson, Jane Fonda and practically every female artist in the business had flashed their bosoms when necessary, I really thought that was all too ridiculous for words.

◇◇

TIME THING
I delight in absolute silliness. I was sitting in The Wolseley with my lovely fiancée Geraldine Lynton-Edwards and she said, "What's the time?" I looked at my watch and said, "9.30." She said, "Time for your baff" and slapped me on the cheek. This is a game she plays. So now we try and trick each other into "What's the time" and "Time for your baff". We were laughing so hysterically at this (which shows our state of mind!) that a nice gay couple a few seats away started crying with laughter too. Try it. Say to your friend, fiancée, girl-friend, male, female, "What's the time?" and when they tell you say, "Time for your baff" and give a pat on the cheek, not heavily of course. They or may not find it amusing. But every little bit helps. Or possibly hinders.

◇◇

RICHARD HARRIS

Elizabeth Rees-Williams was nineteen when she married the actor Richard Harris. She went on to marry another famous actor, Rex Harrison. Everybody said she did that because with two husbands with the initials RH it meant she didn't have to change the embossed towels or bed linen. She later married Jonathan Aitken, the MP who went to prison and came out a born again Christian. When she was with Richard Harris she lived with him next door to me. Richard, like all heavy drinkers, was absolutely marvellous when he wasn't drunk but a bit of a pain when he was. He had a very famous tailor called Douglas Hayward, the man they said Alfie was fashioned upon. Hayward at one point, when he was starting, used to visit people at home. If Richard was drunk he'd lock him in the house and it took him hours to get out! My mother adored Richard Harris. He was very polite to her, she was a real lady. To her he was the perfect neighbour.

I once went to the theatre to see Richard in a play. As I was entering the theatre, everyone else was coming out. I thought, "This is odd the play hasn't begun yet." What had happened was that another actor had slammed a chair onto Richard's foot in the matinée and he couldn't go on for the evening show. I went backstage where he was in considerable pain. We adjourned to the Savoy Hotel where Richard was staying, and a Jewish doctor turned up to examine him. I thought, "Richard's in trouble here." I'd known that particular person since his youth and he'd failed the medical exam twice. He also once came out with a great line to me. I was ill and he came to see me, and I must have said something to which his response was, "I'm not here for the good of your health." Meaning he wanted money. I thought that for a doctor to say he wasn't there for the good of his patient's health was a fairly droll remark!

LA RÉSERVE DE BEAULIEU

I was at the hotel La Réserve de Beaulieu in the South of France last year. It has a small jetty where people can come in by motorboat and then go into the hotel for lunch. There was the most horrific noise. A boat which sounded as if its exhaust had blown was going to and fro trying to moor, and it took forever. Everyone was extremely annoyed at the terrible noise, which shattered the peace of this lovely view of the Mediterranean, and the rocks, and all the other stuff that's around there. Then the boat stopped and two burly men tried to help off a man who appeared to be considerably crippled. The boat kept moving in order to get a securer position, with accompanying cacophony. Eventually it gave up and went away. About half an hour later, the man from the boat was having lunch alone on the balcony above the pool area. My lovely fiancée Geraldine has a son, a French actor called Fabrice, who said to me, "That man sitting there is Larry Flynt. Flynt, of course, is the famous American publisher of pornography and semi-pornography who was shot and crippled by a white supremacist in Georgia who was outraged that a photo in Flynt's magazine *Hustle* showed a black and a white girl together.

I thought: "How can Fabrice know?" I said, "I don't think it is Larry Flynt." That was the end of the matter. In fact it was Larry Flynt. He sat on the balcony for a very long time on his own. I could have had an incredible conversation with him. His career was absolutely historic. He was also the subject of an important movie biography called *The People vs Larry Flynt* in 2005 in which he was played by Woody Harrelson. That was a conversation that I deeply regret having missed!

At the same hotel I missed another conversation the year before with Robert De Niro. I would have liked to have had that, because when we were making *Firepower* in New York with Sophia Loren, the casting director Cis Corman, who then became Barbra Streisand's partner in her production company, said to me, "Robert De Niro would love to meet Sophia Loren, is that possible?" I said, "Of course he can." So we fixed up for De Niro to come on the set when we were filming in New York. Cis Corman advised me, "Whatever you do, don't call him Bobby or De Niro, he wants to be known as Robert Jones."

Evening came and the scene was being lit and I could see in the distance through the cables and the crew a limousine turning up. Out of this limousine got Robert De Niro. As he walked through the New York crew they were all shouting out things like, "Hi Bobby", "How are you Bobby?", "Haven't seen you for a while, Bobby", "Great to see you Bob." Eventually, Bobby De Niro got to me and Cis Corman said, "This is Robert Jones." I said, "Very nice to meet you Mr Jones. I'll just go and check if Sophia Loren is free." I went into Sophia's caravan, came back and said, "Yes Mr Jones, Sophia will see you now." Robert De Niro duly went in to Sophia Loren. When he came out, he thanked me and I said, "Goodbye Mr Jones" and he walked off through the New York crew and who called out, "See ya Bobby! Good to have seen you kid", and all that sort of thing. De Niro got back into his car. I considered that an absolutely Kafkaesque moment. Here was I calling him Robert Jones and everyone else was calling him Bobby because they knew him well.

Years later I'm sitting in same hotel La Réserve de Beaulieu. A few tables away from me is a tall person who keeps looking at me, a very beautiful African American lady and a rather scruffy looking man. When they left I said to the restaurant manager, "Who was that group?" "Oh, that was Bono with Robert De Niro and his girlfriend", he replied. Another opportunity missed. I'd love to have gone over and said, "How are you Mr Jones? Long time no see."

MARGARET LOCKWOOD

Margaret Lockwood was one of the great British movie stars of the 1930s and 1940s and went on acting for many years thereafter. She was famous for her beauty, her dark hair and a beauty spot she had on her face, which she never had removed.

I was brought up on Margaret Lockwood. She was one of my screen heroines. Who can forget her in movies such as Alfred Hitchcock's classic *The Lady Vanishes*?

By the time I made *The Wicked Lady* with Faye Dunaway in 1982, Margaret Lockwood had become a recluse. She suffered from agoraphobia and never left her house in Richmond. She had played the original lead role in *The Wicked Lady,* as the highwayman Lady Skelton, with James Mason in 1945. I thought it would be fantastic publicity to get her to come to the movie's premiere at the Leicester Square theatre along with Faye Dunaway. Margaret's agent gave me her private number but assured me she would not go to a premiere. She would not leave the house and that was it.

I started phoning Margaret and we became great tele-phone pals. She clearly and emphatically agreed to come to the premiere. Before this I arranged to have dinner with her at my house on the night the Oscars ceremony was on tele-vision. I sent a car for Margaret, who gave me very detailed directions as to how to get from her house to mine. She turned up looking very much like the Margaret Lockwood I knew and loved from the cinema in the 1940s. She wore a headscarf. Her face looked identical and the beauty spot was still there. She arrived on time. We had a very nice dinner and then we settled down to watch the Oscars. It was like watching them with an old time movie star who was utterly disillusioned and bitter about everybody and about the fact that stardom had passed her by. She made caustic remarks about everybody who got an Oscar or was nominated, or just happened to be in the audience! It was great fun, but boy was she bitchy! Then she went home.

The next day I said to her agent, Mrs De Leon, that Margaret Lockwood had been with me to dinner the night before. Mrs De Leon said, "I don't believe it." I said, "What do you mean you don't believe it?" She said, "She has never left the house for years. She will not leave the house." I said, "I assure you Margaret Lockwood was sitting in my living room. I have a Polaroid picture of her sitting there last night."

As the premiere came closer, Margaret suddenly no longer took my phone calls. I just could not get through to her. They were building a stage at the Leicester Square theatre for her and Faye Dunaway to stand on. We'd announced to the press that she would be there. But the lady had vanished! I realised that what Mrs De Leon had told me was true. The fact that I got her to my house for dinner was a miracle and she wasn't coming out again! In desperation, on a rainy weekend, I bought a very large bunch of flowers and some chocolates and drove to Margaret's house. She had told me she never left the house and that her neighbour used to do the shopping for her. I arrived at the house in the rain and rang the bell and knocked on the door. I knew Margaret was there. But there was no sign of her and no sign of her answering the door. I felt rather like that scene at the end of *The Heiress* where the suitor comes to the door and knocks but the father has prevented the girl from seeing him. So the door was not answered. Margaret's door was not answered to me. The rain ceased a bit and the lady next door came out into her garden; I assumed this was the neighbour who did Margaret's shopping. She said, "Margaret doesn't want to see anybody." I said, "Could you be so kind as to give her these flowers and this box of chocolates?" And then I thought: "Oh this could be clever." I said, "Would you like to come to a film premiere? Because Margaret's coming and I'd like you to come with her." I think the neighbour said, "That would be fine" but of course Margaret did not go to the premiere, the neighbour did not go with her and I never saw Margaret again.

I did speak to her after the premiere a few times. She was very bitter and concerned that she'd fallen out with her daughter Toots, and that Toots, who was going to originally put a granny house in the garden for her, was no longer going to do so. Margaret led this lonely and desperate life and died aged seventy-three having moved to a flat because she could no longer afford to keep the house in Richmond going. A tragic end to a great and radiant star. These things happen. That, as they say, is show business.

MARLON BRANDO

Marlon Brando and I used to chat on the telephone for hours at least twice a week. Marlon loved telephoning people. Once I was between girlfriends and Marlon went into great detail about how I should get a girl in from Thailand. He said he knew someone who did it and you got a nice, subservient, charming person who was no trouble. That's more than Marlon ever got in his life! His last big association was with Maria Christina Ruiz who used to be his maid. He had three children with her. Marlon always had a lot of gadgets in his house. He was always working on some "mad professor" type scheme. Once he showed me, in his office quarters, a machine he was working on to take steam out of the shower. It was all completely dotty but likeable. Marlon said to me, "Do you know my bedroom, Michael, I've got all this electrical hi-fi and other equipment. One night I lost a tiny screw and Maria was bent down on all fours on the floor looking for it under the bed. That's when the relationship changed." This led to Maria being put in a separate house and giving birth to three of Marlon's children.

Marlon and I got on very well from 1970 – when I met him – until his death. But he had a habit of falling out with all his friends. Even his agent, Jay Kanter, who first met Marlon when he was a post boy and was sent to Kennedy airport to pick up the actor from the plane, suddenly didn't hear from Marlon for two years. And he was Marlon's best friend! Marlon's make-up man, Philip Rhodes, had been with him since he acted with him on the New York stage in *I Remember Mama* in 1944. His wife Marie was Marlon's stand-in even though Marlon was tall with blonde hair and Marie was short and with dark hair. Marlon came to see me one day and I asked about Philip Rhodes. Marlon said, "He's not the man I thought he was." I said, "Marlon, you've been with this man for over fifty years, you can't just throw him aside." But apparently, for a very long time, Marlon did not speak to Philip because of some supposed indiscretion when they were making *The Score*, a film shot in Canada. When Marlon had to write his autobiography he took an enormous advance but was too lazy to do it and couldn't remember much anyway. So he rang Philip and said, "I'll pay you $150,000 to come and help me write it." Philip said to me, "Marlon stopped speaking to me because he said I was being indiscreet and now he wants me to remember everything so he can put it in his autobiography. It's too painful. I can't do it." Then his wife Marie came on the line and said, "Marlon is the cruellest man I've ever met." This was not true; he was a lovely man, but he did fall out with everybody. I'm not sure if he fell out with me or not. I seem to remember there was a time when he didn't call me for a year, but since there were sometimes gaps it didn't worry me at all and I wasn't aware that anything had happened. Indeed, maybe it didn't!

When Marlon came down to shoot the first *Superman* movie he spent the evening before in his house in Shepperton where I visited him for dinner. We had a bet on the pronunciation of the word integral, which he said was "intigral". The loser had to sell French ticklers (male condoms with bubbles) in Piccadilly for an hour. To my great surprise I lost the bet. I still have the gold medallion from Asprey's that Marlon sent to commemorate my defeat. It has "intigral" (which was the only correct pronunciation at the time) on one side and "The Loser is also a Winner, MB" and the date on the other side. When I went to Piccadilly Circus we had a whole lot of photographs taken of me selling these French ticklers from a tray. I sent them to Marlon who said he used to take them out at one in the morning and get a laugh out of them. When he died it turned out Marlon had kept every letter I had ever sent him. He'd kept the script of *The Nightcomers* with his handwritten notes on it and he'd kept the photographs of me in Piccadilly. His personal effects were sold at Christie's in New York. An entire page was taken up with the items relating to me. They were only estimated at $1,500. Like an idiot I did not bid for them, I simply forgot, so I didn't get them. A few months later, I was in Puerto Vino and the executor of Marlon's estate, Mike Medavoy, was there. I told him that I wished I had bid for those items and he said, "You wouldn't have got them. Everything went for massively over the estimate."

What I do have around the house are dozens of letters from Marlon Brando which suddenly turn up in drawers because I haven't filed them properly. Marlon could be a tiny bit tricksy, occasionally, even with me. When I had my seventieth birthday he was making *The Island of Dr Moreau* in the Philippines. I had a very big gathering at the party and asked his lawyer and his ex-agent Jay Kanter if Marlon would just send a fax saying "Happy Birthday Michael" or something I could read out. This never came. A few months later I got a letter from Marlon Brando saying, "Oh dear, Michael, if thou didst ever hold me in thy heart absent thee from Felicity awhile and in this harsh world draw thy breath in pain and please make an effort to get me four tickets to the Euro '96 final. I will not only sell condoms in Piccadilly, I will demonstrate how to use them with a rubber doll. There is a good lad – you can perform this service for me – I'd be ever so grateful and I promise that I will never, repeat never, sell those pornographic films that I took from your house to anyone in Fleet Street. I will be in England shortly and I look forward with eagerness to hearing your chortles and idiotic comments about this tangled life we live. Love Marlon Brando." Marlon's reference to selling condoms in Piccadilly refers to the bet we had some years earlier over the pronunciation of the word integral. Which, sadly, I lost

and the loser had to sell French ticklers in Piccadilly for an
hour, which I actually did and sent him the photographs, as
I have said before. So I got on to Johnny Gold, the owner
of Tramp, who can do anything and he got four tickets for
Marlon and his party. As it happened, England was not in
the Cup Final so the tickets were very easily available but
I didn't know that at the time; neither did Marlon because
the final games before the Cup Final had not been played.
Then I got a phone call from his lawyer who he was staying
with, saying, "Marlon wants to know whether you think it
would be awkward for him because of the public going to
Wembley Stadium." I said, "It will be a bloody nightmare.
There's a long walk into the stadium and a long walk out and
he'll be recognised and he'll hate it. Where is he?" The agent
said, "He's here in my apartment." Her apartment was about
half a mile from my house. I said, "Has he lost his voice? Can
he no longer talk? Why isn't he talking to me and asking me
these things himself?"

The agent said, "I'll see if he's available." But apparently
he wasn't so I did not then speak to Marlon. I'd started the
conversation by saying, "It's a bloody cheek for Marlon to
ask me a favour to get him into the Cup Final because when
I wanted a very few words on a fax for my seventieth birthday he didn't send it, so quite honestly, I shouldn't get the
seats for him but because I love him, I will." So Marlon did
not speak to me. Instead, I got a handwritten card with his
name embossed at the top, which I still have, saying, "Dear
Michael, that it should come to this! Injured feelings over
forgotten birthdays overlooked! Very well – congratulations! Welcome to the unhappy environs of the ever nearing
hooded one. Be at home with the fact that you have irre-
versibly entered the realm of permanent enfeeblement
punctuated with uncontrollable blasts of fruity flatulence –
the withering of your powers and the winnowing of hopes
and daring dreams. Our friendship has weathered the storms
of life and for that, much gladness. When do we meet again

for cheery remembrance and chortling? Warmest regards, Marlon. PS: thank you for your help with the tickets. Your advice was sound. We are not going."

Well that was absolutely typical of Marlon who I adored but who from time to time was a bit nutty. Here he is talking in this card about "forgotten birthdays". There was nothing forgotten about it at all. He was reminded with a phone call from Jay Kanter and a phone call and fax from his agent to please send me a few words of greeting by fax but he declined. Now suddenly he realises. This was typical of Marlon, to behave rather churlishly and then want to make up for it. He was very childish but, nonetheless, adorable for it. I miss him greatly.

In one of Brando's conversations with me about a year before he died he said, "You know Michael, I now realise that all my friends were good-time friends. I think I have only five real friends left in the world and I like to think you're one of them." I said, "Of course, I'm a real friend to you Marlon, but if you've got five real friends you're doing very well, most people don't have five real friends."

Marlon was always very childlike. I remember he rang me one night and said, "You know Michael, I've got this island off Tahiti and I'd like to sell it. How should I do that?" I said, "Well Marlon, why not give it to an estate agent?" Marlon said, "That's a good idea, I hadn't thought of that." But he never gave it to an estate agent because I know Marlon. Whatever anyone offered him for the island, he would think he was being swindled because if that's what they were prepared to pay it must be worth more. So he never sold the island at all. As he grew sicker and sicker, people said he was broke and that he was in terrible financial trouble. I knew he couldn't be broke. He had an island worth millions of dollars, he had real estate. He left some $12m, which may not be a fortune but it certainly wasn't a figure that you could say left him broke. Now a hotel has been built on the island which Marlon was keeping as a kind of sacred spot.

His island was called Tetiaroa. The island was sold when he died for $2m to Richard Bailey, a Tahiti-based hotel developer who had courted Marlon, without success, for many years. The deal was that Marlon or his estate would receive $100,000 a year rent and $400,000 a year or 4.75 per cent of the new resort's gross revenues. So it was not a terrible deal for Marlon and his estate. Now it's called Marlon Brando's Tetiaroa and tourists go there to spoil what Marlon saw as an eco heaven.

Once when I went down to Brando's house in Shepperton, which had been rented for him by a movie company, Marlon greeted me, hugged me, and I felt a lot of newspaper rustling under his clothing. I said, "Why have you got newspaper under your clothing, Marlon?" He said, "Because in this house if the heating is on you can't get any cold water and if the hot water is on you can't get the heating. So at the moment the hot water is on and there's no heating. I remember when I was a tramp we used to put newspaper round us." I thought to myself, "Marlon has never been a tramp, what on earth is he talking about." I said, "Do you mean, Marlon, when you were a tramp you put this newspaper round you to keep you warm?" He replied, "Yes." I said, "Marlon, you've told me many stories about your life but I don't recall you telling me that you were once a tramp." Marlon said, "I'll tell you another time." He never did.

In 1971 Marlon came from Los Angeles to London for *The Nightcomers*, I met him at Heathrow airport. Marlon was not going through a period of great success at the time. He'd made eleven films in a row that flopped dreadfully and quite honestly, despite being a legend within the industry, nobody cared about him. I managed to get to the gate of the plane by the simple device of buying a ticket to some country I did not intend to fly to, getting through customs and immigration, meeting him at the plane, walking him out and then, as I didn't use the ticket, I got a refund from my travel agent. I always impressed American stars when I got to the doors of the plane when their publicists and agents and other important people could not.

So we were walking through the airport, me and Marlon Brando, and when we came out of immigration into the public part of the airport, there was only one photographer! That showed the lack of interest in Brando. This photographer walked ahead of us taking shots. Marlon looked down to the floor. Now if you're looking down to the floor you cannot see where you're going. So I more or less had to guide Marlon like a blind man along the necessary route. When we got to the glass exit doors he bumped into them. I retrieved him from that and we then walked to my large Rolls-Royce. Marlon sat in the back. He continually put his hands over his face so the photographer couldn't photograph him. As we drove off, I said, "Marlon, what do you care about one photographer? I don't understand. What difference does it make to the world? There you are bumping into doors, fumbling your way through the airport, turning from side to side in the car with your hands over your head – for what?" Marlon said, "You're absolutely right, I've always been totally paranoid about photographers; I hate them and I know it's irrational, Michael, but that's how it is."

Later in New York he was surrounded by paparazzi and Marlon hit one of them and broke his jaw. My friend Burt Lancaster, who also hated the paparazzi and had been known to knock about anyone who was taking his photograph, whether they were a member of the public or professional, rang me up with glee. He said, "Well your friend Marlon's done better than me. He broke that cocksucker's jaw in New York."

In 1978, when Marlon Brando was in England, I visited him many times at his house in Shepperton. His eldest son Christian, who was twenty years old at the time, said to me, "Will you ask my father to give me permission to go to Tramp?" Tramp was a very "in" discotheque in London then owned by my friend Johnny Gold. It was a perfectly respectable place. I said, "Christian, of course you should go there, there's nothing wrong with it. I will speak to your father." I said to Marlon, "Marlon, let Christian go to Tramp. It's perfectly OK. Let him have a bit of fun." Marlon said, "I don't want my son to mix with people like that." I replied, "Marlon, what people are you talking about? It's just the sort of place you would have gone when you were young. The clientele are perfectly respectable. Let the kid go out on the town occasionally." But I totally failed to convince Marlon about this. So I went back to Christian and said, "I've got news for you, Christian. You ain't going to Tramp!" He was a charming and very handsome young man. Tragically, twelve years later in 1990, in Marlon's living room, he shot Dag Drollett who he thought was being abusive to his half sister Cheyenne. She was pregnant with Dag's child.

Cheyenne never turned up to give evidence against him so Christian couldn't be tried for murder but he pleaded guilty to manslaughter and spent five years in jail. When he came out he worked as a tree cutter and a welder and then retired to try and get a life, living in a number of places and getting a number of jobs. He died of pneumonia in 2008, thirty years after I met him, aged forty-nine. It's strange that you have a meeting with somebody who seems absolutely normal, content and delightful and then something happens and they go on to have this extraordinary life. I shall always remember him as a very pleasant young man.

I also met another of Marlon's sons, Tuki. He went on to work for Michael Jackson and when Michael's hair caught fire during a Coca-Cola commercial Tuki put the fire out! Marlon said to me, "I've met Michael Jackson, my son Tuki works for him." Marlon and Michael Jackson became good friends. Tuki worked for Jackson until his tragic death and gets a screen credit on the movie of Michael Jackson's rehearsals for his O2 comeback, *This Is It*.

Marlon changed the whole style of screen acting. Before Marlon Brando, actors acted. After Brando, actors behaved.

ME

A few years ago I had a girlfriend called Vanessa Perry who had been a very successful dancer. She had danced in the chorus of *42nd Street* with Catherine Zeta-Jones and appeared in many other shows. Vanessa suddenly became very ill. She was perpetually tired. She felt as if she had lead in her veins. It was so bad that she couldn't get out of bed. At one point when she tried to walk, she couldn't. She experienced a tingling down her back and arms and was suffering from headaches. I was describing this to a publicist who I knew and he said, "My son had that. Its called ME." It's also called Chronic Fatigue Syndrome. The publicist said, "My son cured himself." I said, "How did he do that?" The publicist said, "Well he got a lot of pills together somehow or other. I don't know how but they worked." So I spoke to the son and he gave me a list of the pills, all homeopathic or health pills, none of them medicinal so they could do no harm. I bought them and gave them to Vanessa. Within five weeks she was cured. ME will always come back occasionally but basically she was cured.

I later added one other pill which I'd heard was very successful in the treatment of ME. So this combination of pills, rather like the combination of pills you take for Aids, rebuilds the immune system and is an unbelievable relief to ME suffers. I've offered them to many people, including some seriously major stars, and on each occasion they have produced a cure. ME is not a disease the doctors understand at all. Quite a few of the people I gave these pills to had been seeing doctors for five years and had got absolutely nowhere.

A few years ago, I read in a newspaper that Barbara Windsor had to come out of *EastEnders* because she was continually tired and in pain and couldn't get about. I wrote to Barbara and said, "Barbara, you have ME in my opinion. If you take the pills on this list I'm sending you, you will recover." Barbara wrote back to me and said, "Thank you for the pills. I'm going to ask my doctor." I wrote back saying, "Doctor, schmockter! Just take the fucking pills!" I heard no more except that Barbara remained out of *EastEnders* and out of operation entirely. A year later, Barbara rang me and said, "Could I please have your pill list?" I said, "I gave it to you a year ago, Barbara, and you told me a lot of nonsense about the doctor and obviously you didn't take them." She replied, "No I didn't, but I'm in a terrible condition and I'd like to try them now." I said, "I'm going to send you the list again, Barbara, but don't send me a stupid letter about seeing the doctor because they don't know what they're talking about in respect of this illness. Just take the fucking pills."

Barbara then took the pills and within three months she rang me to say, "They've absolutely cured me. I'm so much better. I'm going back into *EastEnders* in a few weeks. Would you mind if I told the press that you're the person that cured me?" I said, "Barbara, I rather fancy being known as a healer, of course you can tell the press."

So Barbara went back to *EastEnders* and indeed told the press. It appeared in many newspapers that I had cured her. Well, it wasn't actually me, it was the list of pills which I'd got from somebody else. But they're unbelievable effective.

I will not name the major celebrities and stars who've taken these pills as a result of my intrusion, or being told of or reading about their illness. But they are household names. In every case they could afford to go to, and went to, the finest doctors but got absolutely nowhere.

ME is a terrible, debilitating illness. It used to be considered a total fake. Doctors would just say, "Don't be silly. Get up and get on with it." Some of them now believe it exists but they have no idea how to cure it. I just mention this so that you realise that I could be a saint.

MICHAEL GRADE

S ome years ago I had my own television show called *Michael Winner's True Crimes*. This was made for London Weekend Television. The director was Jeff Pope, who has gone on to do some of the most important TV films as a producer. The producer was Simon Shaps who became head of ITV. They were a very nice and professional pair, unlike the people I had working with me on *Michael Winner's Dining Stars*! *True Crimes* was an unbelievable phenomenon. It went out around 10 p.m. and lasted for half an hour. The series dealt with a well-known crime and showed the police investigating it and how they successfully brought the criminal to justice. It should be still running today! The reason it is not is because of a highly unpleasant human being called Michael Grade, now Lord Grade (although why I do not know!), who behaved disgracefully.

Michael Grade is a man who typifies the phrase "he failed upwards". Somehow or other, Michael Grade was considered, although he certainly isn't now, a great guru of television. His other works included noticeable disasters. He took over his uncle Bernard Delfont's company (First Leisure) when Lord Delfont died and made a complete mess of it. The company vanished without trace. Lord Delfont's widow gave her view in no uncertain terms of what she thought of Michael Grade's management abilities. When he took a job briefly in Hollywood with Embassy Pictures it was not a success and didn't last long. He managed a year as Chairman of the BBC Board of Governors and left them in the lurch at a difficult time to take more money as Executive

Chairman of ITV. That job lasted two years. On both occasions he was applauded as he entered the building in his red braces puffing a cigar. The view of many people, particularly at ITV, was that he was pretty useless. When he left there, was no applause; just a sigh of relief that he was going to be replaced.

My particular dislike of Grade stems from when he stabbed me in the back in no uncertain terms. We were quite friendly and frequently lunched and spoke. The series which I told you about, *Michael Winner's True Crimes*, was an enormous credit to Jeff Pope and Simon Shaps who created it and were the main force behind it. But when Grade was giving a speech at the end of the Edinburgh Television Festival he suddenly, out of the blue, said that *Michael Winner's True Crimes* was just the sort of programme that should not be on television because it was exploitative and irresponsible.

How a documentary show which revealed how the police detected, found and successfully prosecuted criminals was exploitative, I do not know. There was certainly no serious violence in it, no sex. It was just a documentary. The kind that is now extremely popular on all channels.

In those days what went onto the network was decided by a small group of people from various TV companies. They were all terrified of Michael Grade. It was alleged that as a result of his intervention *True Crimes* was taken off the air. They actually believed that the emperor was in his clothes when he was stark naked. Grade continued to fail upwards and became the Chairman of Pinewood and Shepperton Studios. One of the senior investors in that organisation tried to get rid of him but he was brilliant at holding on by his fingernails, and survived. In 2009, he successfully sued the brilliant television executive Greg Dyke over allegations of improper conduct. This related to his move from BBC to ITV in 2006 and the allegations of improper conduct had to be withdrawn. A man whose charm far exceeded his talent, Grade segued himself into a number of jobs including a non-executive position at Ocado, the food delivery company. What he knew about food delivery I would think was little more than going to the supermarket and pushing a trolley. You can see I am an extreme non-admirer of Michael Grade. This may sound bitchy, but that's my view of the man. Anyone who diminishes the work of Jeff Pope and Simon Shaps in making one of the most successful TV programmes ever, in my view is not a very worthy person. A close member of his family once said to me, "Well that's typical of Michael Grade. He'll say anything for publicity." Other people said, "He hadn't got that sort of programme on Channel 4 [which at the time he was the head of] so he knocked it." This may or may not be true. Either way, to stab a friend in the back for no great reason I found utterly horrible. Loyalty seems to me quite important and there was nothing about the programme that deserved this attack anyway.

Although Michael Grade was made a Lord – one of the strangest decisions I've ever heard of – his career has largely petered out. He was a marvellous example of charm exceeding talent. Even the charm was paper-thin. Beneath it lurked a very strange man with a knife!

◇◇

DAVID HEMMINGS

David Hemmings, a very good actor, did a number of movies for me starting when he was completely unknown, before he went on to fame in *Blow Up*. He was also an extremely good conjurer. He'd be talking to you and say, "Could you tell me the time?" Then people would look for their watch and it had gone! Because David had taken it without them even knowing. He was an immensely handsome young man but the last time I saw him, shortly before he died, he was fat and sweating and out of breath. Very sad.

◇◇

MRS MERTON

Many years ago you may remember that Mrs Merton was a wonderful TV interviewer with her own programme. She was in fact a young girl called Caroline Aherne who played this old northern housewife brilliantly. They were having difficulty getting guests onto her show because she was so rude to them. Didn't worry me. Therefore they paid a remarkably high fee for those days. I got £8,000 to go to Manchester and be on her show, which I did. I turned up quite early because there's nothing else to do in Manchester. I'm in the dressing room and I hear endless calls to get Caroline (aka Mrs Merton) her Wincarnis, which is a kind of alcoholic wine drink. Then we go on the show and we do the first half and I thought she was absolutely brilliant. Her first question to me, in that wonderful northern voice, was, "Michael, did you mug a young person on your way here to get those clothes?" Later on she said, "Michael, you know in the video shop, the videos are £6 each but as you leave there's a bucket by the door where they're only £1 each. All yours are in the bucket." I replied, "Well Mrs Merton, that means you've got to buy six of mine so that I get the same money as anybody else." None of it fazed me. I thought she was terrific.

This was an hour-long show. Normally when you record an hour-long show for television, you record it in one go. You go right through and do the hour. But not with Caroline Aherne. After my section of the show, which was the first, she stopped everything, left everybody, and went back to the side behind the curtains to drink some more Wincarnis.

I stood there with her and she sloshed this Wincarnis back like crazy. It was rather like watching some fading old movie star who was on the bottle and needed alcohol in order to carry on. I thought to myself, "This woman, however brilliant she is, is going to be in big trouble later." Then Mrs Merton said to me, "Come on, Michael. Let's go back on the show." So we appeared from behind the curtain, walked back and did the second section of the show where we both interacted with the audience of mainly elderly people from the north who were a total delight. I went round and kissed a great many of them. It was a nice section of the show. After that section, Mrs Merton did the same thing. She said, "Let's stop now," and we went back behind the curtain where she knocked back some more Wincarnis. And I don't mean a little. I mean a lot. I could see she was getting a tiny bit less coherent and a tiny bit wobbly. This time when she said, "Come on Michael, let's go back," I thought: "Well she'll manage to get through it but she's not the same person she was when the show started."

The last guest was a socialist MP, I forget who she was, she was some MP from Essex. When I looked closely at the show afterwards you could see that Mrs Merton's timing and persona were not quite as sharp as they had been at the beginning. As everybody knows, Caroline Aherne became famous for dreadful drink and psychological problems, which is a great pity because she was, and still is, a marvellous talent. But she's fighting her own demons. Thus it is so often in show business that the very talented people find the whole thing very stressful. The idea that if you get to the top and get a lot of acclaim you sit back and bask as if in some balmy wind by a beautiful sea with the palm trees waving is not true. Storms gather. They gathered over Caroline Aherne.

NATALIE: MY AMAZING, LOVELY AND WITTY PA

The lady who typed this book for me from rather incoherent dictation tapes is called Natalie Wright. She is unquestionably the best PA I've ever had. Not without faults. Only I am without fault. But she's terrific. Natalie is a single mother who lives in Essex. Coming from Essex to the splendour of my presence and the luxury of the surroundings and typing, as she does, all the notes of my various travels, not unnaturally produces in her a feeling of "why am I not getting more out of life when I'm so close to a lifestyle I'd like to have?"

Like many people, Natalie found it difficult to meet someone whom she really liked and wanted to spend her life with. Faced with that situation she decided, as it later turned out unwisely, to check a website called sugardaddie.com. On this site she came across a man who appeared to be rich, had a yacht, a wonderful job, travelled. She felt, not unnaturally, "this is worth having a go". Natalie, therefore, met up with a chubby gentleman (I use the word loosely) called Mark Casperman, real name Cas. She and Mr Casperman (which she called him) hit it off very well. He was charming, witty, attentive and seductive. Natalie appeared in my office quite shortly after her first meeting with Mr Casperman with a very impressive looking diamond ring. She also had a pair of diamond earrings.

Apparently he had given them to her. I was suspicious from the beginning. I phoned up Sotheby's and got the head of the jewellery department ready to examine the ring and the earrings. Natalie agreed that my chauffeur could take them in. The following day when the chauffeur was due to take them in, Natalie decided, in a moment of love and delusion that she couldn't let the ring off her finger. That if it was to be examined, she would go herself to Sotheby's and let them look at it while she was there. Since my largesse did not extend to giving her a couple of hours off work to do that, I said, "No the chauffeur will take it in, he'll come back and you'll have a report." Natalie refused. The head of the jewellery department at Sotheby's, who I knew well, very kindly offered to come to the house and look at the ring and the earrings. I wish now that I had taken advantage of that. Instead, I was a bit put out that Natalie refused to go when I had made an appointment at such a high level and said, "No, don't bother, if she won't let us bring the ring to you, forget it. But I thank you very much for the offer."

The relationship between Natalie and Mr Casperman continued to go splendidly. He got on well with her parents. In view of the fact that she felt she had met a decent and loving person, she took the huge step of having him meet her son. He got on well with her son and he brought the boy toys. The next thing I heard was that he'd bought Natalie a brand new Range Rover. This I also viewed with great suspicion. I kept saying to her, "Have you seen your name on the log book?" Natalie said, which sadly was not true, "Yes." I think he'd rented the car for the day or simply borrowed it for a day because there was always some reason why it wasn't there any more. Furthermore, he bought a house. This was also somewhat mysterious. He would go there and say, "Oh, the agent forgot to bring the keys" or, "Oh, the agent didn't turn up." At one point, he had balloons tied all round the railings of the house to welcome Natalie, but he couldn't actually get in the gate. These things only slowly reached the ivory tower in which I live.

The crunch came when Natalie's parents, even more

suspicious than me about the situation, and certainly prepared to do more about it, checked on Google and discovered this man was a well-known confidence trickster. He had been to jail on a number of occasions and was being charged again for defrauding Olympic athletes by telling them that if they gave his company £500–£1,000 he would get them sponsorship worth far in excess of that amount.

Natalie is now wiser and sadder. Such things have happened to me. I know many famous celebrities who have been massively conned. Natalie confronted Mr Casperman with the clear evidence of his dubious past. He took back the ring and earrings which were obviously not real. But Casperman remained, even though fully exposed as a crook, desperate to keep in touch with Natalie. He sent her love letters, he harassed her with emails and telephone calls. The whole thing became a nightmare. And worst of all (worst of all, as far as I was concerned and not good for her), he had offered to pay her far more money than I pay (and I'm a very generous payer for staff) to go and work for him for three days a week, getting more than she was receiving from me for five days a week. So Natalie came to me, this is when she still believed everything, and handed in her notice for a job that she greatly liked. So she ended up with no money, no job and, in fact, minus money.

As it so happened I had replaced Natalie with a very good PA who became ill. So Natalie had the chance to get the job back. Mr Casperman in the meantime was charged with fraud and given a jail sentence of three years. To get a three-year jail sentence in this country you practically have to kill off an entire village. You have to go with a machine gun and mow down large numbers of innocent people. But he had been done many times and off he went to High Down Prison in Sutton. From there he continued to bombard Natalie with letters assuring her of his everlasting love.

When a decent citizen, someone who is not used to the ways of the world and certainly is not used to a professional confidence trickster meets such a person, it is, to put it mildly, unfortunate. After all, this man had conned an enormous number of people. It was unfortunate that Natalie became one of them.

There is a happy ending to all this. Namely that Natalie and I are back together! There may be people who would say that someone who is working for me could not be enjoying the normal description of a happy ending. But Natalie has regained her wit and her full level of charm and vivacity which had been severely depleted by this unfortunate event. At least I managed to put her on to the *Daily Mail*, which paid her a few thousand pounds for her story. That is why I feel free to tell it here because it has already been massively exposed in the press.

I asked Natalie, having finished the main bulk of this piece, "Do you think anything good came of this association?" To which Natalie replied, laughing because she's got a great laugh, "Never trust a man." I pointed out that this would not be considered by many people as something good. I said, "Did you learn anything from it?" She said, "Never trust a man." Well I hope she does find someone she can trust because she most certainly deserves to. Next time, I will be even more assiduous in checking out prospective husbands and sticking my nose in where it is not required. For which you never get any thanks. But on this occasion, had I insisted on having the jewellery examined in the beginning, I might have got some thanks. She's a marvellous person. Natalie's now going to type this out and doubtless will make some very acid remarks about it. I did nip in before amending this with further corrections and say, "I want to look at your chapter again Natalie, because I think we should include the story about your orgy on the London Underground." Natalie laughed and said, "Why? Were you there?" She's back on form is our Natalie.

NATIONAL POLICE MEMORIAL

After many years of placing local memorials to officers slain on duty, I decided what the country needed was a National Police Memorial in The Mall where there are a number of memorials dedicated to just army divisions and units, let alone an entire force. This I thought would be easy. Boy, did I have a wrong number. No new memorial had been placed in The Mall for over 100 years. A number of designs for the Police Memorial Trust tribute were presented to and approved by me. They were designed by distinguished architects, including some by Norman Foster. They then had to be approved by the Royal Fine Art Commission under its sarcastic, belligerent and utterly ridiculous chief, Lord Fawsley, otherwise known as Norman St John-Stevas. He made asinine remarks about all of them and all but one was rejected. How Norman St John-Stevas had the cheek to reject Norman Foster I do not know. But he thought he was Mr Know-It-All, Mr Genius when in fact, he was a blithering idiot. Not surprisingly, after a while the Royal Fine Art Commission was disbanded and Fawsley was put where he deserved to be – nowhere.

The one design approved was by an architect called Theo Crosby who did the Globe Theatre. He was a very difficult man and started to interfere with every aspect of the memorial, including telling the sculptor to charge more for a sculpture that was going up. So I fired him. The bronze sculpture was a wonderful piece done by Ivor Roberts-Jones (who produced the statue of Winston Churchill which stands in Parliament Square). It was to go on the side of the memorial. It showed a grieving policeman standing over a stranded, dead policeman.

Norman Foster agreed, when he took over the memorial, to put Ivor's sculpture on his memorial. But it didn't really suit. When Ivor died, I paid for it to be placed elsewhere. He was a wonderful man, Ivor Roberts-Jones. He'd come to my house, get wonderfully over-excited in a Welsh way, swear at me using the F-word frequently. He was a terrific person. Norman Foster, who was working for nothing, had a habit of showing me a design which I'd approve. Then he'd say, "I need a couple of months to refine it." A year later I'd say, "What's going on?" He'd ask me in and show me a totally new design. This happened again and again. Eventually, I got a bit snappy about it and he took his finger out and we settled on the current memorial.

When the Royal Fine Art Commission was flushed down the toilet, the only organisations we had to deal with in respect of the memorial design were the Westminster Council, English Heritage and the Royal Parks. English Heritage and the Royal Parks were no problem. Westminster Council, by contrast, was a total pain. I suggested a site on the corner of Horse Guards and The Mall. It was finally approved in a letter to me from the Secretary of State for the Environment. But of course, there's always a clause that gives them a get out. Westminster Council decided it didn't want it there. Unbelievable! There was one particular lady working on the council who turned up at all the meetings and was utterly against the idea of a National Police Memorial. She said at one point, "There's no need for another National Police Memorial, we've got one. The Queen unveiled it the other day." I responded rather icily, "The Queen unveiled a memorial for the Metropolitan Police only, in the private grounds of the Metropolitan Police College at Hendon. That is not quite the same thing as a memorial to the police of the nation in The Mall." Westminster Council was as obstructive as possible. They asked me to find other sites and suggested a few themselves. So I had to go round other absurd locations, which were totally ridiculous, and make out a report on why they were ridiculous. I continued to persist with them regardless. The council then brought in a lot of local preservation groups. I mean, what was there to preserve? On the area of our intended memorial, known as Cambridge Green on the corner of The Mall and Horse Guards, there was a ghastly brick building, which housed an air vent for the London Underground. As I perpetually said, "A dead horse and three ping-pong balls would look better than that." One of these idiots from the preservation groups said of the Underground vent, "It looks to me like a Tuscan church." This man must have been on funny pills. Another one said, "I think the National Police Memorial should be in Manchester." It was beyond belief, pathetic. That instead of wishing to pay tribute to the police of the nation with a beautifully designed memorial by Norman Foster, these people objected to anything happening at all. It's not as if there was anything there of any worth and we wanted to put something up in its place. There was something there that was hideous and we were proposing to improving it beyond belief.

Foster's design was simply to clad the underground shaft building (which couldn't be taken away) and add a small additional section on the front in black marble, with a lit area behind a glass window for the book of remembrance of police officers slain while on hazardous duty. At the side, there would be a glass tower some 40ft high. I said to Lord Foster, "Everyone keeps asking me what this glass tower means; what has it to do with the police?" Lord Foster replied, "It's a piece of architecture. I sat in The Mall and looked at the area very carefully. I sat there for hours. It blends in with the citadel behind and the various buildings around it. The height and composition are perfect for that spot." I said, "Norman I've got news for you. This glass tower will be lit blue and will therefore represent the blue lamp that is on outside every police station to show the police remain on duty twenty-fours hours a day." Lord Foster did not object to that. The glass had a slight blue tint anyway.

Then the design started to go through the Westminster planning committee. First, they asked for three feet to be lopped off the top of the glass tower. I told Sir Norman, "Norman, I don't care if you sat on a stool and looked at this area for 200 years, the fact is it ain't going to pass unless we knock three feet off the top of the tower. So we're going to knock three feet off the top of the tower. As far as I'm concerned, if Westminster Council wants three monkeys and an elephant sitting on top of your tower, they can have it. I've taken ten years trying to get this memorial passed and we're not going to fall down now." So Norman agreed we could knock three feet off the top of his glass tower.

The next thing Westminster Council said was, "We'd like a water feature." I said, "Norman, this tower is coming out of a little pond. It will make no difference to anything. There will just be a little pond around it with water in it. If Westminster Council wants water, it can have water. If they want beer, they can have beer. If they want Scotch whisky, they can have Scotch whisky. If they want a waterfall with naked nymphs running up and down it, they can have that as well. But at the moment they only want a water feature at the bottom." Norman agreed to that as well.

The design was then passed. I thought it would be easy to collect the £1.5m which it was to cost. Boy, did I have another wrong number. I did indeed get some money. My friend Sir Phillip Green coughed up £100,000. To my surprise another friend Gerald Ronson wrote to me and said: "When you get to £1,499,000 I will pay the last £1,000." I wrote back: "Dear Gerald, I was sorry to receive your rude and silly letter." Ronson went ballistic and wrote me a very long, rude letter. We have since made up and are friends again, although I never got any money from him, in spite of the fact that I had been at a Jewish National Fund lunch that he gave at Claridge's as the main speaker and host, and had also been down to Ford Open Prison where he gave a charity reception after he was let out. Ford Open Prison, believe me, is a long drive. It doesn't matter. Ronson's a nice fellow. Everyone's entitled to be nutty occasionally. In the end, I got so fed up with not getting the money from people I had expected to at least give me something, that I put up the rest of the money myself. I ended up putting in £300,000. Unlike almost every other building in the history of the world, the National Police Memorial came in £400,000 under budget.

It was quite obvious that the Queen should unveil the memorial. So I contacted the Palace and met with a lovely man called Edward Young who was, as it were, in charge of the Queen's activities for that day. When I asked him about his job, he said he got the job by answering an advertisement in *The Guardian*! I thought it rather amusing that the Palace should be advertising for staff in *The Guardian*, an extremely left wing and probably anti-monarchist newspaper.

I was at Buckingham Palace having tea and biscuits with Mr Young I explained, "This is what will go on at the ceremony. I speak first and act as chairman of the event. Then a Pakistani detective inspector from Manchester will speak because that is where more police officers have been killed than anywhere else. Then the Prime Minister (Tony Blair at the time) will speak, then Tim and Queenie Fletcher, Yvonne Fletcher's parents, will say a few words. Then the Queen will speak before she unveils the memorial." Edward said, "Oh no, the Queen will not speak. She's just going to unveil the memorial." I said, "Excuse me, have I got a hearing problem? I can't believe what you just said. The Queen unveiled the memorial to the Metropolitan Police in the private grounds of the Police College at Hendon and she spoke. So why should she not speak when she's unveiling a National Police Memorial paying tribute to the police of the entire nation on The Mall which is a few yards from her front door? I mean how much bad publicity do you people want? There'll be hundreds of mothers, widows and children of slain police officers and you're seriously telling me that they can get stuffed because the Queen refuses to speak at the unveiling of the memorial to their loved ones? Please, Edward, go back to Her Majesty and make it quite clear that it is best if she speaks." Edward phoned me a few days later and confirmed that the Queen would speak.

The event itself was absolutely magical with hundreds of widows and children of police officers who had been killed. Unfortunately it rained a bit but not seriously. And unfortunately in the middle of my speech, as it was being broadcast on television, some idiot turned the generator off thinking it was making too much noise and drowning the speeches. Michael Caine was watching at home. He told me afterwards, "Suddenly the screen went blank. We couldn't hear any sound." The TV never bothered to come back to me when it was fixed. Another big moment snatched from me by fate!

On the platform was Tony Blair, the police Inspector from Manchester, Tim and Queenie Fletcher, myself and the Queen. In the audience were the leaders of the opposition parties, Michael Howard of the Conservatives and Charles Kennedy for the Liberal Democrats. Charles Kennedy had declined to accept the invitation to the unveiling of the memorial. About five days before it, I got on to his office and I said, "Does Charles Kennedy not realise how stupid he is? Does he not understand that there are going to be hundreds of police widows and orphans there and that all the other political parties are attending? If the Liberal Democrat leader does not attend he will look like an idiot. Totally unsympathetic and not very bright." Now I know Charles Kennedy moderately well. He's a very nice person but this was just ridiculous. His aide at the Liberal Democrat office said, "He is with the police. He's visiting Bournemouth and some police stations that day." I said, "Come on! Get into the real world. A police station in Bournemouth is not quite the same as the unveiling of the National Police Memorial by Her Majesty the Queen. Get on to him at once and knock some sense into him." As a result of that, Charles Kennedy came and was, as always, very charming.

I was asked to meet the Queen on the dot of 11.30 a.m. I stood at the edge of the red carpet placed on the grass. There was light rain. The Queen was holding a plastic see-through umbrella. When she went to unveil the memorial I took the umbrella from her so she had more freedom with her hands to deal with the unveiling. William Rees Mogg, in *The Times*, said it was absolutely disgraceful that I took her umbrella and held it over myself leaving the Queen in the rain! I mean how daft can these people be? She was given the umbrella back within seconds of unveiling the memorial. We walked to a tent that had been erected for the reception and I said, "Your Majesty, I'm told that you're very lucky with the weather. In my movies I have always been very lucky with the weather. I think our luck ran out here because it's been raining." The Queen laughed. In fact she laughed at a number of my remarks which places her even higher in my esteem than she was before.

During the reception I had to introduce the Queen to the various police mothers, widows and orphans. On three occasions I called the Queen "darling" because that's what I tend to do. Either she didn't notice or she did notice and decided that silence was the best reaction to it. Either way she was a delight. A great professional. She stayed longer than her schedule showed. Then I walked her back to the car and she sailed off to Buckingham Palace while I went back and had a cup of tea.

Following the unveiling there was further joviality and I say this without being disrespectful to the police or the memorial itself. My idea was that the glass tower would be lit blue to represent the blue light outside police stations. For this we had to have the permission of the Westminster Council. So a large group of people, including the leading planning officer for the council, turned up at the site to decide on the level of the light. Shortly thereafter, Mark

Wasilewski, who runs St James's Park for the Royal Parks (and was a bloody nuisance the entire time), decided the lights had to be sunk into the ground and covered with glass because otherwise it was too difficult for the Royal Parks to mow the grass around them. A pathetic statement if ever I heard one. So the lights were set into the ground and a piece of heavy glass was put over them to protect them. Whereupon the blue light more or less vanished.

After a while I thought: "This is ridiculous. There's no point in going back to the Westminster Council or anybody else for that matter, I'll just do it myself. We have approval for light, so I'll get some more." The memorial was being looked after by Richard Lewis representing the firm Lend Lease. I said to him, "I want to put some extra lights on the tower." We had a meeting at the memorial and I said to the electrical company he found, "Get a ladder. Do it at four in the morning when nobody is looking. Climb up to the top and stick one of those very good lights that people put outside their houses that light up when they sense burglars are coming. Direct it on to the glass tower! I don't intend to ask anyone's permission or I'll be dead before we get it." So they put the light up and it was very effective. It lit the tower, not massively and no more than the buildings around it, but it at least you could see it at night. After a while it occurred to me that it was only lighting the top of the tower. It needed a second light for the bottom of the tower. So I got these people back and I said, "Look, see where that light is, get up on a ladder at four in the morning and stick another light next to it for the lower half of the tower." So that was done.

The Royal Parks had been the most helpful throughout the whole preparation of placing the memorial, but were now going totally berserk because I hadn't signed a licence for the site which they controlled. My charity, the Police Memorial Trus , apparently had to sign this licence on behalf of the Royal Parks and London Underground to confirm our duties regarding the site and what we would do at various times. One of the clauses in this contract said that any damage would be mended by us within seven days. I said, "Fellas, what world are you in? You'd be lucky if you if get anyone to turn up within seven days just to look at it let alone to do it. We'll guarantee to repair any damage as quickly as possible. Which is what we want as much as you." There was a lot of nit-picking over that and other parts of the agreement. Eventually the wording was all re-done to my satisfaction but I still didn't sign the licence because I knew these lights were going up. I finally said to them, "I'll sign the licence but you've got to acknowledge that we have two lights on the tower and that's perfectly alright with you otherwise I'm not signing anything." So the Royal Parks said, "We will give you a side letter saying we have no objection to these lights but we expect you to ask permission from Westminster Council." I thought, "That's good enough." I signed everything and never bothered to go anywhere near the council. The lights have now been up for well over a year. Nobody cares. I don't intend to open a can of worms by going to Westminster, knocking on the door and saying, "Would you please give me a written document that these lights are a thing of beauty and a joy forever". They obviously are. There's a famous saying "Let sleeping dogs lie", or another one, "If you move you're a target". I ain't moving.

Within the window of the main "building" which is the adapted London Underground vent there is a book of remembrance listing all the slain officers. When an officer dies his name is added to the latest page of the book, so it joins the record of other slain officers. We get a lot of requests from families coming up to London asking if we could turn the pages of the book to show their husband, son or father but I'm afraid this is not possible. It would mean going into the building once a week or more and changing the pages. The less the book is messed around with the better. So we just assure them that their loved one is there. I change the pages about four times a year so different names are on view.

A very helpful man called Sergeant Anthony Rae who runs a separate charity called the Police Roll of Honour, which has a memorial to the police in the north of England, updates the pages for our book and keeps us abreast of who is killed if I don't read about it in the newspapers.

ESTHER RANTZEN

I can't stand Esther Rantzen. She's just ridiculous. I mean look how she turned up at Luton to contest the seat in the House of Commons, dressed in her boating hat like she was on the River Thames at Eton, prancing around and posing in the supermarkets with nothing of value to say about the political situation. She may have got a few rubbish words together later but I felt it was just a joke.

My particular dislike of her stems from a time when she had an afternoon programme on television where she interviewed people and debated certain subjects. I was plugging a book. When I'm plugging a book I'll go anywhere. I'll do ten minutes in the toilet to an audience of one if I have to. So we agreed to do this programme. As is absolutely normal for television, my representatives had a discussion with the BBC and basically said that Mr Winner did not wish to be sitting in a row of people who, compared to him, were unknown and without the same level of achievements! If he's on the programme he wants to sit in front of the audience as some sort of individual guest. In any event, this was agreed. We also said to them, "Mr Winner will not wait about for an hour and a half in advance just so you feel comfortable. He'll come half an hour before, have his make-up done and then go on, and if you start later than 3 p.m. which you've just told us is the time you're going to start, he will walk out."

So I duly arrived at the BBC before 2.30 p.m. because I'm very professional. I was in the make-up room and ready to go on by 2.40 p.m. I could see on a television in the make-up room that they were doing more than one show that afternoon and Esther could be seen on the screen doing the previous show. I said to the make-up lady, "When does this finish?" She said, "Oh, it'll finish in a few minutes." In fact it was 2.55 p.m. when Esther came into the make-up room to bask in the usual phoney load of crap everyone says. "Darling, you were brilliant." Darling, the way you handled that question was fantastic." And a whole lot of other sycophantic rubbish. I said, "Esther, I'm sorry to interrupt this hymn of praise you're getting from your own staff but I was assured I'd be on by 3 p.m. It is now three minutes to three. I suggest you stop poncing about and get me on speedily, or I won't be there." Esther flashed a look of absolute hatred because she thinks she's a big star and nobody should talk to her like that. She went out and at approximately 3.15 p.m. I went on and the show started to be recorded. Esther said, "Ladies and gentleman, tonight's show is about manners; good manners and bad manners. I would like to give you an example of bad manners. Sitting in front of you is Michael Winner. He considers himself too important to sit with you so he insisted that he should sit in front of you where he now is. On top of that, I was in the make-up room a few minutes ago and Michael Winner was there and said, 'If you don't get the show on immedi- ately I shall walk out.' Now that is an example of appalling manners." The audience were a bit embarrassed but they clapped. I thought: "Well, if I walk out of this show now this will give Esther enormous publicity. She'll milk it to the nth degree that Michael Winner walked out of her TV show." So I stayed and I said, "Esther, for all the people in the world to make the speech that you've just made, it becomes the most ridiculous possible from your lips. You have been known as the prima donna of British television. You have been known to argue every detail of what size your name should be on the billing, what should happen to you, from where you should be photographed. You're known as a total monster. So I suggest that you should not be talking about me, you should be talking about yourself as an example of appalling manners." That got a big round of applause. Then we did the programme which was, of course, a total bore because Esther is very boring on television now, and we went back and wrote a solicitor's letter to the BBC and her producer which said: "If Mr Winner's response to Esther Rantzen is not included in the broadcast you will receive a writ for libel." So they included it. Since then, I have bumped into her from time to time. I look the other way.

NIGELLA LAWSON

I have often dined with Nigella Lawson and her husband Charles Saatchi and very nice people they are too. For a short time Nigella had her own TV programme that went out around 2 p.m. in which she interviewed people and did some cooking, or something. They asked if I'd go on it. I didn't have a book to plug and I don't bother to do these daytime shows unless I do. But as I knew Nigella I said, "Yes." Now what regularly happens on television is that they ask guests to come in at least an hour and a half before they need you because they then feel secure that they have you in the building. This may be great for them but it's no fun for me. They push you toward an airless room and expect you to sit in a cubbyhole which makes Auschwitz look like a holiday camp. I once made that remark to an audience of Jewish people at Jewish Book Week. It didn't go down very well, to put it mildly. Somehow I got out of it. Anyway, when they asked me to come to the studio at 1 p.m. I asked, "When do you record the show?" They replied, "3 p.m." I said, "Well then, why on earth am I coming at 1 p.m.?" The production assistant replied, "You have to have make-up." I said, "That takes five minutes." She said, "And then you have to rehearse." I asked, "What do I have to rehearse? Is it a sketch?" She said, "No, it's an interview." I said, "I've been doing interviews on television for over fifty years. I don't have to rehearse anything. Don't have me there more than thirty minutes before you start recording or I'll turn round and walk out." So I got to the studio at 1.30 p.m. because they now told me they were now going to record at 2 p.m. I carried with me some little present in a plastic bag which they were going to auction, or give to charity, or some nonsense. The studio is in Wandsworth which is quite a way from my house so I was missing lunch. I got to the reception desk and said, "Michael Winner." The girl behind the desk looked up as if she was totally bored and said in a rather terrible accent, "Do you want to wait in the canteen?" I said, "No I don't. I've come to be on the show." She said, "Oh. Do you want to wait in your dressing room then?" I said, "No I don't. I want to get on the air. When does this programme start?" She said, "3 p.m." I said, "I was told it's recorded at 2 p.m." She said, "Well it doesn't, it records at 3 p.m. and probably later." I think she could see from my expression that trouble was brewing. She said, "I'll call Anna." Anna was the production assistant. All these female television production assistants wear almost a uniform: a pair of tight, light blue jeans, a white shirt and they carry a clipboard, as if that makes them important. So Anna bounces down towards me in the reception area as if she has such charm she will manage to get out of anything and says, "Oh hello, Mr Winner, how are you?" I said, "Excuse me Anna, why am I here an hour and a half before the recording when I said I would walk if I was here for more than half an hour before?" She said, "Well you have to go into make-up". I said, "We've had this conversation Anna. Make-up takes five minutes." She said, "And then you have to rehearse." I said, "No Anna, I don't have to rehearse. It's a talk show and I've done them for fifty years. I've never had to rehearse any of them. So why am I here?" Now Anna was looking a little uncomfortable. I was getting extremely angry. I raised my voice. I said, "Anna, do you see that door?" I indicated the glass door through which I'd come. I said, "I am 98 per cent out of that door right now." Anna looked somewhat worried. I continued, "And now I've just gone through the other 2 per cent. I'm out altogether and I'm leaving." I walked through the door and back to my car, where the chauffeur was waiting, with Anna running after me. She said, "Would you like to see Nigella, Mr Winner?" I said, "If Nigella runs very quickly she'll get here in time to wave goodbye to me." Then I got into the car and drove off. My office, because I hadn't given them my mobile number, proceeded to get various messages that I was in breach of contract and that I should go back, and this, that and the other; a load of old nonsense. I hadn't even signed a contract. Well, I did not go back. And why should I? After that I never got asked to any more Nigella and Charles Saatchi dinners.

Actually my problems with Nigella started considerably earlier. Many years before I'd been on a TV programme with her and I thought she was very snooty. She treated me as someone who wasn't worthy of being on television with her. I remained polite and before I left the studio I went over to her, she was sitting behind some sort of desk, and I said, "Bye Nigella, nice to have met you." She just looked up at me as though I was total rubbish and said nothing. I thought: "What a bloody rude cow."

Then I became quite friendly with Charles Saatchi before he was going out with her. One day I was in a children's clothing shop just off Sloane Street getting some clothes for a friend who had a small child. Charles Saatchi was there and greeted me effusively and we were having a very nice chat. Then Charles went to one part of the shop and I went to another. At this point in came Nigella Lawson. She saw me and said absolutely nothing, just looked frosty and frozen. Charles Saatchi called out, "Look who's here Nigella, it's my friend Michael Winner." At that point Nigella changed completely and said, "Oh Michael, how nice to see you." She obviously didn't think it was nice to see me but as her new husband was greeting me in a friendly way she thought she should.

To say I'm not mad about Nigella Lawson is to put it very mildly. In fact, rather offensively (and I don't mind being

offensive from time to time) I call her the Fat Cow with the
Mixing Bowl.

O. J.

Imade a film, *Firepower*, with O. J. Simpson and was friendly with him and Nicole before the double murder. I saw O. J. quite a lot after the murder and again after his trial. I decided to telephone him in prison. O. J. Simpson got a 33-year sentence for trying to nick his own clothes back from a dealer who stole them and then tried to sell on to punters from a hotel in Las Vegas. Thirty-three years for that! Whatever one may think of O. J. Simpson, that sentence looks grossly unfair. Over here, the most anyone would have got is six months and they would have been out in two and a half weeks and given a holiday in the South of France. I discovered that O. J. was at the Lovelock Nevada Correctional Center at 1200 Prison Road, Lovelock, Pershing County. It's what is known as a male/medium security prison. From the photographs on the web it looked like a reasonably posh hotel where families would go for holidays in the desert. I rang the prison and asked to speak to O. J. Simpson. A very charming official said, "I'm not allowed to reveal what inmates we have in this prison." I protested, "It's all over the web. Everybody knows O. J. Simpson is there. It's been reported in dozens of newspapers." The prison official said, "In order to speak to anyone on the phone in this prison you have to have written permission from the prisoner and also from the prison authorities." I said, "Well if I drop you a line could you sign it and then I'll have permission?" He added, "I'm not even saying Mr Simpson is with us." I insisted, "I'd like to write to him." He said, "If you write to him you need his prison identification number." I said, "I haven't got that. Would you give it to me please?" He said, "I don't accept that O. J. Simpson is in this prison at all. But I'll tell you what..." and he started to give me website after website to trawl through to get to the Nevada prison inmate system. After a while I said, "It's very nice of you to help me like this. I really don't think an English prison officer would go to all this trouble." To which the prison officer replied, "It's a very quiet day here sir." Eventually we came to a site on which there were two O. J. Simpsons, one of whom was the wrong age. I said, "I've got the site now and this one looks like the real O. J. Simpson because he's stated to be sixty-three years old and that's what O. J. is." The prison officer asked, "Is there a number by his name?" I said, "Yes." He said, "If you write to him and mention that number he will get the letter." I said, "Are you sure?" He said, "Yes, he will definitely get the letter." So I wrote a very charming letter to O. J. to find out how things were going, suggesting a general chat and asking if he could put me on the list of those who could phone him. I'd read that O. J. was beaten up in prison by a skinhead, but he denied it. That he was unbelievably fat. That he was crippled by arthritis (which he was last time I met him) and various other things. I thought I'd like to know about all this. We were together for a very long time in the Caribbean on a movie and I went to his house one New Year's Eve and met nearly all the people involved in his case including a very charming ex-football player called Al Cowling who was his stand-in in the movie and who drove the getaway car in his famous chase in the white Bronco down the super highways of Los Angeles with 123 police cars following him! I'm sad to report that O. J. did not respond to my letter. He didn't phone, he didn't write.

At the beginning of 2010, I was in Los Angeles sitting in a restaurant with a group of people including Jack Gilardi, O. J.'s theatrical agent at the time I employed him. Jack said rather regretfully that after the murders his agency said that he had to let O. J. Simpson go. They could no longer represent him. But he did see Al Cowling quite regularly. I said, "Give Al my best, he was a lovely fellow." What I should have done was get Al Cowling's number and phone him, and he could have taken messages to and from O. J. That's the sort of nonsense I find quite amusing. I will get Al Cowling's number and sort this out. As the saying goes, "Little things please little minds while bigger fools look on."

OLIVER REED

Imet Oliver Reed in 1962 when casting a film. I wanted him but the producer refused to have him. Oliver was very sensitive. He'd written a script about two men carrying a wardrobe up a hill which was symbolic of something but I don't remember what. I helped him get his part in *Gladiator* and spoke to him a few days before he died in Malta in 1999. I was sending over an important journalist from the *Daily Mail*, Alison Boshoff, in relation to the film *Parting Shots,* which Reed had just made with me. I said, "Oliver, please, whatever you do don't throw her in the swimming pool." Oliver had a penchant for throwing people in swimming pools. He assured me he'd behave very well. He was very excited about his future. He was going to play the lead in Uncle Silas on television. He was full of life and at his most wonderful. He was very sober and spoke very rationally, as he always did to me. The conversation was a delight. Two days later, before the journalist had gone out to Malta, I received a telephone call from the *Daily Express* asking whether I had any comment because Oliver Reed had died. I literally shouted out in pain. Later, his brother Simon said to me that when he was telephoned and was told Oliver had died he roared with laughter because he assumed it was Oliver playing a joke by getting someone to call him and say that he was dead. It took a while before Simon realised the truth that his brother really had died.

I have to smile at the ludicrous entry in Wikipedia (one of many), which says that Oliver Reed's remains were buried in the thirteenth-century cemetery in the heart of Church

Town village. I was at Oliver's funeral. It was preceded by a service in a church at Mallow, County Cork. After the ceremony, a number of cars followed the hearse through little Irish villages to the village with Oliver Reed's favourite pub. At the side of the pub was a rough track leading to a field where Oliver was to be buried. This story I have told before but I think it's so good I'll mention it again. I was with Oliver's first wife Kate, a beautiful red-headed Irish lady. As we walked down this track and into the field everyone was saying, "What a marvellous field, what a wonderful place. See those elm trees and the Irish countryside beyond? What a perfect spot for Oliver to be buried". Kate said, "What a load of shit; what a crappy place. It's full of cow shit and flies and dung. Only Oliver could be dumb enough to want to be buried here."

I speak to dead people. I clearly envisaged telephoning Oliver the day after the funeral and saying what a wonderful funeral it was and then telling him what Kate had said. He would have replied in that very quiet voice with a beautiful British accent, "Did she really, Michael? She always had a marvellous sense of humour did Kate."

I finally got to employ Oliver Reed in 1963 on the first of six movies, in a film called *The System* which we shot in Torquay. Oliver had something of a drink problem even then. He didn't drink in the day and he didn't drink in any way that affected his performance or prevent his turning up on set, immaculately on time, which he did for me for the next many years. But I did hear about his drinking. He also took terrible risks. He and David Hemmings became great mates. They were staying in a hotel in Torquay overlooking the bay. There was a ledge outside the hotel windows with a sheer drop below. Oliver would play a game of creeping along the ledge and then climbing into someone's bedroom and frightening them at night. Since he was drunk at the time, the fact that he survived at all is a miracle. He could easily have fallen to his death.

Even then Oliver was determined to become a star. He had a little Mini car and I noticed something in a pocket on the inside of the car door. I said, "What is this Oliver?" He said, "They're my fan photographs. The lady who runs my fan club is coming down soon." It was a surprise to me that Oliver had a fan club, which he well deserved, so I'm glad he did. I wouldn't say Oliver was more interested in women than drink. It was Hemmings who was the great sexual raver and who had an affair with Jane Merrow, the leading girl in the film. Another actress in the film was a wonderful cockney girl called Barbara Ferris. I remember her saying, "I don't see how Jane Merrow could have David Hemmings, his fingernails are so dirty." I couldn't quite see what that had to do with sex but it was a remark I always remember.

Oliver's drinking increased and although it never interfered with his work, taking him on location was a nightmare. Whatever hotel he was in you knew he would switch the shoes around outside the doors (those were the days when they cleaned shoes), throw flour over the diners and generally cause chaos. When we were in Austria he pissed on the Austrian flag and screamed "Heil Hitler" all over the place. I don't think Oliver ever stayed in a hotel more than one night because after that they wanted him out. On *Hannibal Brooks* we were on location for nine weeks. So you can imagine the number of hotels we had to use for Oliver alone. He would come to the set the next day very sober, very quiet and very professional. When I'd say, "Oliver, we've got to change your hotel again because you were pissing on the Austrian flag, throwing flour all over the people in the dining room and changing shoes around outside the doors" he would look like a naughty school boy who had been caught and say, "Did I really, Michael? I was so drunk I don't remember."

Oliver and I used to play a rather naughty game. He loved little bets. When we were making *I'll Never Forget What's'isname* in Cambridge, we used to take books from the shelves of the university library and we had to guess what date the book was published; the closest guess got £1. That's not much, but by the end of the day one or the other of us had to pay up £200 or £300. When we got to Austria there were no books to guess the dates of so we would play a rather vulgar game, which we didn't consider vulgar at all in those days. If we saw some girl passing by we would say, "How much would you pay to fuck her?" Or if she was really ugly, "How much would you have to be paid to fuck her?" No money passed hands but it amused us in the many hours we would sit on a set while the shot was being lit. I'm sure we should have been talking about very intellectual stuff, but we weren't.

Later Oliver went to live in Guernsey to save money. I always felt that was a bit odd because his brother, who managed him and got a fraction of his salary, was living comfortably in England whereas Oliver had to go and live in Guernsey. Oliver himself mentioned this to me but he was so loyal to his family, the implications, if any, did not trouble him. He handled his money poorly. He once said to me, "My brother invested for me in building some apartments. I must be the only person who went into property and lost money on it."

Oliver was unbelievably generous. He went to Barbados and met a taxi driver and financed him to open a car service with a fleet of cars. He was always giving out presents to people. He was just a wonderful and very warm, giving person. The idea that he was some sort of drunken lout was ridiculous. I felt particularly aggrieved when some of the newspapers wrote, after Oliver's death, that he'd had a wasted life. The idea that some journalist, contributing very little to society, should put him down in that way, I found it appalling. Oliver was a very fine screen actor, starred in many of the most important films over many decades, was immensely kind and led a wonderful life both on and off the screen. The only trouble was, any time he was on a television talk show I was asked to attend because they thought I would keep him sober. Most of the time I declined because the one time I did turn up he was just as drunk as he would have been if I wasn't there. Although he was very nice to me.

Who knows what demons compel someone drink that much. It certainly harmed Oliver's career later on. In particular, on a big US pirate movie, *Cutthroat Island*, directed by Renny Harlin in which Oliver was to star with Geena Davis. At the pre-shooting party Oliver rushed round the room and showed everyone his penis on which, apparently, (I never saw it) he had a tattoo. This did not go down well with the Americans who were rather strait-laced. Renny Harlin immediately replaced him.

ORSON WELLES

Orson Welles was a great, great genius. I've told many stories about him in my autobiography and in the press, so I've got to be careful not to mention them again as this is all meant to be new.

I went to see Orson about our movie, *I'll Never Forget What's'isname*, and next thing I got was a letter from him:

Dear Michael, yesterday evening I didn't wish to enter into any serious discussion with you in the presence of the gentleman who was with us, and whose position and responsibilities are unknown to me, however, I must insist before shooting starts, that there is a clear understanding between us regarding working hours.

Only under exceptional circumstances do I ever consent to work more than the normal shooting time of 9 a.m.–6 p.m., or its equivalent if night shooting is required [we always shot 8 a.m.–6 p.m. and that was quite short compared to what some people did]. The interpretation of quite "exceptional circumstances" is something that we will have to work out together, if there is some single day or night in which you expect me to work longer. I say "single" because this seems to me a fair portion out of a proposed period of nine days filming.

I must also tell you that I was rather alarmed by a remark of yours which, at least I understood, to signify that your lunch break is often only a half hour duration. Here again, I didn't wish to enter into anything resembling a dispute in the presence of a third party whose position I didn't understand, but I must be quite firm in insisting on a full hour lunch break – or the equivalent to a lunch break during night shooting. I cannot function efficiently, or do justice to myself, or to your film under any other working conditions. I have always insisted upon, and received, these conditions, and I think it's important that this be clear between us, and that you make your plans accordingly. Please forgive the formality of this grim little note, but its content is important to both of us and I would be grateful for your assurance in these matters before starting work tomorrow.

I can't remember if I agreed to all this nonsense or not but I do know that Orson was the most cooperative, marvellous, helpful and giving person you could possibly wish to have on a movie set. Other directors have hated him. Lewis Gilbert who made a film with Orson, *Ferry to Hong Kong*, said when he spoke at the National Film Theatre that he still had nightmares about him. Other directors have said how impossible he was to direct or to have on a movie set. Quite the contrary; Orson was helpful, always cheerful, with a wonderful, kind nature and never, in spite of what he wrote to me, was he worried about timekeeping. He was just a total delight and we remained friends until he died.

I have another handwritten letter from Orson, dated 1 June 1967, in which he wrote: "Your very kind letter chased me to Greece; it's just caught up with me here in Paris where it is much appreciated, believe me. How's our picture? And what about the next one? Affectionate regards, Orson." I don't know what letter he was talking about actually because my filing system seems to have failed me there. The next thing I know is that on 7 June 1967 Orson sent me a script he wrote called *Dead Reckoning*. It was beautifully written and Orson, as always, was having great trouble getting any film going because his record as a commercial filmmaker was a disaster, even though he had made some of the most important films in the history of cinema. I have a telegram from him regarding my movie *The Jokers*, sent to the Leicester Square theatre where the film was premiered. It says: "Dear Michael, I know it's a great hit because I've seen it. So will millions more. Fondest, Orson." This was a man who was meant to be difficult or unpleasant. He just wasn't. He was marvellous.

He was always financing his own films and he was always sending me telegrams seeking help. Here's a typical one but I don't know the date:

> Dear Michael, urgent I have immediately young, bright cameraman to replace French cameraman called away on other jobs. No lamps, no reflectors, only natural sun. We have been photographing at apertures hitherto unheard of and need adventurous youth to continue. French man was also camera operator. If two men need operator also must be very talented. Important picture, Jeanne Moreau, Laurence Harvey and others on small boat requiring newest novelle vague [sic] performance. Must have cameraman cum operator or team. Immediately repeat immediately for three weeks. Can you help?
> Fondest, Orson Welles. Hotel Adriatic HVAR tel. 74164.

Orson's reputation for not making money included *Citizen Kane*. He once told me when I asked him what he would like to do before he died that he had never done he said, "Make one movie that shows a profit." At an enormous tribute to Orson in Los Angeles at which the American Film Institute presented him with their lifetime achievement award, he went up to the podium and said, "In this room there is every important studio chief in Hollywood. There are all the great producers, all the great directors, all the great studio executives. You have all come here to pay me tribute. But none of you will give me a job." I thought that was immensely sad and so true of the industry. They all applauded him like mad. None of them gave him a job.

CALL ME PETE

For a period of four years and three months between 7 December 2000 and 23 March 2004 I was under criminal investigation by the Inland Revenue. I greatly enjoyed it. It came about because I had a moment of what can only be described as heavenly guidance or gross stupidity. Around 1968, tax rose to 98p in the £1 for money you had earning interest and 75p in the £1 on ordinary income. The country seemed to be sliding into total chaos with endless strikes and disasters and many people, including me, thought this was absolutely ridiculous and put some money aside in Switzerland. This was illegal.

My money stayed there until at one point a backer of one of my movies collapsed and I brought it in to pay the crew and cast. So none of that money was spent on holidays, dancing girls, orgies, drugs, yachts or the normal frivolities.

The account was closed in the early 1980s for a good reason. There was no money left in it!

In 2000 I was having a normal tax investigation over minor matters, none of which were in any way incorrect and I decided, in a moment of madness or deep humanity, to say to the Revenue that I once had money in Switzerland. The Revenue was represented by the most marvellous man who was an ace investigator and worked like a tiger on their behalf. His name was Peter (call me Pete) Thackeray. He had long hair and looked as if he belonged on one of the old 1960s "ban the bomb" marches. He had a great sense of humour and was a very nice person. I mentioned to a Christian lawyer and a Jewish accountant that I was revealing these matters and that they should represent me in any further investigation.

That was a bit of a laugh. The Christian said he didn't want to work with the Jew because he could do it all himself and the Jew said he didn't want to work with the Christian because he could do it all himself. I said, "Come on fellas, I'm about to be investigated on a criminal charge, let's all pull together. Never mind all this prima donna nonsense." So they worked together and within seconds greatly loved and respected each other.

I had not, actually, at that point told the Revenue what happened in Switzerland but I was about to do so. Whereupon Mr Thackeray who at the time was just looking into these other minor matters, came to the office of the Jewish accountant in St John's Wood with the Christian lawyer who said, "Mr Winner wishes to make a full disclosure but we would like you to put him under Hansard." Hansard was an option the Revenue could, if they wished, adopt. It meant that they would listen to the full confession, as it were, and if in further investigations nothing was found to be dishonest and everything that the criminal (me!) had told them was true then they would guarantee not to prosecute the taxpayer in the courts but to do a deal that would be outside of the judicial system. This way there was no chance of me seeing a newspaper placard: "Winner charged with tax evasion!" Although most people would have thought, "Good for him!"

When Mr Thackeray was told that I wished to be under Hansard, he said, "I will have to go back to Bristol and ask my team leader." At which point the Jewish accountant said, "Well there's a telephone in the room here, Mr Thackeray. Why don't we leave the room and you can phone your team leader in Bristol and see if he agrees to put Mr Winner under Hansard. If so, we can continue." Mr Thackeray did get approval for Hansard. He came to my house on 7 December 2000 where and I made my statement. The statement was basically that if any country in Europe, or any other well-run country, operated a tax system which took 98 per cent of earnings interest away and 75 per cent of earned income there would be a riot. The miners wouldn't stand it. The bus conductors wouldn't stand it. Nobody would stand for it. Therefore, although it was improper of me to move money out of the country, the circumstances were such that it was quite clear that the law of the land was behaving like an ass so that's what I did.

I explained that the Swiss account was closed. In these circumstances, the Revenue could only go back twenty years. Anything you did before that they cannot touch. But as the accounts had been closed eighteen years previous to this meeting, and as there was no evidence about it, Mr Thackeray took the view that something might have been going on and wanted to penalise me. I don't blame him; he was working for the Revenue.

There followed – I tell you this in case it ever happens to you – a meticulous examination of every penny my companies and I had spent during the last twenty years. This was not carried out by the Revenue. They are very clever in this respect. They save money on staff by insisting that the taxpayer has this detailed examination done by an accountant; the accountant being unlikely to falsify anything or he'd be in big trouble. Then the Revenue looks at the accountant's report and spends some considerable time going over it and asking questions and dealing with it.

During this four-year period, a report of five thick volumes was produced by my accountant.

When Mr Thackeray first came to my house, my lawyer said, "You'd better give him something." I said, "What do you mean give him something?" He said, "You'd better put something down for the Revenue as a sign of goodwill." I said, "Would £20 cash would do?" My lawyer said, "No it won't. You've got to give him £800,000." I knew I was in the poo so, what the hell, I'd have to do it. Mr Thackeray came for the meeting where I duly made my speech. It was taken down by a Revenue stenographer. It was later produced for me to sign and Mr Thackeray wandered off with a cheque for £800,000.

My lawyer and accountant did not wish me to speak to Mr Thackeray after that. They said they would deal with it. But from time to time I did write to him and he wrote to me. By mistake I once faxed a letter from Thackeray to a private house in St John's Wood instead of my accountant. I had obviously pressed the wrong number on the fax machine. The person who had received it very kindly sent the letter back to me writing: "This is the first time I've seen a tax inspector with a sense of humour." Dealing with Thackeray was a delight. He fought like a terrier for the Revenue but he seemed a very good human being.

The report into my affairs ground on and on and on. Eventually, some four years later, the Revenue were given the Report and when they had queried everything, it finally came to what Thackeray said at the beginning – "a horse trade". The whole thing was so confused as no one knew what interest I'd made in Switzerland on the money or anything because there were no records. Thus it was finally agreed that I should pay the Revenue £3m less the £800,000 they had already received. I said to my lawyer, "Ask if I can pay it over two years." The lawyer said, "I'm not prepared to ask that. We've agreed a settlement and that's it. If you want to change it you call Mr Thackeray." I said, "Mr X, you have been telling me throughout these entire four years not to talk to Thackeray under any circumstances. You're taking enormous fees, and now you tell me I should speak to him because you don't feel like it. Bollocks! Call him up and say I want to pay over two years." The lawyer said, "He won't accept it." I said, "You don't know he won't accept it until you try it. Tell him that's what we want. Then, and only then, will we know whether he accepts it." The lawyer called me back ten minutes later and said, "He's accepted that.

You can pay with two cheques. One dated now and one in a year's time." So on the 23 March 2004, at 11 a.m., the lawyer, the accountant, Pete Thackeray (he'd always said "call me Pete") and his boss Mr Maggs turned up at my house for a settlement meeting. They also brought a Revenue stenographer so everything would be noted. By now Thackeray, who I hadn't seen for over four years, had gifted himself with a haircut. He wasn't the long-haired "ban the bomb" marcher I first met. In fact, I didn't really recognise him because Mr Maggs, his boss, looked much the same.

In this settlement meeting I said, "Excuse me I would like to say something on the record. I would like it taken down and I would like it to be in the Revenue files. I've met many people in my life but I've never met anybody I admire more than Peter Thackeray. He is a marvellous public servant of this country. He is a great representative of the Inland Revenue. He has fought like a tiger on behalf of the Revenue and I do not even agree with the settlement. I think it is far too one-sided for the Revenue. But that is Peter Thackeray's job and he has done it superbly. I think this nation is very lucky to have him as a public servant." Whereupon Mr Maggs said, "I've been with him for four years." As if to say count me in too.

On reflection I think this probably destroyed Thackeray's career. To have the "criminal" making a speech praising the investigator could be seen by some people as rather odd, as if something untoward might have gone on, which it certainly did not. The meeting continued and I signed off various documents for the Revenue. When that was done Pete Thackeray said to me, "Now, Mr Winner, you are respectable." I said, "That's the only thing that worries me, Pete. I'm not sure I want to be respectable."

I still speak to Peter Thackeray occasionally. When he retires I will pay him a glowing tribute in my column, in the *Sunday Times*. You would have thought having handled this matter so well, by getting for the Revenue £3m which they were not expecting to receive, that he would have been given some sort of a promotion. Even my lawyer and accountant said he should have been made team leader. But Thackeray was not made team leader. He was pushed into another office in another part of the area and when I asked him whether that was an upgrade or a downgrade he said rather bitterly, "It's a sideways move; I'm just waiting for my retirement." This is an exceptional man. Bright, totally dedicated, fair within the realm of his work in that he has to claw back as much money as he can for the Revenue. An all-over good person is Pete. So I was very sorry to see him not receive recognition for having got a few million quid out of Winner. Of course, my accountant and lawyer got a few quid too; £500,000 to be exact. So it all cost me £3.5m. What I only get into!

There is a very funny story that goes round in accountancy and tax adviser circles about a very famous person who was also put under Hansard and assured the Revenue that everything he was saying was right and true. When they finally made the settlement, this celebrity gave them a cheque from a bank he hadn't told the Revenue anything about! As a result, that Hansard was blown apart and he went to prison!

Another great case was Ken Dodd. The Revenue took him to court for what they claimed were hundreds of thousands, if not millions, of pounds of unpaid tax. It was revealed he had money under the bed, money here, money there and had not declared an income from interest from investments in Jersey and elsewhere. He had bank accounts everywhere! Ken Dodd was brilliantly represented. I'm sure he himself was an incredible witness in the box because the jury sympathised with him. He was found not guilty by the court. That doesn't mean that he did not have to pay an enormous amount of back tax but at least he avoided going to prison. Ken has brought the Revenue case against him into his act. I understand he does at least half an hour of Revenue jokes about the inquiry that he underwent. Good for you Ken Dodd.

NIGHTS AT THE COMEDY

In the 1950s I had a poky little office in Dean Street, Soho. I was under contract to a bad-tempered producer called Daniel M. Angel as an associate producer. In fact, I never did that. I was directing movies. But in the gaps between (which were not uncommon), that is to say when I was not shooting, I would have lunch almost every day at the bar of Wheeler's restaurant in Old Compton Street. I sat always with the same people: Francis Bacon, the painter; Lucian Freud, the painter; and a TV person called Daniel Farson. We chatted every day. We ogled the girl (Carol) behind the counter who had enormous bosoms. She now owns the French Horn at Sonning even though the bosoms have diminished. She was Catholic and she married a Jew (Ronnie) who was selling toilet rolls from a barrow outside the restaurant. His parents objected. Her dad, owner of Wheeler's, had a gin and tonic and then approved! Behind the bar was a beautiful water-colour painting personally signed painting by Walt Disney, which today would be worth at least £200,000. I never knew what happened to it. Nor did Carol when her father, Major Walsh, sold the premises.

In 1963 I put on my first theatre show. I was junior partner with another producer called William Donaldson. It was called *Nights at the Comedy* and was a pub variety show with an incredible cast of the day. It was Jimmy Tarbuck's first West End appearance and there was a legendary comedian called Jimmy James, a drag act called Mrs Shufflewick who was extremely funny, and a man called Bob Tray who sang "Mule Train" and accompanied himself by hitting himself on the head with a tin tray. It got rave reviews but was a total disaster. My senior partner, William Donaldson, who was meant to be very rich because he was part of the Donaldson shipping family, suddenly ran out of money. He vanished. Leaving the cast unpaid. They were all going totally berserk. I was in the dressing room with Jimmy James who was a real old timer and he said to me, "You know, Michael, I've seen this many times before. I'm used to it."

The show was compered by Daniel Farson who I sat with at the Wheeler's bar. He wasn't meant to compere it. There was (and is) a very brilliant actor called Nicol Williamson. Williamson had a habit of leaving shows. He did the first few previews of this show extremely well and suddenly was gone! His agent said to me, "He's gone to Glasgow where he thinks he's a reincarnation of McGonigall", a very famous Scottish poet. The agent said, "You'll have to go and get him back." I said, "I'm not working for British Rail. I'm certainly not going up to Glasgow." So we replaced Nicol.

William Donaldson went broke a number of times with further shows. He was eventually penniless on the beach in Ibiza where he met his ex-secretary who was there as well. They went back to London where she worked as a prostitute and he and she ran a brothel. Donaldson wrote a brilliant book about this called *Both the Ladies and the Gentleman*. Being rather dodgy, William Donaldson sold the book to two different publishers! I got him out of trouble by recommending an agent who smoothed it all over. Then I found in his next book he was quite rude about me! Which illustrates perfectly the well-known saying, "No good turn goes unpunished."

I now return to the days of the bar at Wheeler's, in particular to Lucian Freud. Lucian who recently died aged 86 was still painting brilliantly. In fact, at the time of his death, he held the world record price for a living painter, £17.2m for a picture that was sold at auction.

I saw him from time to time, and, of course if you go back

sixty years there is a bond. Lucian was a very private person, so when I saw him, which was largely at The Wolseley restaurant, I'd have a brief chat with him but not impose on him. He was always absolutely charming, normally with a very beautiful lady, often one of his family. I said to him a few weeks before he died, "Lucian, you look so wonderful. Do you do any exercise?" He said, "No." I said, "You don't jog round the block from time to time?" He said, "No. But I have a bath every day." Then Lucian paused for a second and said, "Some days I have two baths." He had a wonderful sense of humour. He was one of the great British people ever to be born. People often said to me, "If you know him, why has Lucian not painted you?" The answer to that is very simple. He obviously didn't want to. And I don't blame him. I shall greatly miss him.

◇◇

TRAVELLING MAT

There was a wonderful Jewish film cameraman called Otto Heller. He came from Czechoslovakia and worked on some of the most famous films in England including *The Lady Killers, Alfie, Funeral in Berlin* etc. He did two films for me, the first being *West Eleven,* which was set in Notting Hill Gate. I was forced by the producer to build, in the studio, a small bed-sitting room that was meant to be in Notting Hill Gate. The film camera is often mounted on what is called a dolly which people push so the camera can move during photography. A very tense scene was being shot when the camera dolly got caught up with a mat on the floor and pulled it along. To which Otto, who had a habit of talking during takes and therefore destroying the sound, said, "Look Michael, travelling mat." That is a reference to a technical device used in movies to superimpose one image upon another, called travelling matte. Otto was an incredibly good cameraman. He would enter a set or a room that he had to photograph, and with his white hair and short stature, he'd put his hand on his head as if in agony and say, "Michael, how I do dis? How do I do dis?" Then he lit it brilliantly. He lived in Baker Street. When he met people he always said, "Otto Heller from Baker Street." I don't think we've ever had a better cameraman in England than Otto Heller, God rest his soul.

◇◇

DRIVING MR WINNER

I once had a marvellous chauffeur who was very big and burly. He drove my Rolls-Royce Phantom V which had a glass division. When he came to see me for the job he said, "I drive with dignity, sir. That is one of the key points in my favour, I drive with dignity."

When we were driving along, if someone pulled out in front of him, even if they were a long way ahead, he would scream with hysterical road rage, "You stupid fucking cunt. You arsehole..." Eventually I pushed the button, lowered the glass division of the car and said, "It really is a bit disturbing, particularly when I have friends sitting in the car with me, to hear you screaming and swearing all the time." To which he said, "They don't make Rolls-Royces like they used to, sir. That division is meant to be soundproof." He was the most wonderful man, this chauffeur. He sold stolen goods from the back of the car. One day my friend, the famous film director Lewis Gilbert, came up to me and said, "My watch doesn't work." I said, "Oh really, Lewis?" He said, "Yes, my watch does not work." I said, "What's that got to do with me?" He said, "Well I bought it from your chauffeur." On another occasion I had my car radio nicked. I said to the chauffeur, "I won't bother to claim; it's only a radio." He said, "I had three TVs nicked from the boot!"

At the time I had a very high-pitch-voiced bookkeeper who was moving into a new house and wanted some carpets. The chauffeur said, "Don't worry, sir, I'll get you the carpets." He duly provided some carpets at a fraction of their normal cost. My bookkeeper said, "But they're not the colour I wanted." The chauffeur said, "You can't choose the colour, sir, they nick whatever is nearest the door."

On another occasion, he was driving down Mount Street (not with me in the car) after which I got a letter from a lady saying that my chauffeur had chased her down Mount Street and then deliberately reversed into her Austin Healey causing a lot of damage. I showed him this letter. I said, "Mr X, apparently you chased this woman down Mount Street and smashed into her. You can't do that sort of thing. You'll go to jail." He said, "I could do with a rest, sir. Jail won't worry me." I handed the letter over to him, declining to put it through my insurance. Later I said, "What's going on?" He said, "Don't worry, sir. The case is coming up. I'll handle it." A member of my staff went to the court. When the case came up the corner of Mount Street and North Audley Street was said to be full of people who spoke in cockney accents like him. They came as witnesses and all swore blind that the women drove into the back of his car. So my chauffeur got off.

There was another wonderful moment with this chauffeur. He was garaging my Rolls Phantom in his block of flats. He lived in a council flat in the middle of Mayfair! The richest area in London and he had a council flat there. He said to me, "We can't use my garage anymore, sir." So I found a garage just off Grosvenor Square. I said, "Go and look at that garage Mr X and make sure it's OK." He came back and he said, "Yes, it's a very nice garage, sir." So I paid for this communal garage where we had a space. After four months, one weekend I'd run out of Havana cigars. I foolishly smoked fifteen to twenty Havana cigars a day. I knew there was a box of cigars in the car. The chauffeur was off. And I couldn't get him on the phone. So I rang the garage and said, "Excuse me, you have my Rolls-Royce Phantom V parked in your garage. I'd like to come and get something from it." The man at the garage said, "We've never seen a Rolls-Royce Phantom here. It definitely isn't here." I said, "That's not possible. I've been paying for the space for three months." The man said, "Well you may have been paying for the space but I can assure you there's no car here." The following morning when Mr X came in I said, "Excuse me, where are we parking my Rolls-Royce Phantom?" The chauffeur replied naming the hotel just north of Grosvenor Square. I said, "We're not parking it there because, needing some cigars, I rang them over the weekend and they said they've never seen the car at all." The chauffeur said, "You're absolutely right, sir. The car is still parked in the garage in my council block." I asked, "Then why am I paying for this garage in Mayfair when the car has, in fact, not left your garage?" I should point out here that he was not paid for my using his garage. I was paying for the garage at the hotel, which obviously he was not getting anything from. I said, "I told you to check the garage out very carefully and see if the car was OK there." The chauffeur said, "I did check the garage out, sir. But I didn't take the car down. When later I tried to get the car in it's such a large car we couldn't get it down the ramp into the garage. So it's back in the garage in my block of flats."

The chauffeur was also in charge of the respray of my car. I'd bought the car from Harry Saltzman, the famous James Bond film producer. The problem was he had his initials in gold on all four doors. Also it was getting a bit scratched. So I said we would have it resprayed. I chose a garage but the chauffeur advised, "I've got a much better garage than that, sir" and he named a very large repair company. He said, "You're going away. Leave it with me, sir. I'll put it in there. They're meant to use six coats of paint on the car. I shall go in every day and I shall see the coat of paint put on and then I shall put a little pencil mark on the car and go in again and make sure that they've covered that layer of paint with another layer of paint."

When I returned after being away on a movie, there was the car resprayed. Except that I noticed embossed under the black respray were the initials HS quite clearly visible on all four doors. I said to the chauffeur, "Look at that Mr X. What can you see on those doors?" He said, "I can see the letters HS, sir on all the doors. It's a disgrace. These modern people don't know what they're doing." I said, "You said you were going to go every day and check that they'd put six coats of paint on it." He said, "They wouldn't let me in, sir, so I couldn't do that." Thus the car had to go back and be resprayed yet again. It's wonderful isn't it, the joys of employing staff!

PETER USTINOV

Peter Ustinov was a raging anti-Semite. I'd known him since I was fifteen when I first interviewed him but it wasn't until 1987 when I employed him on Agatha Christie's *Appointment with Death* that I learned so much more about him. I still liked him – I liked him when I first met him and I liked him until the day he died. But he was not in any way the cheerful uncle type that he put forward as his personality.

We had a press conference for *Appointment with Death* at the Hilton Hotel in Tel Aviv. Other stars of the movie where there, namely Lauren Bacall, Carrie Fisher, David Soul, John Gielgud, Jenny Seagrove and Hayley Mills. We all sat on a platform. One of the Israeli journalists said to Ustinov (who was playing Poirot), "Are you Jewish, Mr Ustinov?" To which Peter replied with a very curt and surly, "No." The journalist persisted. She said, "But we all thought you were Jewish, Mr Ustinov." He said, "I'm not." Nothing like, "But it is a pleasure to be among you, I have many Jewish friends" or that sort of stuff. It was quite clear that he was delighted he wasn't Jewish. In fact, Peter is half white Russian and half Palestinian. He made it quite clear during the shooting of the movie what he thought of the Israelis and the Jews. It became so bad (or good if you think it's a bit of fun) that one day the stars who had a kind of joint dressing lounge while they waited for shooting in the main square of Jaffa, found Ustinov really annoying. Lauren "Betty" Bacall was a well-known Jewess, born Betty Joan Perske, which is why she was often called Betty even later on. She was the only child of Natalie Weinstein-Bacal, a secretary, and her husband William Perske. So there were all the actors in this room and suddenly Lauren Bacall shouted out at Peter Ustinov, "You're an absolute anti-Semite, Peter." He muttered something about, "I have no hatred of any race or religion", which was a load of nonsense. The other actors all walked out of the room leaving Ustinov alone. They sat in the square of Jaffa at a coffee table rather than go into the room with him. Peter eventually came out. There was an Israeli Arab sweeping the road. Peter went over to him and started telling him stories.

Ustinov absolutely had to tell stories. It didn't matter what the audience was. He just had to have an audience. I went once to a Chinese restaurant in Jerusalem which had been recommended to me by Johnny Gielgud. Jenny Seagrove and I walked into the restaurant. There were only four other people there. Peter Ustinov and his wife, and an American couple who Peter had moved to sit next to so that he could spend the evening telling them stories. Mind you, his stories were very good. But enough is enough.

Another thing about Ustinov that was very naughty (and annoying) is that he was absolutely unprofessional. He never bothered to remember his lines. When you're doing an Agatha Christie movie where you have long speeches like, "I put it to you Mrs Boynton that you were not in the tent on the night of the murder, you were out at the terrace of the hotel..." and that sort of thing, you need to get it accurate. We were sitting in a ballroom in Tel Aviv. The film was set in 1935. It was very hot and all the other stars were in evening dress round the table while Poirot delivered his deductions. They were all sweating, particularly John Gielgud who was quite old by then. Peter kept getting his lines wrong because he simply hadn't bothered to remember them. When I pointed out that he had made mistakes in the lines, he would get very snappy and say, "No I didn't. You're not listening properly." I said, "Peter, it's not a case of whether I'm listening or not. Here are the headphones and here is the recording of what you just did and you will see that you said the wrong lines." Which of course Peter did see. He didn't apologise or anything; he just looked extremely grumpy and we carried on.

In spite of all this I continued to like him. Except he's dead now so I can't like him anymore. But I like his memory.

Towards the end of the movie Peter, his wife and I were having dinner in a very nice restaurant near Haifa. Peter said to me, "If you lived in Israel, Michael, where would you live?" I said (not strictly truthfully because I liked Israel), "I'd live near the airport, Peter, so it would be easy for me to get out." Ustinov said, "Why can't I say things like that?" I said, "Because you're a well-known anti-Semite, Peter."

The last time I saw Peter was in 1999. As one of the heads of the Directors Guild of Great Britain I'd arranged that the Directors Guild would give its lifetime achievement to Stanley Kubrick. We asked Peter to come and present the award to him. Sadly, by the time we got to present the award at the Piccadilly Hotel, Kubrick had died. All his family were at the event and we obviously continued to have the award given out. A large number of stars attended. I'd asked Peter to come from Switzerland at the expense at the Directors Guild to give the award to Stanley's wife, Christiane. Peter turned up at the reception prior to the dinner and I was shocked. He had aged massively since I last saw him. He was doddery. It wasn't a case of whether he'd live to make the speech; I wasn't sure he'd live through the main course. For a man who loves speaking nonstop he didn't speak at all; we just greeted each other and then he stayed in a corner very quietly. For the award dinner, Peter was at my table along with Joanna Lumley, Maureen Lipman and various other stars. Again he just sat absolutely quietly not speaking to anybody. I thought, "How on earth is he going to make a speech, he can't even talk at the dinner table."

I made the various announcements of who was there and then I introduced Peter Ustinov. He got up from the table and shuffled toward me. I helped him on to the podium and he got to the lectern. I was dreading what was about to happen. The minute he got to the podium and the microphone, Peter Ustinov became another person. All the old age, the tiredness, the depleted spirit, left him completely. He proceeded to give immaculately, with perfect timing and great wit what was, without question, the greatest speech I have ever heard. He recounted, imitating all the actors perfectly, the first script conference for *Spartacus* which he'd made for Stanley Kubrick. He did perfect impersonations, and put them into a marvellously funny story, of Kirk Douglas, Laurence Olivier, Charles Lawton, John Gavin and Tony Curtis and what they said at that first reading of the script. The audience was in hysterics and so was I. It was a brilliant performance. Peter finished the speech and handed the award to Christiane Kubrick. Then, as if the air had been let out of him, he reverted to being a very old man and wobbled slowly back to our table. He died just over four years later.

It transpired that he had not made a will for years. I understand, although I could be wrong, that the old will made no mention of his wife Helene, who was with him from 1972 until his death and that a lot of the children were left out. I further knew that his son Igor from his marriage to Suzanne Cloutier, which lasted from 1954 to 1971, was left out of the will. Igor sued over it in Paris. Peter's London agent Steve Kennis went over to give evidence although he said to me, "What evidence I could give that was of any use I do not know."

There's no question Ustinov gave great joy to many people with his acting, his directing, his writing and his marvellous one-man shows, as well as his work for UNICEF; the fact that he was cantankerous and in many ways bizarre is irrelevant. I like those sort of people.

He is perhaps summed up by one of his many sayings: "I do not believe that friends are necessarily the people you like best. They're merely the people who got there first." I think this shows the cynicism that lay beneath Ustinov's "jolly uncle Pete" exterior.

POLICE

One of the things I am most proud of doing in my life is to have created the Police Memorial Trust charity which puts up memorials to police officers slain on duty, usually on the spot where they met their death. I also inititated and oversaw the building of the National Police Memorial in The Mall, the first memorial to be erected there for over 100 years.

This all started in a strange way. On 17 April 1984 police constable Yvonne Fletcher was shot outside the Libyan delegation in St James's Square. She was part of a small group of police patrolling around a group of demonstrators. A Libyan stuck an automatic gun out of the window of their legation and sprayed the area. Yvonne Fletcher was killed. Her police hat fell to the pavement and became a poignant symbol of her tragedy. The photograph of this young lady appearing in the press was very moving.

I was in my study at home and I said to my assistant, John Fraser, "You know, it's absolutely ridiculous. No one will remember Yvonne Fletcher's name in a few weeks. Tell me the name of the last police officer who was killed." Of course he couldn't. At that time the police were getting a very poor press (which is not unusual) with the miners' strike particularly focusing the attention of some people against them.

I said, "We should really put up memorials for police officers killed on duty. There are memorials to members of the army, the navy and the air force who fight and die on our behalf but the police fight a war that has no beginning and no end, and their deaths go completely unrecognised by any public monument."

My assistant said, "With the French resistance fighters they put a plaque on the building showing where they had died." I was so incensed about the killing and lack of recognition for the police that I wrote a letter to *The Times* which was published on 21 April 1984 suggesting that a memorial be erected to Yvonne Fletcher and to police officers killed on duty. I wrote: "It would serve to indicate that not everyone in this country takes seeming pleasure in attacking the police in the execution of their difficult duties, but that most of us regard their conduct and bravery, under a whole series of endless and varied provocations, as demonstrably noble and worthy of our thanks."

After the letter was printed, I received donations from the public together with a large number of letters from people approving of my sentiments. I didn't quite know what to do with the money because I was not intending to start a charity or put up memorials. I was simply writing about it. It was for someone else to put up the memorials if they wanted to. Someone more in the establishment than a Jack the lad film director.

A few days later, on 27 April 1984, at the invitation of my friend Sir David English, then editor of the *Daily Mail*, I wrote a long article in that paper on the day of Yvonne's funeral. It finished with the words:

> I can see a day in the future when human memory, being what it is, has discarded the events that now seem so important and the shadows from the trees above sway slowly to and fro on the pavement of St James's Square, the sunlight catching a small memorial. Maybe two people passing by will stop and one will say to the other, "Yvonne Fletcher? Who was she?" To which there is a simple and noble answer. She was a member of the British Police Force.

Further money was sent to me. I was now looking at thirty cheques totalling around £400. One was from Lady Isobel Barnett, the television personality. I thought: "I know what I'll do, I'll get a letter from the Charity Commission telling me how to set up a charity to honour police officers. Then I'll return the money to all these people and send them a copy of that letter and say, 'You form the charity, here's how you do it, and when you form it count me in for £5,000.'" I wrote to the charity commissioners asking how to set up a charity to honour slain police officers by the placing of memorials. The next day at around 10 a.m. I received a phone call. It went like this: "My name is Rao, I'm a charity commissioner. I have your letter before me. Are you telling me, Mr Winner, that you want to put up memorials to mere policemen?" That's what he said, "Mere policemen". When Rao said that, I put my hand over the phone and looked up at my assistant Mr Fraser standing in front of me and said, "Fuck it. We'll have to do this." I returned to the phone and said, "Yes that's right, Mr Rao. I would like to form a charity to put up memorials to police officers slain on duty." Mr Rao said, "We won't allow that as a charity I can assure you. Are you telling me that if a police officer dies you want to put up a memorial to him? The pavements will be full of memorials. It's out of the question." I asked, "Mr Rao, have you ever permitted a memorial to be put up as a charitable event?" Mr Rao replied, "Yes, we have allowed it. We allowed a memorial for President Kennedy and a memorial for Lord Mountbatten but I'm certainly not allowing one for policemen."

To put it mildly, I was getting extremely aggravated. And when aggravated, I'm known to bite and be quite fierce. I said, "Let me tell you something Mr Rao, Yvonne Fletcher died a few days ago and there is a great outpouring of sentiment and regard for her in this nation. I want this charity formed and I want it formed quickly so that I can collect for her memorial while she is still remembered. If you want a public battle with me in the media, you can have one, but you'll personally come out of it very badly." There was a pause and Mr Rao said, "I don't like your attitude." I replied, "We're not in conflict, Mr Rao." He said, "Yes we are. You're trying to bully me." "You're absolutely right, Mr Rao." I said, "I'm trying to bully you. And I'll tell you something else. I have a tape recording of this conversation (which I didn't!) and if this charity is not formed in the next three hours I'm going to call a press conference for 4 p.m. this afternoon where I will play the tape recording. Tomorrow you'll be the most hated man in the land."

That got him! Rao started to splutter, "Well you know, we have to get permission at the Commission and then I have to get Revenue permission and . . .." By now I was really angry. I said, "That's all your problem now, Mr Rao. All your problem. Get on with it." I slammed the phone down. An hour later Mr Rao rang me. He said, "The charity's formed. You can start collecting." I thought: "Fuck me, I'm now chairman of the Police Memorial Trust, a name I've invented and a title I've invented. What the fuck do I do?" Well the answer is I got on with it.

We raised some money for the memorial. But then came the horror of dealing with the people who run St James's Square. That is the pompous, arrogant businessmen who have buildings around the square. I wanted to put my memorial on top of the approximately two feet high wall that runs round the square. I went to a meeting with the St James's Square Committee, or whatever it was called, with a police officer from Scotland Yard. The St James's Square nitwits had the audacity to produce plans of a memorial that they had drawn up. It was very small and just fitted into the wall. I said, "This is the Police Memorial Trust, we did not authorise you to design our memorial. We have our own memorial." Apparently we were not going to have it on their wall. So it occurred to me that we could have it an inch from the wall coming out from the pavement. That needed the permission of Westminster Council. We wrote to the council who just prevaricated and would not give permission. So finally, through a friend of mine who knew her, I got the number of Lady Shirley Porter who was at the time the head of the council. I rang her up at home one Saturday morning and I told her the position. I said, "Lady Porter, I want this memorial approved. It's to a dead police officer who gave her life for the nation. It's highly symbolic of the nation's regard for the police and Westminster is giving me a run around. I want you to step in and do something." Lady Porter said, "What's the deal?" She actually said that to me. She said, "What's the deal?" As if we were talking about a business transaction or bartering or bargaining at a market stall. I thought to myself, "Let's not get involved here. If she wants a deal, I'll give her a deal." I said, "Tell you what, Lady Porter. Instead of the memorial being six inches thick, we'll make it four inches thick." "OK," she said, "done." And thus we got permission to place the memorial and started to do so.

The most amazing aspect of starting the Police Memorial Trust was still to come. My greatest adversaries and the greatest pain-in-the-arse people, putting Mr Rao at the Charity Commission and Lady Porter in the shade as far as gross nastiness is concerned, were the police themselves. They were beyond belief. The police at Yvonne Fletcher's station, Vine Street, wrote letters to police magazines saying they didn't want the memorial claiming that St James's Square was well known for tramps, vandals and drug addicts and the memorial would be defiled within seconds. If there was any place in London not defiled by tramps and drug addicts it was St James's Square. The police at Vine Street, where Yvonne had worked, were placing a cherry tree somewhere in the middle of the square with a little plaque on it. I assumed that they were jealous that my memorial might detract from their cherry tree. Or they were just highly suspicious that a civilian would actually want to honour the police without an ulterior motive. The Fletcher family, who became and remain my dear friends, stuck by me 100 per cent. They wanted the memorial to Yvonne. Tim and Queenie Fletcher were the most marvellous people, and their family were also lovely, and they totally encouraged me to go ahead with the memorial. They were with me all the way.

I visited the memorial with Geoffrey Dear, an Assistant Commissioner from Scotland Yard. He should have been later made Commissioner, but he went a bit nuts and fired the entire detective squad in Manchester and rode around in front of his policemen on a white horse. He kind of boxed himself out of the job. He later was made a Lord. Geoffrey and I went down to look at the memorial site and Assistant Commissioner Dear said to me, "Wouldn't it be wonderful if we could get the Home Secretary to unveil the memorial." I said, "Geoffrey we're not going to get the Home Secretary to unveil it. He will be sitting in the back row. The Prime Minister will unveil this memorial. In the front row with her will be the leaders of the other parties namely Neil Kinnock, David Steel and David Owen. And behind them will sit the current Home Secretary and his three shadow Home Secretaries; all four of them. That is what will happen, Geoffrey."

And of course it did. But I do remember another little comedy. We'd asked the four political leaders, one of whom was the head of the Liberal party, David Steel. It took a long time before I kind of "nurtured" him to come. He was on television with me about a week before the event on a morning programme and the interviewer said, "Mr Steel, are you going to the unveiling of Yvonne Fletcher's memorial?" And Steel (really it was one of the most stupid things I've ever heard anyone say as a political leader) said, "Well I wasn't going to but Michael Winner blackmailed me into it." He actually said that! I said, "David I don't see why you had to be blackmailed into going to the memorial for a young policewoman". Whereupon David Steel said, "No, no I shouldn't have said that. Of course you did not blackmail me I was delighted to be invited and it's a great honour to be coming." What a bloody laugh these people are!

Not one single member of Yvonne's colleagues in the police force, not one single member of the Vine Street police station where she worked, not one single policeman in the police federation that represented her – nobody – came to that ceremony representing the police. But we had Margaret Thatcher, the Prime Minister. We had the Leader of the Opposition, Neil Kinnock. We had David Owen and David Steel the other party leaders and the Home Secretary with three shadow Home Secretaries. It was a massively successful event.

Mrs Thatcher was absolutely marvellous. She was due to go to our reception after she unveiled the memorial to be with Yvonne Fletcher's family, and the political leaders of the opposition parties and various other dignitaries. It was held in the offices of one of the companies which had a building overlooking the memorial. I was told she would stay for twenty minutes. I remember we all got into the lift together, me, Mrs Thatcher, David Steel, David Owen and Neil Kinnock, and I said, "If this lift collapses, it will be significant in the nation's history." But we all got out of the lift safely and went into the reception. As we were looking out of the window at the memorial I said, "You know, a lot of people, Mrs Thatcher, say this memorial will be vandalised." She said, "Well if it is, Mr Winner, we'll repair it won't we?" Indeed, because the police were so paranoid, I had warned Yvonne Fletcher's family that it was believed it might be damaged. To which Queenie Fletcher replied, "You know, Mr Winner, if we worried about that we wouldn't put memorials or statues up for anybody, would we?"

Neil Kinnock, David Steel and David Owen were looking nervously at Mrs Thatcher as she seemed to be overstaying her twenty minutes. It was as if they had somewhere better they would rather be. After forty minutes, Mrs Thatcher left the window where she had been talking with Yvonne Fletcher's mother and father, and I escorted her to the back of the room where she was going to leave the building through a back entrance. As we reached the back of the room a little old lady came up and said, "I've always admired you Mrs Thatcher." I whispered in Mrs Thatcher's ear, "That is Yvonne's grandmother." Mrs Thatcher, who'd already overstayed her time, said to the grandmother, "Come with me my dear. Let's go to the window and look at your grand-daughter's memorial together." There were no members of the press there. Mrs Thatcher was not doing this for public-ity or for effect. She did it because she had a fantastically good heart. Of that I'm certain. She led this little old lady back to the window and I could see the look on the faces of Neil Kinnock, David Steel and David Owen which was as if to say, "Oh my God. She's come back. We'll have to stay here longer." Mrs Thatcher and I stood at the window with Yvonne's grandmother for another ten minutes, then I took Mrs Thatcher back. As we were leaving through some corridors I asked, "Mrs Thatcher, when you stop being Prime Minister what would you like to do?" She said, "Oh I don't want to stop being Prime Minister, Mr Winner. It's a wonderful job. I'd like to have it forever." I said, "Yes, but the chances are you won't have it forever. So what do you think you'll do when you haven't got it?" She said, "I'll do some charity work or something." Mrs Thatcher attended a number of our memorials and I have the highest regard for her. At a time when even the police were not supporting us, she did.

This strange behaviour from the police continued. For a number of memorials that followed Yvonne Fletcher's, the police in charge of the area would say to me, "There's no point in putting up this memorial, Mr Winner, it will be vandalised within half an hour." They never were.

When we put up a memorial to PC Keith Blakelock, not

on the estate where he was stabbed to death, but on his home beat, the Area Chief Inspector Alan Stainsby, said to me, "I don't want this memorial anywhere, Mr Winner. It will only cause trouble." Later he became my dearest friend. He came up to me after the ceremony with tears in his eyes and thanked me for putting the memorial there. That was on the Muswell Hill roundabout where Keith Blakelock patrolled his home beat.

At that memorial it became quite amusing because however serious these tributes are there is often something amusing that happens as well. The family of Keith Blakelock consisted of his wife Elizabeth and his mother, a lovely white-haired old lady called Amy, and their children. They all came to the memorial which was unveiled by Neil Kinnock who was Leader of the Opposition and had been at the time of Blakelock's death. I always ask the family to bring flowers to place at the memorial during the ceremony. Neil Kinnock and I left the podium after the speeches. Neil unveiled it and put his flowers down by the memorial. I looked to Mrs Blakelock who was next to put down her flowers. She was sitting there on the podium and not moving. Everyone thought something had gone wrong with the ceremony or that she was overcome with grief and couldn't move. I went over to her and said, "Liz, where are your flowers?" She replied, "I put them at Keith's gravestone this morning." So I promptly grabbed my flowers, which were at the podium, gave them to Elizabeth Blakelock and she went and laid my flowers. The next lot of flowers were meant to be laid by Keith Blakelock's mother, Amy. I looked to the platform and Amy just shook her head from left to right as if to say, "I haven't got any flowers, too bad".

The other interesting thing about that ceremony was that shortly after Blakelock was killed, the police investigated the house of a black lady called Cynthia Jarrett, during which she fell over and died of a heart attack. Bernie Grant, who was the leader of Haringey Council, totally opposed the memorial.

I only got it put up because a Conservative member of the council gave me secret memos between Bernie Grant and the socialists saying how dreadful to have a memorial to a police officer and what could they do to thwart me. I went to see Neil Kinnock at the House of Commons over this matter. He said, "I really don't have much control over Bernie Grant, Michael, but I'll do my best." Neil Kinnock then decided, I think very rashly, to attend a memorial ceremony for Cynthia Jarrett who'd had the heart attack just before he went on to unveil Keith Blakelock's memorial. I wanted to ask Bernie Grant to our memorial ceremony because it was the proper thing to do but Liz Blakelock said, "If you do, I won't be there and nor will any of my family." She was totally appalled that Neil Kinnock placed Cynthia Jarrett, who died of a heart attack, on the same level as her husband who was stabbed thousands of times by a mob. She was a game lady was Elizabeth. She went up to Neil Kinnock at the reception after the ceremony and he obviously thought, "I'll go for my usual speech," you know, "How nice to see you," and "I'm so sorry about your husband." But Liz let him have it. She reduced him to an oil slick. She said, "Mr Kinnock how dare you go to this other ceremony for Cynthia Jarrett a few minutes before you come to my husband's ceremony." Did she carry on! Neil Kinnock went white. I thought it was extremely amusing. I said, "Liz, you're wonderful dear. If you ever need a job come to me." Liz later married her childhood sweetheart and went to live in the north. Sadly, that marriage failed. One of her children has joined the police force. I saw them recently at an anniversary ceremony at Keith's memorial where they all came along.

On that occasion I was sitting quietly on a chair in the street waiting to make my speech when a policeman came up to me and started talking. I said, "Who are you?" He said, "I'm the Commissioner of Police, Sir Paul Stephenson, we met before." Well how am I supposed to know if he doesn't wear a badge?

We now have thirty-three memorials throughout the land to police officers slain while on duty. The mother of one of the slain officers – her son had been killed about two years earlier – was with me on the podium and as we walked to the reception area, she said to me very quietly, "You know, Mr Winner, they say time heals. It doesn't." The families have been immensely grateful that there is a permanent tribute to their son or daughter who otherwise would have been unrecognised. These memorials are now greatly appreciated by the police. The Police Federation gave me an award two years ago at their conference in Bournemouth.

What I really want is to be made an honorary police constable; I'm not sure who to ask about that!

STEPPING UP TO THE PLATE

After some years of placing local memorials at the sites where police officers had died, I decided to put up the National Police Memorial. It was suggested to me by the Commissioner of Scotland Yard that I have a meeting with the various police associations, none of which I knew much about. There was the Police Federation that represents ranks up to the grade of Inspector, the National Association for Retired Police Officers, the Superintendent's Association and possibly a couple of others. They all came to my house to lunch. Now, believe me, the police can out eat and drink anybody. If there was a contest for eating and drinking the police would definitely win it. If it became an Olympic event, they'd get a gold medal. So these important people sat down and got through God knows how many bottles of wine and liqueurs and all that sort of thing! Then we adjourned to my sitting room. At the time, the chairman of the Police Federation was a man called Leslie Curtis. He crossed his legs and said, "Now Mr Winner, I have an important question for you regarding the Police Memorial Trust. My members want to know whose hand is in the till?" I said, "That's very easy for me to answer, Leslie. My hand is in the till. It's in the till of my property companies and it's putting money into the Police Memorial Trust. It's in the till of my movie companies and it's putting money into the Police Memorial Trust. It's in the till of my personal account and it's putting money into the Police Memorial Trust. I suggest that tomorrow you send round here an accountant to closely examine our books and when you've done that you can put

a statue up for me outside the Police Federation head-
quarters." The next day Leslie Curtis personally sent me a
cheque for £100. From him, not from the Police Federation.
Up until then they'd done absolutely nothing to contribute
towards memorials for their own members. It is only fair to
say that this changed when the National Police Memorial
came along, and the Metropolitan Police Federation made
a most generous donation – since then, I not only became
friends with Leslie Curtis but with all the various Chairmen
of the Police Federation who followed him. And after the
first few ceremonies the President of the Federation always
attended. Also, the Police Federation agreed to undertake
upkeep of the National Police Memorial.

A VILLAGE GREEN

Behind each of the memorials I put up to slain police officers is a tragic story. We all criticise the police a great deal, sometimes necessarily. But they are out there dying for us. My second memorial, the one after Yvonne Fletcher, was to the three police officers killed by an IRA bomb at Harrods. We always fly the families from wherever they are to get them to the ceremony. On this occasion a police dog was also killed. The letters I got about the dog! Endless! They wanted me to include the dog on the memorial or put up a separate memorial for the dog. I greatly sympathised with the death of the dog but I pointed out to them my charity was restricted to placing memorials for police officers slain on duty and it did not include dogs. I suggested to the writers that they set up a charity and I'd contribute to it so they could put up a memorial to the dog. Needless to say, none of them did. It's very easy to talk. Not so easy to do. The memorial to the three Harrods police officers was unveiled by Princess Alexandra. Mrs Thatcher came along later and laid flowers, as did the Home Secretary, Douglas Hurd, and the leader of the Labour party, Neil Kinnock.

Our next memorial was to PC Brian Bishop in Central Avenue, Frinton-on-Sea. There was a great kerfuffle at the time because the police had shot somebody without apparently giving him due warning and it turned out to be somebody who was innocent. The knock on effect of that incident was that police were terrified to shoot even when threatened by a man with a gun unless they went through some rigmarole of saying, "We are police officers. Put your gun down otherwise we may have to shoot you." I'm surprised they didn't ask the police to give them a visiting card and a signed photograph as well. PC Bishop was on duty in the seafront area of Frinton. A gang was being chased and one gang member turned on him with a gun; PC Bishop, I'm sure, was influenced by the recent goings on and did not fire quickly enough. Therefore he was killed.

We put up a memorial to DC John Fordham in West Kingsdown, Kent. That had its bizarre side. The house of one of the people who received money from the gold bullion robbery in London's Heathrow airport was in West Kingsdown, Kent. The man's name was Kenneth Noye. The police were mounting a major operation to apprehend people all over the country. So Kenneth Noye, in this little lane with a big garden in front, had two policemen crouched in his garden waiting for the word as to when they should go in. Noye had two very ferocious Rottweiler dogs. They smelt something was wrong and led him to Detective Constable John Fordham who was crouched behind a bush. Fordham was under instructions not to reveal himself. So he just sat there with black paint all over his face. Noye came up and stabbed him to death. All because he wouldn't break the vow of silence, as it were, that he was under as a police officer. Noye got off when he was sent to trial for the murder of Fordham because he said, not unreasonably really, "What would you do if you came into your garden and there was a man with black all over his face hiding behind a bush? I assumed I was under serious threat and so I intended to wound him but I ended up killing him." Noye was sent to prison for a number of other matters since then, including receiving some of the proceeds of the Heathrow bullion robbery.

When we do these memorials I often go myself to the site and work out where to put the memorial. Noye's house was in a very narrow country lane. I stood outside the house. Noye was, at this point, in jail. The police had obviously taken down a lot of the bushes seeking evidence, so there was a fairly clean run up to his house. My car was parked some way away because I didn't want it in the photograph if I was going to photograph the area. In the car was my girl-friend, waiting for me. Suddenly these two Rottweiler dogs, famous from the court case, came rushing down the garden making a terrible noise. The only thing that separated them from me was a two-feet-high brick wall at the end of the garden, which they could easily get over. I could also work out, even knowing the danger I faced, that if I turned and ran for the car, the dogs would catch me, and a running man was like a red rag to a bull, or in this case, a red rag to two dogs. So in a rare moment of being compos mentis, I stood stock still as the dogs leapt over the fence and came up to me. For a second they stopped and faced me. I said, "Where have you been? You're a bit late. What have you been doing then?" The dogs were so nonplussed by this apparent lack of fear that they kind of sniffed around a bit and ignored me. When they went back into the garden I returned to my car.

The memorial was unveiled on the nearby village green by Lord Denning who was Master of the Rolls. He was a great character, very old and a wonderful fellow. We flew Fordham's family over from New Zealand.

Most of our memorials remain untouched by vandalism. By a sheer coincidence (I'm sure it was not more than coincidence!!!) on the day that Noye was first released from prison for a day off, Fordham's memorial on the village green was smashed with sledgehammers and pulled out of the ground by a powerful four-wheel drive vehicle.

We replaced it and it has been there untouched ever since.

MEMORIALS

As late as 1988, the police were still telling me every time I suggested a memorial that there was no point as it would be vandalised. This happened when I wanted to put up a memorial to the most famous police slaughter in this country, when Sergeant Christopher Head, PC Geoffrey Fox and PC David Wombwell were killed in Braybrook Street, Shepherd's Bush. As a result, the Police Dependants' Trust to help police families was founded. I was assured by the local commanding officer that there were gypsies in the area and the whole thing would be destroyed within seconds – there was no point in putting a memorial up at all. As usual, I ignored this rubbish. We flew the families back from all over the world for the ceremony. The memorial was unveiled by Harold Wilson, then a bit doddery. His "secretary" Marcia Falkender (then Lady Falkender) said to me, "Harold has no idea what to say. Would you write his speech?" So I wrote a speech which praised the officers and Harold read it brilliantly. He was a great actor/statesman. Although he was definitely descending into senility he did a very good job on this occasion. A year or so later, I read there'd been a riot on the large grassy area outside Wormwood Scrubs prison where the memorial was situated. The next day I said to my assistant, "You'd better go and look at the memorial because if there was a riot going on and anti-police protests, God knows what happened, there's a chance the memorial may be damaged." It was totally undamaged. Indeed, after Harold Wilson unveiled the memorial, it became the norm for everyone to bring flowers. There were hundreds of flowers around the memorial. Far from damaging the memorial, the local people, who the chief police officer of the area thought were against it, removed the cellophane wrapping from the flower tributes so that the flowers were able to live longer.

One of my other memorials was to PC Frank Mason who died in Hemel Hempstead, Hertfordshire. He was off duty walking his dog. He saw some bank robbers outside Barclays Bank. He intervened, not armed, as none of our police are armed, and in my view should be. Frank was shot and killed. His memorial was unveiled by Cecil Parkinson, now Lord Parkinson, who I happened to have been at Cambridge University with. In those early days, Cecil Parkinson spoke with a northern accent and later went to work with a friend of mine for a firm called Dexion, who did shelving. Cecil Parkinson was extremely active in the Cambridge University socialist club. He later acquired a very posh voice, became a Conservative and a cabinet minister, and a great friend of Margaret Thatcher. He was always a very nice person and it was good to meet him at the memorial ceremony. It's funny how you meet these people from time to time in unusual circumstances.

A memorial to PC Duncan Clift was unveiled in Hexham, Northumberland. PC Clift had been on holiday in Northumberland. He was in a car park when a local young villain stole a car and came charging out. PC Clift stood in the way saying, "Stop. Stop." He was run over and killed.

The resulting trial was absolutely typical of how people can get off. They found fingerprints all over the car of this young villain. He was well-known locally. He was charged with the murder of PC Clift. In court his story was, "Yes I did get into the car and I did intend to steal it. But I then decided not to steal it and I got out and went away." So he was basically saying, "Prove that I was driving it at the time PC Clift was killed." As there were no witnesses who could attest to that or attest to seeing him getting out of the car later, he got off!

A memorial to PC Laurence Brown was unveiled in Hackney. Here was a place, if anywhere, you would expect a police memorial to be vandalised. It was not. Years later I was told of a strange incident. Flowers were continually laid at this memorial and every night the police would go by and see the flowers had vanished. They eventually found out that the flowers had been taken by an 80-year-old lady who worked in a local hospital. Fearful that the flowers would be nicked overnight she took the flowers home, put them in water, and put them back the next morning. This was absolutely genuine and she was well known for doing it with the approval of the widow of PC Brown. Two policemen turned up at her door at midnight frightening the poor old dear almost to death. I wrote about this matter saying this was really not the way to handle it. First of all, if you take something and do not keep it and do not intend to keep it then you are not committing theft. This lady was obviously doing what she and the widow of the slain officer believed to be a good turn. No action was taken against her.

Detective Constable Jim Morrison was the subject of a memorial just off the Aldwych in London's West End. When I arrived for the ceremony in my Rolls-Royce the police had cordoned off the area, as they always do. This time they refused to let me through. I said, "Have you gone totally crazy? The only reason you're here is because I'm placing a memorial to your slain officer. Get out of my way." I went absolutely berserk. Sometimes the police are not terribly bright in these matters. When I do these ceremonies I always ask the local liaison officer, appointed by the police to work with us, if I can have his home address because I find if I send letters to police stations, the chances of them reaching the person they are addressed to are slight. This memorial was unveiled by John Major. I have a Marlon Brando question that I ask people: "On a scale of one to ten, how happy have you been in the last year?" It always provides an interesting response. Sometimes not an honest response but it is always revelatory. When I asked Major he said, "Well I've been up and down." I said, "No, no. Never mind up and down, John. I want to know a precise number between one and ten which represents your happiness over the last year." He said, "You know Michael, I don't need the despatch box to take home every night. I don't need the bulletproof car. I don't need to be at 10 Downing Street." He went on with a whole series of things he didn't need as if to say, "I've got one foot out the door and I wouldn't mind having the other foot out." He finished by saying, "I'm very fond of cricket and the theatre and I'd like to spend more time enjoying those." Of course, was true that he was not terribly interested: after a short time further as Prime Minister, he wasn't PM any more.

We had a memorial unveiled by Tony Blair, who had just been made leader of the Labour party, to Sergeant William Forth who was killed on a council estate in Gateshead, Tyne and Wear. Forth was standing with another officer. The officer he was with went into one of the buildings to see somebody and while Forth was waiting for him members of the public, presumably who lived on that estate, came and battered him to death with sticks, bricks, pieces of wood or whatever. The people on the estate declined to have the memorial where he fell so we put it just outside the estate. Tony Blair came to unveil it. I asked him my usual question, "Tony, on a scale of one to ten, how happy have you been in the last year?" Blair immediately said to me, "Four." I said, "Four's absolutely dreadful, Tony. You've just become leader of the Labour party. Surely this is a triumph for you." Blair said, "Yes, but it's a nightmare, Michael. I've got to modernise the party and bring it in to the current era and it's very, very difficult. I'm fighting a lot of old timers who object." I said, "I thought Neil Kinnock had modernised the party for you, Tony." He said, "No, Neil Kinnock did very little. I have to do all the work now." That was in 1995. I became very friendly with Tony Blair. I have great regard for him. He brought peace to Northern Ireland. It is true that going in to Iraq was a disaster, although at the time most thought it was a marvellous idea. I think Blair has been very badly treated over his decision to send troops to Iraq. Ten minutes after Blair and I left the canvas-covered podium, a wind blew the whole thing down!

Tony Blair then came to unveil a memorial for us in 1997 to PC Philip Walters who was killed in Ilford. Sometimes the police liaison officers we have working with us are very good and sometimes they're not. The policeman who had been assigned to help us on that day was ridiculous. The memorial was in a long street called Empress Avenue. Obviously, my car and the Prime Minister's and the family's vehicles had to park right near the tent we put in the street for the reception and by the memorial. But this silly police officer acting as our liaison said, "You'll have to park in the crossroads at the bottom. You and the Prime Minister." I said, "It's a 200-yard walk. Are you telling me if it's pouring with rain the Prime Minister has to walk in the rain for 200 yards up Empress Avenue? Why can't he park in Empress Avenue? You're closing the street off. It will be completely deserted." This policeman said, "Yes but we told the people in the houses that no cars would be parked there." I said, "Just a minute, you mean there's a tent up, there's an area cleared for the memorial, there are 300 people going to come to a reception in the tent and you think they're going to worry about the Prime Minister driving his car up to be near the event, or the family of the slain driving up to be near the event? Don't be so ridiculous. If I have to get on to the Commissioner of Police I will. If I have to get on to the Home Secretary I will. The road is empty so we can use it for the ceremony. It's not empty so we can have a roasted pig and a cup of tea." Then he caved in.

This was shortly before the election when Tony and the Labour party were put into power. His people, not unnaturally, wanted Tony to be seen and not only at the ceremony but talking to police officers. And why not? After the ceremony there was a walk of about fifty yards from the podium to the tent where the reception was to be held. All the police who were at the ceremony were going to the tent for snacks and a cup of tea and that sort of thing. Tony and I stood together and Tony started to speak to some police-men. Another police officer from Scotland Yard came up and said, "You must not talk to the Prime Minister in public." This was beyond belief. They'd put out an instruction that Blair was not to talk to the police in public because it was quite near an election. So I said, "Tony, you're not going to get anywhere here, you'll have to talk to them in the tent" where of course there were no TV cameras or anything. I thought that was very surly of the police, that when a senior politician came to unveil a memorial for them they wouldn't even talk to him unless he was in a tent.

Shortly before this ceremony I'd made a decision, having voted Conservative for forty years, to switch to Tony Blair. He seemed to be a very forward-looking and rather right-wing politician. I said to Tony in the tent, "You know, Tony, I voted Conservative for forty years, but in a couple of weeks I'm going to vote for you." He looked absolutely amazed as if he was thinking, "Well, if Michael Winner's turning round to vote for me we may well have a chance because he's the sort of person we need to get to switch established voting patterns." Tony Blair looked at me and said, "You are really going to vote for us, Michael?" I said, "Yes absolutely, Tony. I think you'll get in. Have you bet any money that you'll get in because if you've put some on, I think you'll do well." Tony said, "I have not made a bet, no." I said, "Well I tell you what I'll do, Tony. I'll lay £5,000 for you and if I win I'll send you the winnings for a charity of your choice." So I put £5,000 on Labour winning and of course I won the bet. The odds were very small and I think I ended up sending Blair £750 which he and Cherie gave to the NSPCC.

In October 1998 Tony Blair unveiled a memorial to PC
Nina Mackay in Arthingworth Street, London E15. Nina
Mackay had been with a group of officers trying to arrest
a criminal. They had to break the door down. It was Nina's
turn to break the door down but unfortunately she was not
wearing a bulletproof vest. Standing just the other side of
the door was the criminal with a knife. The minute Nina
burst the door open and came in, he stuck the knife into her
and she died. Here is a typical case that, had the police been
armed, they would have been able to shoot the man before
he knifed Nina. I've never understood why the police of this
country are not armed. The villains are armed. Police all
over the world are armed, so why not our police? The ridiculous suggestion is put about that if they were armed bullets
would be flying everywhere and everyone would be getting
shot. Well I don't see everyone getting shot in Switzerland,
Belgium, France, Italy or any of the other hundreds of countries where the police are armed.

Another memorial we had was to Jeffrey Tooley who
was killed in Shoreham-by-Sea. Tony Blair arrived rather
shaken because his son had been found drunk and asleep
in Leicester Square or some nonsense and he'd had a very
bad press about it. He said to me, "Have you read the papers
this morning, Michael?" I said, "Well it's irrelevant, Tony.
You know, young people are entitled to have a good time. I
wouldn't worry about it."

In October 2010, the current Prime Minister, David
Cameron, unveiled a memorial in north east London to PC
Gary Toms. Boris Johnson the Mayor came as well. I like
Cameron. I voted for him with considerable trepidation
but he seems to be standing firm and as much as anyone
can be a great Prime Minister in these very difficult times I
guess he's doing very well. Boris, of course, is always amusing. Before he got the job as Mayor, I said to him, "If you
are elected as Mayor, you've got to change the traffic light
system at the bottom of The Mall leading into Trafalgar

Square. It's absolutely ridiculous. It's on red for fifty-seven seconds and green for eight seconds." Boris said to me, "No it's not. It's on red for one minute five seconds and on green for six seconds." When he got in he didn't change it at all. It's absolutely impossible to get past Admiralty Arch at the bottom of The Mall if you're going towards the Strand. Even on a not particularly busy night or day, it takes quarter of an hour just to get through that one gate. Made even worse by the fact they've taken one lane away for cyclists. I wrote to Boris after he got the job and reminded him of what he said and asked why nothing had been done about it. His response was that they'd done some ridiculous testing and if they made the lights longer on green, there would be a tailback (of course I'm exaggerating) all the way to Wiltshire. Well since the lights used to be properly timed there, I don't recall any major tailbacks. I think the traffic in London is worse under Boris than it was under Ken Livingstone and they're both people who hate cars. Boris goes about on a bicycle and Ken used to walk. The fact is that most people drive cars. While we expect to have red lights and delays, the delays now are absolutely beyond human belief. It's worse than it was in World War II with the bombing.

RACHEL WEISZ

I went to see a play called *The Shape of Things* by Neil LaBute who wrote one of my favourite movies ever, *Nurse Betty* starring Renée Zellweger.

The play was at the Almeida Theatre. They had moved from their normal premises in Islington to an enormous barn-like place near King's Cross while the Islington venue was rebuilt and improved. One of the stars of this play was the beautiful actress Rachel Weisz, who had already done very well starring in the film *The Mummy* and was later to star in *The Mummy Returns, The Constant Gardener,* both the film and play of *The Shape of Things,* and many other projects.

I found myself sitting next to a lovely, short, old lady who drew me into conversation. She had a marvellously lilting Jewish, middle-European accent. She told me that she was Rachel Weisz's mother. She was naturally very proud of her daughter. She said to me, "You must come backstage and meet Rachel after the show." I hate going backstage to meet actors and actresses. After the play is over I'm ready to go home. The dressing rooms are crowded and there's not much you can say except, "Darling you were wonderful," whether they were or not. In this case, Rachel was wonderful but I really didn't want to go and meet her in those circumstances. But her mother, Edith, insisted that she take me to Rachel's dressing room to meet her. So I duly followed her up some stairs along a welter of corridors and eventually to the door of a dressing room. Edith knocked but there was no answer. So she opened the door and there was no one in the room at all. Rachel had obviously gone elsewhere! I said, "It doesn't matter Edith, dear, I'll go home now. I wish you well and it was lovely to meet you. Congratulate your daughter for me." Edith would have none of it. She said, "No, we'll find Rachel." We then went back along the various corridors and through a maze of places and ended up in the very large bar area, now largely denuded of public. In a group of five men stood Rachel Weisz, talking to them. I think they were probably something to do with the play, though not Neil LaBute, who had greeted me when I came in and told me how much he had liked my movies. As we approached the group Edith handed me the bunch of flowers that she had got for Rachel and said, "You give them to her, Michael. Say they're from you." I said, "I can't possibly do that, Edith, because they're not from me." We then went up to the group and Edith said to her daughter, "Look Rachel, it's Michael Winner." This went down like a lump of lead. Nobody cared, including Rachel. They were engrossed in their own conversations. I hung around a bit and then, as they used to say in the *News of the World* when they got into brothels, made my excuses and left. Edith followed me a bit and wrote down something on a piece of paper. She said, "This is Rachel's address. Send her some flowers tomorrow." Rachel at the time was living in Haverstock Hill, north London and for all I know she may still be living there today, because that is where Daniel Craig lives. To my eternal shame I did not send Rachel flowers the next day or any other day. Will God ever forgive me?

This incident further confirmed my utter belief that one should never go backstage. I remember John Gielgud's last West End appearance in a play. One of the worst plays I've ever seen in my life, called *The Best of Friends*. It was a two-handed piece in which Gielgud continually forgot his lines. So I did not go backstage on the first night. The next day I spoke to Johnny Gielgud on the phone (he was a dear friend and the most marvellous man) and told him how good I thought he was in the play. Which he was when he remembered his lines. Gielgud said to me, "Why didn't you come backstage, Michael?" I said, "Well I didn't want to disturb you, John, I always find it difficult going backstage." Gielgud said, "You should have come. I was hoping to see you." I felt absolutely terrible at that point. Here was one of the greatest actors in Great Britain, one of the greatest actors in the history of the world, doing – as it turned out – his last-ever theatrical performance, and I had not even bothered to go backstage.

My house is full of gifts from John Gielgud including gold embossed telephone notepads and various other things. He was the most marvellous man. After he died his letters were published. I thought it very amusing what he said about me because he was a bit of an old bitch and loved being an old bitch and we had some wonderfully bitchy conversations together. Johnny wrote about me: "*The Wicked Lady* is great nonsense, directed by a mad nut called Michael Winner, a foul-mouthed director with a certain charm – at least very respectful to me, but most unpleasant to his underlings – a restless, maniac mixture of George Cukor, Harpo Marx and Lionel Bart."

Some people thought that was insulting. I thought it was extremely funny, very nice and typical of Johnny Gielgud.

THE ROUX OF ROUX

Without doubt the most lunatic and pathetic meeting I was ever forced to have regarding my life as a so-called food critic was one where I met Michel Roux, then chef and owner of the Waterside Inn, Bray. In June 1994, having previously given good reviews to the Waterside Inn, I had a very poor meal there and so reported in the *Sunday Times*. Some time later, two Jewish television writers, Laurence Marks and Maurice Gran, wanted to go to Le Gavroche, owned and run by Michel Roux Jr, the son of Albert Roux and nephew of Michel Roux of the Waterside Inn. When I rang to make the booking, Michel Roux Jr came on the line and said he would not serve me. He did not give a reason but I assumed (rightly, as it turned out) it was because I'd given his uncle Michel Roux of the Waterside Inn (confusing isn't it?) a bad review. Michel Roux Jr at Le Gavroche continued to get as much publicity as he could by telling the press I was banned. And that I'd asked to come with Joan Collins and Jane Asher! He then had the impertinence to write to me and say that, as far as he was concerned, his banning me was a private matter, when he had (briefly) a column in some paper that has since collapsed and the first one he wrote was all about banning me from the restaurant and the fictitious fantasy that I was hoping to bring Joan Collins and Jane Asher. How he considered it a "private matter" when he'd publicised it everywhere I do not know.

Anyway, back to the main story. I was very friendly with a wonderful man called Nico Ladenis, a three-Michelin-star chef who had a restaurant in the Grosvenor House hotel. I'd known Nico since he was selling advertising space on the *Sunday Times* in the early 1960s. The lady he married lived above me in Cornwall Gardens! I'd tried to seduce her but failed. She was right to succumb to Nico!

Nico was a very close friend of Michel Roux of the Waterside Inn and he said to me, "Why do you not go back to the Waterside Inn and see if you can give it a good review?" I said, "I'd love to. I gave it very good reviews before. It was only that one meal. I remember that Michel Roux provided a terrific meal for your birthday party that I went to, Nico. But how can I go if I'm banned." Nico said, "I'll speak to Michel Roux of the Waterside Inn and get back to you." Nico then rang me and said, "I've spoken to Michel Roux; phone him up and make a booking."

I rang up the Waterside Inn and spoke to Michel Roux and said, "I'd like to book a table for two for next Saturday." Michel Roux said, "I would like to come and see you in your house." I thought: "That's bloody odd, all I'm doing is making a restaurant booking! But I'd better go along with this." I said to Michel Roux, "Of course, be delighted to meet you."

So one morning Michel Roux turned up at my house. We sat for an hour having coffee and biscuits and gossiping about everything. He was my new best friend. I then walked him down the pathway to the wrought iron gate and into the road and said, "Lovely to have met you, Michel. I'll phone up and make a booking." To which Michel replied, "We have to have a family conference. I will call you." I thought: "I don't believe what I've heard. He has to have a family conference! This is the owner of the restaurant! I mean, how much can you build up a non-event?" It was totally beyond belief.

I rang Nico and said, "Nico, you won't believe what happened. Michel Roux says he has to have a family conference before he can let me in. He said he'd let me know the result of it."

Six weeks later I'd not heard the result of this family conference so I rang Nico and said, "When you suggested I phone your friend Michel Roux in order to make peace and happiness, I'm sure you assumed that I would be honoured with a seat at the Waterside Inn. Well, not only have I not been honoured with a seat at the Waterside Inn, I was told there is a family conference on this unbelievably important matter and that Michel would report back to me but he has not reported. I've waited six weeks, Nico. Are they still conferring? What should I do?" Nico said, "Leave it to me." He rang me back the next day and said, "They had a family conference. Michel Roux wanted to let you in but Michel Roux Jr at Le Gavroche did not." I thought to myself: "Well it isn't Michel Roux Jr's restaurant. It's his uncle's restaurant. This whole thing is absolute fantasy land. Do these people not realise how utterly insane they are?" Obviously they don't. So as far as I was concerned that was the end of it. I'd only been to the Waterside Inn three times in my life and whether I went again was not of the slightest concern to me.

Later Nico Ladenis said to me, "Michel Roux wanted to let you in. But his nephew Michel Roux Jr did not. He said you were rude to his receptionist (totally untrue) and that you were extremely rude to his daughter." I said, "Rude to his daughter! I never knew he had a daughter. How can I be rude to her?" Nico Ladenis said, "His daughter used to work at the Hertz counter at Nice airport and she said you came for a car and were very rude to her." I said, "At last Michel Roux Jr has said something truthful. He's absolutely right. I did go to Nice airport and I went to the Hertz desk. I couldn't open the car because it had some sort of new fangled key. On top of that the car was filthy. So I went back to the desk and this lady came to the car and got me in. I moaned to her about the car and I was probably extremely snappy because it was raining – and you don't like to go to the South of France and find rain – and the car was dirty and I was generally fed up with life. If he would care to give me his daughter's address I would be happy to write and apologise."

I heard no more. But about two years ago, Michael

Caine's daughter was getting married. The wedding was to take place in the church at Bray followed by Michael Caine taking over the whole Waterside Inn for his close friends and giving a dinner there. I thought to myself: "This will be interesting. Will the new owner, now Alain Roux, Michel Roux's son, have me thrown out when I'm there as a guest of Michael Caine? I rather doubt it." So I was looking forward to the event.

As it transpired, on the same night I had to be the star guest on the Michael Parkinson television show so I couldn't go. Various people have spoken to me since and said that I would be welcome at the restaurant but they're just customers and I really can't be bothered to find out. If I want to eat in Bray, I go to Michael Parkinson's pub, the Royal Oak in Paley Street, which I "discovered" and as a result of my praising it to the sky, all the critics went down and loved it, and it got the AA Restaurant of the Year award and then a Michelin star. That's good enough for me.

SPEECH 23C

As I was leaving the Palace Hotel, Gstaad, I said to the owner, Andrea Scherz, "Here's £150," (and I gave it to him in Swiss money). Give this out to staff with at least £50 to the concierge." "Ah," said Andrea, "that's what I want to be in my next life, a concierge."

What he meant by that was that in every hotel there is a business running where the profits do not go to the hotel. They go to the individuals running it. The number one group that makes a fortune outside of their regular salary, and I do not just mean in tips, are the concierge people.

You can bet that any restaurant or shop recommended by a concierge is recommended because they are getting a cut-back. They are not recommended for any other reason. This may be a somewhat sweeping statement, and I accept there could be exceptions, but personally I've never come across them. A classic example was at the Cipriani hotel in Venice. In the *Sunday Times* I'd recommended a lovely little restaurant just off St Mark's Square run by five old ladies, the Fiorin sisters, called the Trattoria San Marco. I'd given this a very strong recommendation. I was swimming in the massive Olympic size pool in the gardens of the superb Cipriani hotel when a man, also swimming, said to me, "I tried to go to the Trattoria San Marco because you recommended it in the *Sunday Times* but it was closed." I asked, "Who told you it was closed?" He said, "The Cipriani concierge when I asked him to book a table for me." I thought to myself: "That's strange, it's July. Why should a restaurant close in July?" I was walking around St Mark's Square the next day and there was the

Trattoria San Marco fully open with the Fiorin sisters hard at work. It was quite clear to me why the concierge had said it was closed: because then he was able to point the client in another direction to a place where he got a cut-back whereas he got no cut-back from the Fiorin sisters. On this occasion I went to the concierge and gave them what I call "Speech 23C" which is extremely strong. I said, "Don't you dare tell people restaurants are closed when they're open. And particularly if I've recommended them! We all know why you told Mr so-and-so the restaurant was closed. It was because you wouldn't get a commission from them. It's there. It's open. And you knew perfectly well it was open." The concierge just looked guilty and said nothing.

I've known concierges send people to shops where they charge twice as much as another shop. A friend of mine, Barry McKay, was sent by a concierge of a Venetian hotel to a glass factory. All he asked for was a boat to take him to Murano. It turned out the boat took him straight to this glass factory and shop where he was fawned over and seduced and ended up buying a chandelier for €40,000. Later on he walked around and found he could have got an identical chandelier from a shop nearby for half as much. He told me that he was going to sue the hotel for misrepresentation and for God knows what. I said, "You can't. You were the buyer. There's a very famous saying 'buyer beware'." Well, this man is marvellously terrier-like when he feels he has been misled. He told the chairman of the hotel chain he'd sue them; he told the glass factory he'd sue them too. He did eventually get 50 per cent of the cost back from the glass people because otherwise he would have sued them and the publicity would have been dreadful for both them and the hotel. So well done Barry! You did what few do. Stood up and gave 'em hell! That is very rare. In general, if you are recommended anything by anybody who is not a close friend, and even they can be wrong, check it out very carefully. If you spend anything more than a few quid for trinkets check, check and check

ABOVE Michael Winner with Charles Bronson on location for *Death Wish* in New York.

BELOW Michael Winner with Burt Lancaster on location for the movie *Lawman* in Mexico.

ABOVE Marlon Brando and Michael Winner on location for
The Nightcomers.

BELOW Michael Winner and Oliver Reed on location for *The Jokers.*

ABOVE Faye Dunaway and Alan Bates with Michael Winner on *The Wicked Lady* location.

BELOW Oliver Reed, Michael Winner, Orson Welles on location for *I'll Never Forget What's'isname.*

ABOVE Michael Winner on location for *Bullseye!* with Michael Caine and Roger Moore.

BELOW Michael Winner, Diana Rigg, Chris Rea and Bob Hoskins on *Parting Shots*.

ABOVE Michael Winner and Tony Blair at a police memorial ceremony.

BELOW Michael Winner with Boris Johnson at a police ceremony.

ABOVE HM The Queen unveils the National Police Memorial in The Mall with Michael Winner.

BELOW Michael Winner with David Cameron at a police ceremony.

ABOVE Michael Winner at the St John Hotel with chef Tom Harris, Therese Gustafsson and general manager Matthew Rivett.

BELOW Michael Winner with Robert Earl and son Robbie outside the Earl of Sandwich.

ABOVE Michael Caine given award for 'Best Home Chef' by Michael Winner; Shakira Caine on left.

BELOW Michael Winner and Geraldine Lynton-Edwards at The Ivy restaurant, Los Angeles.

again. And always bargain. It doesn't matter where you are. You can say, "I want 20 per cent off or I'm not buying it". You'd be surprised in how many places, including high street shops in England, you will achieve that discount.

THE CASE OF THE
MISSING EARRINGS

One of my most ghastly hotel experiences took place in May 2010 when Geraldine and I, plus theatre supremo Adam Kenwright and his lady friend Sarah, visited the Château de Bagnols in Bagnols near Lyon. This is an incredibly preserved eighteenth-century château, painstakingly restored by Lady Helen Hamlyn and paid for by her husband Lord Hamlyn. The hotel never made money even though it was so beautiful. Shortly after Lord Hamlyn died Lady Hamlyn sold it to the von Essen Group. It was appallingly run, terrible food, but beautiful beyond belief. The staff was rude and incompetent.

The really extraordinary occurrence started on a Saturday morning when Geraldine could not find her diamond earrings. She was quite certain she'd left them in the bathroom of the suite on the Friday night before, in one of her containers to hide them. She didn't worry because she assumed she would find them when we got back on Saturday evening. We returned to the suite around 4.30 p.m. and Geraldine commenced a very major search for her earrings. This caused increasing distress for both her and me! Because she couldn't find them and as they were not insured, I too was less amused as time went on. It seemed to me that they had been nicked. So the evening was blighted by the disappearance of Geraldine's earrings.

The following morning, a Sunday, Geraldine went down around 10.30 a.m. to have a run. On her way back she went into the reception area and said, "I've done something very silly." The receptionist said, "You've lost your earrings. We have them." Geraldine said, "Where were they? In the rubbish?" The receptionist said, "Yes." Geraldine was so happy to get the earrings back she really didn't care how they'd gone or where they'd gone. Although later, thinking about it, she became quite irate, as was I. During the day, my friend Adam Kenwright and I, driving to a restaurant, conjectured as to how the earrings could have possibly been in the rubbish, a small bin in the bathroom. How could they have fallen neatly into the wastepaper basket! I took photographs of the bathroom to show how impossible this would have been. Both the sink and table had rims on them; Geraldine thought maybe she put them under a flannel which was loose on the table and then they fell when she moved the flannel. We tested that theory with two Smarties kindly provided by the hotel and, of course, they did not go neatly into the basket. As Adam Kenwright said, "She'd have to be the greatest professional ball thrower of all time to get two diamond earrings into a basket." Also, how could the hotel possibly find two diamond earrings in among the general refuse from that room and, possibly, other rooms? I remained highly suspicious of this remark about the earrings being found in the rubbish.

On the morning of Monday 31 May, I telephoned reception. The lady who had apparently received the earrings was not on duty. But the lady who was on duty said she would call her. I said, "I want to know how these earrings got from Geraldine's room to the reception and what time did they get to reception?" I was telephoned back by the lady on duty who said, "The cleaner handed them in on Saturday evening." That I find hard to believe. They clean the room in the morning or certainly not very late. So why were they sitting with the cleaner until the evening? When handed in they apparently stayed with reception. The receptionist on duty said, "The cleaner said they came from Geraldine's bathroom and she'd found them on the floor." I said, "Well if she found them in Geraldine's bathroom why were they removed at all? And as they were removed, why did you not immediately call up and tell Geraldine her earrings had been found? Or if she was not in the room, leave a note? Or as you saw us both going out on Saturday morning and coming back on Saturday evening, why did you not tell us then?" To that the receptionist had no answer.

It seemed to me that if Geraldine had not gone into reception on Sunday morning and asked about her earrings, or asked about them by intimation, since no one was bothering to tell her the earrings were in reception why should they tell her in the days ahead? I took the view (perhaps cynically) that they would have kept the earrings, waited until we left and then sold them and divided the spoils. That may be rather ungenerous but it seems to be a reasonable deduction in the circumstances. When I went downstairs on Monday 31 May, I asked to see the Manager, Franco Mora. Not a very good manager anyway. He was in the kitchen. There was no work going on in the kitchen so I stood with him and said, "Mr Mora, I've been going to luxury hotels on the continent for years, starting with the Palace Hotel Lucerne in 1945. I have never known such a disgrace or such incompetence as in the matter of Geraldine's earrings." I then told him what happened. I said, "Mr Mora, if some earrings were found, do you not feel it was the duty of those who found them, particularly as they knew the room they came from, to immediately inform the guest in that room?" Mr Mora then went into a story about how he had found someone else's jewellery in the dining room, had gone round to all the guests to check at once and then had given it back. This had no relevance because it didn't happen on this occasion. He seemed highly uncomfortable.

I then asked Mr Mora, "Did you know about these earrings?" Mr Mora said, "Yes, I was told about it on Saturday afternoon." "This matter gets more ridiculous by the second," I thought. Here is the general manager of a hotel who knows that diamond earrings have been handed in at reception and presumably was told they came from Geraldine's bathroom. Whether he was told or not, no attempt was made on his instruction, or by anyone else, to check with guests whether they had lost any jewellery. No attempt was made to tell Geraldine her earrings were at reception. As a result, long after they had reached reception Geraldine spent a very fraught time looking for them. I spent a fraught time worrying about it and the evening was considerably less pleasant than it should have been. As we were leaving on that Monday, I said to Mr Mora, "Why did you not, when you knew the earrings were in reception, do something about it?" His answer was beyond human belief. He said, "The cleaner was not sure whether they belonged to the current occupant of the room or the one who was there before." As if that made any difference! Mr Mora had been told diamond earrings had been found in Geraldine's room. They were found over twenty-four hours after we took occupancy of the room. Why did everybody remain totally silent on this matter? Perhaps I have a suspicious mind but I repeat my assumption that it is possible the staff would have kept the earrings and when we had left, not having asked for them, would have sold them and then divided the spoils.

I could be completely wrong. But the facts of what occurred leave me with no alternative but to believe that.

The hotel has since changed hands because von Essen Hotels went into liquidation. At the time of writing it's run by the liquidator.

◇◇

LOST RESTAURANT

I had one of the greatest meals I've ever eaten in a tiny private house turned into a restaurant on the ground floor on a journey back from Manchester with Jenny Seagrove. I have no idea where this was place was except I remember Seagrove and I signed the visitors' book. There a lady was making the food in the kitchen. It was absolutely fantastic. I went into the kitchen to look at the desserts and she'd baked five incredible-looking cakes which actually tasted marvellous. Cakes frequently look good when you see them displayed in shop windows, but they taste bloody awful. These were sensational. I have been trying to find the name of that woman and the name of the place ever since. But I have not been able to. It was probably twenty years ago. If anybody knows of such a place and what it was called I would love to be told about it. I'm sure it doesn't exist anymore as a restaurant but I'd like them to know that it was one of the great dining experiences of my life.

◇◇◇

DANCING ON MY FEET

One of the most unusual moments I ever had when eating a dinner was at a dinner party given for Sir Michael Parkinson. His portrait in oil by Jonathan Yeo had been put on show at the National Portrait Gallery. A number of people were asked to go there and then on to a party given by David Ross, the co-founder of Carphone Warehouse. At the party there was a large studio room set out with two tables of twenty people on each table. It was quite simply too many for the room. The noise was deafening. It was all hard surfaces and the sound of forty people talking echoed off them. I sat next to Mary (Lady Parkinson) and more or less opposite Michael Parkinson, with Geraldine on my right. After the main course, I said to Geraldine, "I'm going to leave." She said, "You can't leave." I said, "Watch me, I'm going to." Michael Parkinson said he'd walk me to the door; he didn't object if I left early. So I got up to go.

Then I was the only person in the room standing because I was about to head for the door. Geraldine knocked her cutlery against the glass making a clinking sound, the sort of noise that people make when they want everyone to fall silent because a speech is about to be made. Normally this doesn't work the first time and people have to keep clinking the glass and calling "Sssh" before people shut up for the speech. On this occasion Geraldine clinked the glass and the entire room fell silent. Thirty-nine people were suddenly looking at me intently, waiting for my brilliant speech. I had no idea this was going to happen. I had no idea what to say. But I danced on my feet and spoke about Michael Parkinson having a photo not only in the National Portrait Gallery but he should have one in the Playboy Club, at the Raymond Review strip club which was reopening and various other places. I then went on to say, "Actually I'm normally at this time watching Hitler but you have detained me from that. I watch Hitler every night but tonight I had to give him up." This actually went down rather well although it was a fairly bad taste remark. It happens to be true.

After I left a lady said to Giles Coren, the food critic of *The Times* who was there, "I thought the joke about Hitler was in very bad taste." To which Giles Coren replied, "What do you think of Muslim jokes?"

Since we're on the subject, I'll talk about Hitler. I do find it fascinating to watch the goings on of the Nazi party and the World War II stuff because I lived through World War II. I have two photographs of Hitler on my mantelpiece. I also have two photographs of Winston Churchill because at the time of the war the two great adversaries were Churchill and Hitler. One represented goodness and the other represented total evil. So I watch Hitler documentaries every night. Once he wasn't there and I had to watch Mussolini. That was a disappointment I can tell you.

◇◇

HOME-MADE

A restaurant moment I always remember was in a tiny place I visited with the famous film director Lewis Gilbert and his very grand wife Hylda. It was way out of London and I forget why we were even there. We dropped in for tea and cake on a long journey. It was a small place run by a woman who served these cakes which were absolutely dreadful. Hylda took a bite and pulled a rather imperious "hate it" face without saying anything. The woman said, "These are home-made you know." Hylda's expression I will always remember. She didn't actually say anything but the expression said quite clearly, "Home-made? So what!" And she's absolutely right.

The fact that something's home-made does not mean that it's good. It just means that it was made at home.

◇◇

RICHARD LITTLEJOHN

One of the moments I'm most proud of in my spotty career on television is when I was on a Richard Littlejohn show some years ago. Littlejohn had with him two lesbians who had some senior positions in the London County Council, I think. He was literally baiting them like you would bait a bear. He was saying, "You have children? How did you have children?" and then he would shake some liquid about in a plastic container and squirt it at them and say, "Was it squirted in you like this?" It was beyond belief. I sat there getting absolutely furious because the children of these lesbians were in the audience and they looked extremely nice and spoke very well. It was quite clear the lesbians had been wonderful parents to the children. Finally, Richard Littlejohn turned to me, thinking I was rather right wing and would agree with him. What then happened is played frequently on the *100 Most Famous Moments in Television*, one of those compilation shows put out from time to time. I said, "Richard, I have just witnessed the most horrible sight ever on British television. That television should sink to the level of baiting and humiliating a lesbian couple who are perfectly decent, good, upstanding citizens in order to get a laugh from the audience is just beyond belief. It is disgusting. The lesbians and their children are beautifully behaved and are clearly very nice responsible people. You, Richard, are an arsehole." The audience clapped like mad. Littlejohn was kind of left gasping.

RICKY GERVAIS

Many years ago I got a telephone call asking me to be on a talk show with some new stand-up comedian who I'd never heard of. The studio was way down in Kent which is a very long way from my house in Holland Park. So I'm driving for hours and hours to Kent through terrible East End traffic. The whole thing is a nightmare. Eventually, I get to the studio and a small man with dark hair opens the door of my Rolls-Royce and says, "Mr Winner, welcome." I thought: "This fellow will go far." He's standing on the steps of the studio and he's opening the car door for me. He continued, this comedian, I had no idea who he was, by saying, "I do hope you enjoy my show, Mr Winner." I said, "Well, as long as you're nice to me, I'm sure I will enjoy it." To which he replied, "Well I may not be nice to you." I thought: "Oops, I better come off autopilot here and be ready for anything." I never mind if people try to be difficult or rude to me on television because that immediately makes the audience feel sympathetic towards me. I've handled it a million times before and I knew whatever this fellow slung at me, I could deal with it.

So we do the show and while he was very outrageous, I thought it was a very entertaining time. Now guess who that was? It was Ricky Gervais. Three years later he was on the Parkinson show. He'd become a TV star. Parkinson said to him, "Ricky, you had a talk show didn't you? What happened to that?" Ricky Gervais replied, "I was so rude to all the guests we couldn't get any guests. So after twelve shows we had to finish it because nobody would come on the air with me." Parkinson said, "Well of the twelve guests you had, who was the best?" Ricky Gervais said, "Without doubt, Michael Winner. He didn't mind any of it. Whatever I said, however rude, he just laughed and got on with it. He was the best of them." I've never seen Ricky Gervais again from the day he opened the door for me and we did the show together. But when I do, I'll remind him that he owes it all to me.

As it happens, I do quite a bit on Twitter, which I find very entertaining, and one of my Twitter followers said, "I found your show with Ricky Gervais and here is the link to it and if you click on it, you'll see it." So I clicked on the link and in came Ricky Gervais doing his stand-up act at the beginning of the show. It was absolutely brilliant. There's no way you'd get away with one word of it today. He referred to Stephen Hawking being unlikely to be in an Olympic race and there were various other things all in extreme bad taste (if you think there is such a thing as bad taste) and all totally politically incorrect. It was a very, very funny opening monologue. The first guest, who I'd forgotten because I probably didn't even do the show with him and he recorded it separately, was Antony Worrall Thompson. I thought: "I can't be bothered to watch that," and I never got to see my interview on it again. Didn't matter, I've done so many I don't bother to keep them or store them in any way at all. I think Ricky is at his greatest when he's coming out with somewhat offensive one-liners or doing stand up comedy. I haven't seen all of his films by a long way so they may or may not be good, I don't know. *The Office* was a certain type of programme, which for me was certainly not a laugh aloud programme. But I appreciated the skill of it and the cleverness and wit. As far as I was concerned, it was not a patch on the monologue he performed at the show which we did together so many years ago. That was really funny and outrageous and funny, funny, funny.

ROBERT MITCHUM

Robert Mitchum was not the laconic, easygoing tough guy that he portrayed on screen in his private life. He was a very complex, somewhat schizophrenic man who I greatly liked. We became very good friends. If I ever went to Los Angeles he would come up from Santa Barbara, where he lived, to have dinner with me. When he came to London we would meet frequently.

Working with Bob was interesting. He was a long time professional. The first moment when he showed, quite rightly, his slightly steely side, concerned his transport. My co-producer of the film *The Big Sleep*, Elliott Kastner, had provided his own Range Rover and driver for Mitchum so he could get some money off the budget. All the other stars had a Daimler limousine. When I asked Elliot why he was providing his own Range Rover and driver he said, "Bob Mitchum loves Range Rovers. He particularly wanted it." After a few days, Bob said to me, "Why am I in a Range Rover when everyone else is in a Daimler limousine?" I replied, "Bob, Elliot Kastner assured me this was your chosen vehicle." Bob said, "I don't like it. Can I have Daimler limousine like everyone else?" I immediately switched the car. Mr Kastner then asked me to sign a cheque on ITC (Lew Grade's Company) for the entire price of a new Land Rover. I complained, "I can't do that, it's not right." Elliott said, "It's producer's perks." I didn't sign! Elliott did not get the outrageous payout, although he insisted I sign an "OK" for him to get the cost of hiring the Range Rover for ten months, which in those days came to about £3,000. Mr

Kastner was not a nice man! These disgusting con tricks of getting money into the hands of those it should not be in from a movie budget are not uncommon.

Bob was immensely professional during the shooting but I wouldn't say that he was a totally happy human being. He started an affair with a nude model, who by chance, I'd photographed with three other girls that afternoon in order to use the photo as a book cover in the movie. Then suddenly Bob turned up with her! How he met her, I don't know. Also, an extra on the film decided to make a beeline for Bob. These two girls naturally didn't like each other. One evening the extra turned up at Bob's flat above the Caprice restaurant in Arlington House that we were renting for him, hammered on the door and the two girls had an almighty fight in the corridor outside, egged on by Bob and his friends, who were doubtless somewhat inebriated.

Bob would always say to me, "I wanted to have a quiet night but all these people came and I ended up having too much to drink." I said, "Bob, just a minute, what do you mean came?" He replied, "Well, they just knocked on the door and turned up." I said, "Bob, you're very strong. You're very tall. The doorframe is not that big. You could have stood in front of the door and stopped them coming in. Are you telling me that they knocked you down and rushed over you like a cartoon figure, flattening you out and that you then rose and joined in the drinking?" Bob just shrugged. In fact, he was a very educated man. When he wasn't being a bit of a Jack the lad he was more like a university professor. He was very well read, he wrote poetry – he was always falling in love with somebody and sending them poems. In the meantime his wife was at home reading about his latest exploits in the press.

Bob said to me one day on the set as a horse went by, "The only difference between that horse and me is the horse can shit in the street." The implication being that Bob was worked like a dray horse. I said, "Bob, I want to ask you something. I know what you don't like because you frequently tell me. Can you tell me what you do like?" He replied, "Yeah, I'd like to be sitting on a beach in Tijuana, Mexico smoking marijuana."

When sober, Bob was as delightful as anyone can possibly be. He was highly intelligent, very lucid and very witty. When he gave his lecture at the National Film Theatre he said, "Michael Winner keeps the crew in order. If they don't do as he says, he threatens to throw them out of their homes. He owns so much property all the crew are living in it."

When Bob got drunk, which was not totally unknown in the evening, he became impossible. He had a very crisp voice on the screen but when drinking, it got less and less clear. He rambled. He told very complex stories of things that had happened in his past, naming studio executives and other people; the stories eventually became totally incoherent. If you said, "Who was so and so, Bob?" He would growl, "I've told you already. Aren't you listening?" It was impossible to listen to him when he was drunk and I avoided it. Rather like I avoided Oliver Reed in the evenings.

There was no question Bob was a great actor and an enormous personality on the screen and off. He had terrific presence. When he entered a room you certainly knew he was there. When he was on the screen you certainly knew he was there.

He was always moaning about what his son cost him to keep. I said, "Bob, it's quite normal for a father to look after his son and give him financial assistance." Bob responded, "What, when he's forty years old?" I said, "Bob, you just won the argument."

Eventually Bob went into the Betty Ford clinic for treatment for alcohol addiction. He said to me, "I didn't want to go but my family insisted I went. I couldn't even go as a residential patient because my wife was in there." I never knew his wife had a drink problem at all. Being married to Bob, I'm not surprised that she did.

Bob stayed on the wagon for about four weeks. And then we went to lunch at the Waterside Inn. They announced their special was a Raspberry Bellini and I said, "I'll have that." Bob chipped in, "So will I." I said, "I thought you were on the wagon." He replied, "Yes, well I'm not anymore." He was a great companion and a very warm person. He was a highly respected citizen of Santa Barbara. He tragically got cancer. I didn't see him at that point but the actress Sarah Miles went to visit him. She said he was so thin it was like he wasn't there at all. Bob never took himself too seriously. When I said to him once, "That walk of yours is so famous, Bob, it's really fantastic." He said, "People think I have an interesting walk. I'm just trying to hold my stomach in."

He pretended not to care, but he was the hardest working person I have ever met. Always word perfect, even when he was drinking and smoking a lot of cigarettes. I said, "Bob, this will not do you any good. You really ought to cut the cigarettes out." He said, "Well you've got to die of something." He carried on smoking until he died, aged seventy-nine, of lung cancer in Santa Barbara. You could say with absolute certainty regarding Mitchum: they don't make them like that anymore.

◇◇

MICHAEL AND SHAKIRA CAINE

Michael Caine is rightly known for his marvellous sense of humour and his superb skill in storytelling. Perhaps not so well known is his marvellous wife, Shakira, who is Indian. Michael tells of when some local people came round to his house and said, "We have a petition protesting against too many Asians coming to live in the area." To which Michael said, "I can't sign that, I've got my own one here at home. I married her."

Shakira came up with something most telling. I was saying to her, "Shakira, you know I'm having dinner with so-and-so (I mentioned a famous actor), he's a nice fellow but quite boring. He really isn't worth two hours having dinner with." Shakira said, "You can always get up and go." I said, "Let's get this clear, Shakira. You're saying in the middle of the main course, I can get up from the table and leave?" Shakira said, "Everybody knows you're rude. Michael, you can do anything."

I was at a lunch at Michael Caine's house, Joan Collins was there. She said, "I was in The Ivy last night, there was nobody there that I knew." Michael Caine said, "That's because they're all dead."

◇◇◇

ROMAN POLANSKI

In the early 1960s, I received a telephone call from Gene Gutowski, a maverick film producer and promoter. He told me that he was bringing a young Polish film director to London in the hope of getting him a career in Europe and then in America. This was Roman Polanski who had made a film called *Knife in the Water* in Poland, which had considerable artistic success. Gene asked me if there was anywhere I thought he should take Polanski in order to get his films financed in the UK. Polanski arrived and Gene Gutowski failed to find anyone interested in him and called me again. I suggested he try a couple of small time distributors named Tony Tenser and Michael Klinger. They took up with Polanski and he made two films for them, *Repulsion* in 1965 and *Cul-de-Sac* in 1966. I met Roman quite a lot in those early days. On one occasion, we went to see Clive Donner's film *The Caretaker*, which was playing at a cinema in Oxford Street, long since demolished. Although the film had just opened, the audience consisted of only twenty people. Gene Gutowski, Roman Polanski, myself and my girlfriend sat down to see the movie. During the movie Roman Polanski kept getting up and going to another seat. Then he would leave that seat and go to another seat. Then he would leave that seat and go to yet another seat. This he did throughout the film. It was quite easy to do that because the cinema was more or less empty. I never found out why he moved from seat to seat, except maybe he was hoping the film would look better from a different angle. When I asked him what he thought of the film, Roman said, "He got his lefts and rights all wrong." Left and right are rather important in movies. It means that if you have someone on the screen who's talking to someone else and for example, it's a close-up of one person and then the other, it is fairly important that they appear to be looking at each other and not both looking, let us say, to the left of the screen which would be odd. In fact, lefts and rights are not really that important. I always remember Orson Welles saying to me, "I never understood lefts and rights. I just have everyone look straight at the camera." Also Stanley Kubrick would continually refer to what is known as "cross the line". On an over-shoulder shot, instead of the people always look-ing to the same place either left or right according to which angle you were shooting at, he would have them looking the same way. Nobody stormed the cinema. There were not riots in the street. But I thought it was an interesting remark from Roman. Perhaps covering the fact he didn't want to say how dreadful he thought the film was.

I met him a number of times after that. The last time I saw him, or actually didn't see him, was about a year ago in the Palace Hotel, Gstaad, just after Christmas. Roman had been released from a kind of house arrest in Gstaad when the Swiss refused to hand him over to the American authorities for prosecution on child rape charges, and was in the lounge of the hotel giving out CDs of his movie *Ghost Writer* to various staff at the hotel. By the time I got to the lobby, he had left.

STANLEY KUBRICK

One of my great friends was the late and lamented brilliant movie director Stanley Kubrick. Stanley was the most original person in the directing game I've ever met. He insisted on doing absolutely everything himself. He operated the camera, told them how to light the scene, rented the movie company his own cameras, signed every advertisement, however small, that was going into the press (there were no faxes or emails in those days) so the adverts had to be taken up to Hertfordshire by taxi, signed and returned, before they could be published. He knew the light density on every cinema in America and the type of screen. He was just extraordinary in his attention to detail. That is why his films went continually and massively over budget. When Kubrick started *Barry Lyndon*, he said to me, "We're going to make the entire movie within five miles of my house and all the crew and actors will travel by bus." I said, "Stanley, I've got news for you. I did a film with Ryan O'Neal. He's not travelling in any bus." Of course, the whole plan was ridiculous. The film was set in dozens of locations, most of them in Ireland. While Stanley was shooting in Ireland he received a phone call at his hotel. A voice said, "This is the IRA. We're going to get you" and the caller put the phone down. Stanley was absolutely terrified of being attacked personally. He really believed that the world he had created in *A Clockwork Orange* existed. So he very seldom left his house. Faced with what he believed was an IRA threat, Stanley simply walked out of the hotel, got into a car, drove to the airport and was back in London in two shakes of a dog's tail. From London he rang his associate producer, Bernie Williams, and said, "I've gone to London and I'm not coming back to shoot in Ireland. You go on the set and pretend you're me." Bernie Williams looked nothing Stanley Kubrick at all. But he went through this fiasco for couple of days and then everyone returned to England. The film was put on hold for a number of weeks until English locations were found for shooting (and reshooting) all the stuff that was going to be shot in Ireland.

There was a point when Stanley decided the tax in England was too high and he was going to move to Holland. He suggested that I should move too. That the two of us should invest in a TV aerial to be put up at The Hague to get English television. In those days there was no satellite television. This went on for a very long time with memos and letters and details being discussed at length. Like so many of Stanley's schemes, it fell to the ground softly and was abandoned.

Stanley and I could have been English hermits stranded in Holland together. Quite an amusing thought really.

Then Kubrick finished *Barry Lyndon*. He did as he did with all his movies, until they were made public, kept it secret beyond belief. So when the executives of Warner Bros came to see the movie, he had all the windows on the doors to the cinema covered with paper and Sellotape and he had the air-conditioning on cold. He thought that if he kept the air-conditioning cold it would keep everybody awake.

When the film was released I got a copy of it because I was running movies in my home cinema which were on celluloid reels. Whenever I ran a film in my cinema I had to call Stanley afterwards and discuss it with him. He rang me once and said, "One of the great films is the *Texas Chainsaw Massacre*. You must see it, Michael." Which I did, and I thought it was terrific.

Stanley and I shared a projectionist. He was a very nice fellow but invariably drunk. This is not the best position for a projectionist to be in when he's dealing with thousands of feet of celluloid film. On one occasion this charming but unreliable projectionist managed to get a reel of a film called *The Dresser* scattered all over the floor of my projection room. It took him four hours to sort it out and rewind it. These films were what are called the director's copy in which each shot is graded by the director personally to play in the West End of London. It was a hell of a responsibility having them in my house at all. So now I'd seen *Barry Lyndon* and I rang Stanley about it. I congratulated him on the film, which I thought was marvellous, and I said, "Stanley, you know, I saw in the magazine *Films and Filming* a number of shots of naked girls in a brothel. Was that cut from the movie?" Stanley said, "Of course it wasn't." I said, "Well I never saw it, Stanley." Stanley said, "You must have done. It's in the film. You've just run the film." I said, "Stanley, did you hear me? I did not see the scene in the brothel." Stanley thought for a minute. Then he said, "I know what happened. The scene is at the end of a reel. The projectionist obviously turned that reel off too soon and switched to the next reel so you missed that scene. You've got to run it again and see it. Call me when you've seen it." I said, "Stanley, he's going to have to rewind the whole reel, he's going to have to put it on, then he's going to have to, somehow or other, get to the end, it's going to take forever." Stanley said, "Never mind. You've got to see it." So I stayed about an extra hour in the cinema just to see a four-minute sequence (at most) in the brothel. Then I rang Stanley back and said, "The brothel scene was fantastic, Stanley. It really made the whole film. I can't believe I missed it."

I had a bit of a falling out with Stanley regarding his 1980 movie *The Shining*. Before he made any movie Stanley would call me endlessly with questions such as, "What does an electrician get in Switzerland between 6 p.m. and midnight?" or, "What does a make-up girl get in Germany as a basic fee and an overtime rate?" He would go on and on about this. In the case of *The Shining* he was thinking of filming it in Switzerland but of course eventually decided against it and shot it in the studio.

So there was Stanley phoning me five or six times a day at least, asking for facts and figures about the cost of crew and the cost of location rental and the cost of hotels and the cost of travel. Stanley said to me, "This film, I'm going to make in ten weeks and that's it. I'm going to make it in ten weeks." Eventually I said, "Stanley, I don't know why you're calling me with all these requests for information of the tiniest detail about salaries and costs because you know you're going to go five times over budget, minimum, and you know the film is not going to take ten weeks to shoot. With luck it will take about thirty-five." At this point, to my surprise, Stanley became very hurt. He said, "That's very unfair, Michael. Of course the film will be shot in ten weeks." I said, "I'll tell you what, Stanley. I'll have a bet with you. I'll bet you £10,000 it's shot in over thirty-five weeks." There was a brief silence. Stanley did not take the bet. Nor did he phone me for a very long time! But he did call me a few times, particularly in 1999 when he was filming *Eyes Wide Shut*. It was one of those marvellous calls where he started being very ingratiating and wonderful (and I did adore him) and then said, "Michael, you're very well in with the police. I want to close some streets in east London. Only for one night. I'm having difficulty." I said, "Stanley, tell me the street and I'll see what I can do." He said, "No, no, I'll send you great details of the situation." So Stanley's production manager Margaret Adams, who later came to work for me and used to alternate between Stanley and me (two extremely difficult people!), sent round this ring binder full of the most immaculately detailed information. It had maps of the streets he wanted to close – the streets were highlighted in yellow – and details of what he wanted to do. I knew that it was all a load of nonsense. I rang him back and I said, "Stanley, you want to close two of the main arteries running from central London to the east. I may have some influence with the police, although not much, but that is ridiculous. You won't get permission for it from anybody." Stanley said, "Well I only want to close them for one night." I said, "Stanley, come off it. You know that one night does not exist in your vocabulary. These streets, which they're not going close because you won't get permission, you'll need for at least a week. The disruption to London's traffic, to the deliveries that go on at night and to people going home will be beyond belief. I'll write a letter for you which you can give to the police and see if it works."

I sent Stanley a letter saying that he may show it to whomsoever he wished. In it I wrote that he was a very responsible person, one of the greatest directors in the history of cinema, just the sort of person that Britain should support in every way and he wants to close these streets and I strongly suggest that he is given permission to do so.

Needless to say this letter went down like a lead balloon with the police and Stanley did not get to close the streets. He ended up building the streets in the studio.

My final contact with Stanley was very sad. He never, ever left his house in Hertfordshire. The idea of him coming into the West End for an evening was absolutely unthinkable. But as one of the leaders of the Directors Guild of Great Britain, I wanted the Guild to give him the lifetime achievement award which they'd given to many very famous directors such as Fred Zinnemann who did *High Noon* and many, many more. Eventually, to my great surprise, Stanley agreed to come to the Piccadilly Hotel to personally accept the lifetime achievement award from the Directors Guild. He was going to bring his family and he was very much a participant in the arrangements that were being made. Tragically, before *Eyes Wide Shut* was released and before our ceremony, Stanley had a heart attack and died. His family came to the ceremony, which I've written about in the tale of Peter Ustinov who was going to give Stanley the award. Stanley was a unique and marvellous man. And I definitely miss the oddball telephone conversations we had over a period of many, many years.

STEPHANIE BEACHAM

For my movie *The Nightcomers* with Marlon Brando, we had agreed a deal for Vanessa Redgrave who was to co-star. She rang me two weeks before the movie was to start to say that she has filming in Italy with Franco Nero, who she later married, and the film was running over so she couldn't make it. I chose to replace her with a newcomer called Stephanie Beacham. There was some nudity in the film and simulation of intercourse. Stephanie was very concerned about this but eventually signed a contract that she would appear nude. A few days later, she went to the photographer Terry O'Neill to be photographed for the movie for pre-production publicity. When Terry showed me the contact sheets there were a great many shots of Stephanie topless, showing, I might add, the most marvellous bosoms. I said to Terry, "How did you get her to take her clothes off? We had to negotiate for an hour." Terry said, "I couldn't stop her. She just took her clothes off and posed in front of me." Stephanie had this wonderful double standard. She was Miss Prim and Proper one minute and Miss Not Prim and Proper the next.

We took her to the Venice Film Festival where *The Nightcomers* was an initial entry. I was sitting on the beach on the lido with the film's producer, Elliot Kastner, and a few other people when Stephanie suddenly ran along the beach, came up to us and said, "They've just raped me. They've raped me." I said, "What on earth are you talking about, Stephanie? Nobody's raped you in broad daylight. Please make sense." She said, "No, no. I was standing on the rocks and the photographers were taking pictures and suddenly they took my clothes off and they were photographing me with nothing on but my panties." I thought to myself: "Oh this is another Terry O'Neill gag. Stephanie's suddenly turned again from Miss Prim and Proper to Miss Let's Flash My Tits Around and Have a Giggle."

TOMMY COOPER

Tommy Cooper was a member of the Masonic Lodge in Shepherd's Bush which my father went to in the early 1950s. They were a rather anti-Semitic bunch so my father moved to another Masonic Lodge in St James's! Tommy was always very pleasant. I didn't meet him then, but I must have met him sometime later because by 1962 I was employing him in rather a strange movie called *The Cool Mikado*, which featured him and Frankie Howerd. Tommy, like most comedians, was quite dour and reserved when not performing. Later, I was doing a guest column called "Atticus" in the *Sunday Times* and decided I'd have a joke from Tommy Cooper. I went to see him at his house in Chiswick where he lived with his wife Gwen. From time to time he'd knock her about. She herself said, "We fight. I throw things and he'd throw things back." Tommy also ran an affair with Mary Fieldhouse, stage manager and lady who basically managed him on tours. I sat in the house with Tommy and Gwen and their son Thomas and after chatting away said to Tommy, "Give me a joke for this column I'm doing for the *Sunday Times*." You'd think I was asking him to tell me the secret of atomic physics or advanced mathematics and algebra. Instead of coming out with one of the many jokes for which he was famous, he sat there, his brow furrowed and leant with one elbow on the large table. I said, "Any joke will do, Tommy, all your jokes are fantastic." Tommy still sat thinking about it.

Eventually, when I thought I'd be staying there for lunch, dinner, tea and breakfast the next morning, he came out with a joke which was perfectly fine and which I used. I can't remember what it was now.

FRANKIE HOWERD

Frankie Howerd was another extremely morose comic. I employed him in 1962 in a very low budget film which could afford him only because he had recently been "outed" as a homosexual after he'd gone off with an electrician who came to do some work for him in his house. The electrician's wife went to the newspapers. In those days, homosexuality was considered unacceptable so Frankie Howerd went from top of the bill to bottom of the bill, if he could get a job at all.

I begged him not to wear his wig in my movie but of course he did. He lived very close to me in Kensington. On one horrific night I was in a local restaurant with the American actor Peter Falk. Frankie was there with his boyfriend. He came over to us and sat at the table talking endlessly and saying what a great actor he was and basically trying to get Peter Falk to introduce him into Hollywood.

I did like Frankie but he was odd to put it bloody mildly. I remember once I was at a greyhound racetrack (God knows why!) and Frankie was there. He was at another table some way away. He had not seen me. So I wrote a letter by hand saying: "Dear Frankie, I think your greatest performance ever was in the film *The Cool Mikado*. You were really brilliant. I've seen it literally hundreds of times." Somebody took this letter to Frankie Howerd. Frankie read it, then stood up and looked round the room to find out who had sent it. I was a bit hidden behind a pillar so he never saw me. But he spent a long time looking round for this mythical fan. I went over to his table before leaving and told him the joker was me. He was highly unamused.

I first met Frankie at the BBC when he was doing a show called *Variety Band Box*. He alternated as the comic with a man called Derek Roy. When Frankie Howerd was on the audience numbers increased massively from when Derek Roy was on. That's what really made him. He was a great talent but not a happy man.

KENNETH WILLIAMS

In the late 1950s, an American director, Sheldon Reynolds, was making a TV series called *Dick and the Duchess* with Richard Wattis, Hazel Court and Patrick O'Neal. The British unions were getting very fed up with him because they said a British director should have been employed. I knew Sheldon Reynolds socially so he rang me one day and said, "You will come on the set and you will say 'action' and 'cut' and you will go on the call sheet as the director but I will actually do the directing." This is what happened. Eventually the union said that was unacceptable and I was unceremoniously fired. Before I was fired, however, we were doing an episode of this TV show with Kenneth Williams who was quite clearly absolutely brilliant and somewhat bonkers. Sheldon Reynolds had a wicked sense of humour. There was a scene where Williams, I cannot remember why, got locked in a clothes locker in a gymnasium. Of course, he was not locked in, he just went in and the door was closed. It was very near lunchtime. Sheldon Reynolds sneaked up while Kenneth Williams was in the locker and locked the door. Sheldon then had the assistant director call out, "Lunch everybody, back in one hour." We all waited as Kenneth Williams tried to get out of the locker. Which he couldn't, because it was locked from the outside. Thinking he was left alone in the studio and would not only miss his lunch but be in this locker for a very long time, Kenneth started to panic and was banging on the door screaming. After a while we let him out! He had a good sense of humour, Kenneth; I'm sure he said something extremely funny but sadly, I don't remember it.

PETER COOK

Peter Cook was one of my dearest friends. When I first met him he was revolting. He came over to me at a party and said, "You've never employed me, Michael Winner, because you've got no bloody taste and you're an idiot," and walked away. In my experience, when that sort of thing happens, it invariably turns out to be someone you become very friendly with. Later on, I met Peter a few times through John Cleese or at premieres and realised what a wonderful, but tortured, person he was. He was very jealous of the fact that Dudley Moore had got big success in Hollywood and that he himself was really not doing very much. He played around with a few girls, got very drunk, smoked too much; but in a strange way I think enjoyed that sort of life. At least it was his life and he was determined to stick with it. John Cleese gave him a personal trainer as a birthday present. He also gave me the same trainer, a rather dreary man called Josh Saltzman. I was at a premiere with Peter – if ever I was at a premiere and he was there we always sat together – and he said to me, "You know, Cleese gave me Josh Saltzman for a birthday present. He came along to my house and we set off for a brisk walk. We got as far as the cake shop in Hampstead and I went in for a cake and a coffee." And thus the training session continued without doing Peter any particular good.

I said to Peter, "You know you're a brilliant writer Peter, an extraordinary talent. Ben Elton is writing plays all over the place that are going on in the West End. You could do far better. Why don't you do it?" Peter's wife encouraged him.

But Peter never wrote plays. He wasn't going to bother to make an effort.

The last time I met him was at the party to celebrate John Cleese's marriage to Alyce Faye Eichelberger. They got married in Barbados where I not only went to the wedding but also went on their honeymoon with them. But this was the party in London. Or it may have been for one of Alyce's children I can't remember. Either way I sat opposite Peter. We were chatting away and I said, "Peter, lean forward I want to see the top of your head." He leant forward. Normally if people are thinning a bit I recommend them something called Regaine Extra Strength which has remarkable regrowth qualities for hair. Peter had a very good head of hair and I said, "Peter you don't need it you've got a very good head of hair. It will last forever." The next thing I heard was that he had been told that unless he stopped drinking and smoking he would die. I phoned Peter about this and said, "Peter, I hear you're not well and you've been asked to stop drinking. For Christ's sake, don't die on us because you're one of the few intelligent and really decent people I know." Peter said, "Well it's my life and I'm not going to stop. I'm going to keep drinking and smoking and that's it. If I die, I die." And that is exactly what happened. He kept drinking. He was carted off to hospital and on my break in Barbados for Christmas 1994 and New Year 1995 John Cleese said to me, "You know, Peter's in the hospital. He's very close to death. He's going to die." On 9 January 1995, Peter succumbed to his excesses and died at the young age of fifty-eight. He was a great, great loss. His real talent was never totally fulfilled. I think that's sad.

WON TON TON

When I made *Won Ton Ton the Dog Who Saved Hollywood*, it was the idea of my producer, David Picker, to have all small parts played by very famous old-time stars. So we ended up with an incredible cast of stars from Victor Mature to Phil Silvers to Virginia Mayo to Milton Berle; stars from up and down and beyond. There was an American act famous in the 1940s and 1950s, called the Ritz Brothers. One of them, Alan Ritz, was dead by the time we made *Won Ton Ton* but Jimmy and Harry lived on. They were to play, in drag, women cleaners. I called them and spoke to Harry Ritz, who said the part was too small. He assured me they were very famous and had kept 20th Century Fox studios going. Without them it would have been broke. A slight exaggeration. So I had to send the writer down to meet them to increase their part. We arranged that they'd meet the writer, who was young and Jewish, in the Beverly Wilshire Hotel. "Go and see them. Make them happy," I said. The writer said, "But how will I recognise them?" I said, "Just a minute, they've told me they are the biggest stars in Hollywood and have kept 20th Century Fox afloat. That's your problem. You recognise them, find them and talk to them." The writer managed to spot them and added a few lines to their part. At this time they were not doing well. They were playing occasional clubs and cruise liners. It was 1975 and their glory days were well over. But they were legendary in the business and all the great comics paid tribute to them. They were a kind of cut price Marx Brothers. The problem being that the Marx Brothers all looked completely different and the Ritz Brothers looked much the same. When they came on the set they did what we call in the business "schtick" which means a rather music hall type act even though they were in the middle of a film and playing parts. My cameraman was a marvellous chap called Richard Kline who lit many of the most famous films in Hollywood. When the Ritz Brothers had finished their rehearsal Richard turned to me and said quietly, "There's a reason these people haven't been seen for years. They're no good."

On the same film, we had Johnny Weissmuller who was an American swimmer who won five Olympic gold medals and one bronze medal, among other accolades. He became the sixth actor to portray Tarzan in the movies, a role he played in twelve Tarzan pictures. He is the best known Tarzan of all. Johnny, by the time I met him, was quite old. In 1973 he was working in Las Vegas as a greeter at the MGM Grand hotel. *Won Ton Ton* was his last movie. We were sitting in the desert and Johnny was having to wait rather a long time to go on the screen because we were shooting other artists. I turned to him and said as a joke, "Well Johnny, that's it, thank you very much for the day's work." Whereupon Johnny got up and headed for his car to go home. I had to run after him and say, "Johnny, that was a joke dear, you haven't actually done anything yet. Hang around a bit and you will."

We had a very famous Jewish comedian in the film called Henny Youngman, a legend among American comics. He did nightclubs and Las Vegas. Everybody playing small parts in *Won Ton Ton* got paid the same, $500 a day. I rang Henny and told him that was what the figure was. He said, "Absolute rubbish. I've never been so insulted in my life. The minimum I get is $5,000 a day." I said, "Well Henny, I'm afraid that's not what we pay. Everybody's getting $500 a day and that's it. Either take it or leave it." Henny, without drawing breath, said, "I'll take it." He was famous for a great many well-known lines, one being: "My wife said to me one day, 'I'd like to go somewhere on holiday I've never been before.' I said, 'Why not try the kitchen.'" Another one was: "My wife said, 'You're driving me mad.' I said, 'That's a very short journey.'"

Henny met me in Beverly Hills and we were having lunch together. He'd come from New York and brought with him a salt beef sandwich from the famous 49th Street Deli in New York. We went to a posh cafeteria in Rodeo Drive, Beverly Hills. Henny was clutching his salt beef sandwich, wrapped up in brown paper. The maître d' was absolutely furious. I said, "He's an old man, let him bring his sandwich in and eat it here, what do you care? I'll pay for a sandwich from you even though we don't take it." So they let Henny and his sandwich in.

Another famous Henny Youngman gag was, "Do you know what it means to come home at night to a woman who'll give you a little love, a little affection, a little tenderness? It means you're in the wrong house, that's what it means."

Personally I love those one line or short joke comedians who just stood still and delivered the gags. Today they all use terrible language, run about the stage, tell a lot of drawn out stories which are not funny, and think that passes as comedy. They could all take a lesson from Bob Hope, Henny Youngman, Jack Benny and the other real greats of American show business. Or from English greats, like Tommy Cooper. They were funny.

KENNY EVERETT

I met Kenny Everett when he asked me to do some sketches with him on his television show. I would appear from time to time. In a particularly funny one I interviewed him as Cupid Stunt, the lady with the big bosoms, for a movie. We became friends. Kenny was the most marvellous person. He was consumed with being gay. He was secretly proud of being gay and would recount the most horrendous stories of visits to strange places in the East End where people put their penises through holes in curtains and everyone had mass orgies. He took up with a Russian ex-soldier and a Spanish waiter. They were a ménage à trois. This went on for a long time. I remember one horrific New Year's Eve where my car was stuck in a traffic jam in Regent Street and I had Kenny and this Russian, Boris (who was a total pain), and my girlfriend in the car. Kenny and Boris were having a major row. The Russian lived with Kenny, was always drunk and always being sick all over the place. Kenny was very fastidious and neat. He put up with all this I guess because of love, sexual attraction, or whatever.

Some years later, Michael Parkinson was doing a daytime radio show of charades. I was on it. Kenny was the team leader of my little group. Sitting next to him in the television studio, I said, "Is Boris still with us?" meaning was Boris still his partner. Kenny said, "Only just." I said, "What do you mean, Kenny?" He said, "He's got Aids, he's dying of Aids. He's in the most terrible state. He won't be with us much longer." I said, "Are you alright then, Kenny?" Kenny replied, "Yes, I'm fine, I didn't get it."

In fact, Kenny was not telling the truth. It is rumoured, and probably true, that Boris gave both Kenny and Freddie Mercury Aids of which they were both to die.

So as far as I was concerned Kenny Everett did not have Aids until I suddenly saw in one of the Sunday tabloids a big splash that Kenny had Aids. I wrote to him to say that if he needed anything, money, help of any kind, he could look to me. I also telephoned him. At the time he was just doing a radio programme. I said to him on the phone, "Kenny, why did you suddenly decide to come out and tell everyone you had Aids?" He said, "I didn't decide to come out at all. I went to the Chelsea and Westminster Hospital for my usual check-up and someone there must have phoned the press." This does not surprise me. Whenever I've been in hospital, which sadly is more than I would liked to have been, someone phones the press and within seconds journalists are round the hospital and phoning up and checking on things. Hospitals are full of people wanting to make a few pounds from phoning the press and telling journalists things they should not be telling them.

Kenny lived not far from me in Kensington. I asked if he would like to come to tea or come and see me. He was going to come and then he phoned to say he was just too ill to leave his apartment. "Things are falling off me, I'm in a terrible state," he said. A few days after saying this to me, Kenny died. I miss him. Although I certainly don't miss Boris!

STING AND TRUDIE STYLER

In 1982 I was auditioning actresses for the part of a gypsy girl to play Alan Bates's lover in *The Wicked Lady*, a period piece set in 1895. One of the scenes involved this character being in a whip fight with Faye Dunaway. During the whipping, her blouse was somehow or other whipped off revealing bosoms and a few whiplashes! She also had to be nude in another scene, where Faye Dunaway, as a high-wayman, bursts into the bedroom and finds Alan Bates, her lover, in bed with the gypsy girl.

One of the girls I saw for this part was a young actress called Trudie Styler. A very nice person, and still is! I was most impressed with her. Thereafter, she kindly dropped an envelope through my door containing nude photographs of her. I can see one now. She was sitting on a beach against a rock. She had a very good body. I was seeing some other people for this rather important role. I said to her agent, "I'm interviewing people this coming Saturday on a call-back, so I'll need to see Trudie again." The agent said to me, "That will be difficult because she has a very famous boyfriend. He's taking her to the Caribbean with him." I said, "I really can't be bothered about that. I'm recalling a number of actresses for this part on Saturday. If Trudie comes she comes. If she doesn't, her chances of getting the role are very slight." So Trudie put off her trip and came to see me.

The reason she was not chosen for the part is that it was meant to be a gypsy girl and we found a Greek girl who looked like a real Romany, so I chose her. Later I learned that the famous person who Trudie was with was the musician Sting, who she went on to marry and have children with. I see them from time to time. You could not come across more charming people. I also read in a magazine interview with Sting that when he was down and out he composed his first album while squatting in a basement apartment I owned in South Kensington. For which, of course, he paid no rent. I don't think I've seen him since reading that article. When I do I intend to ask him to pay me the rent. Especially as he's now very rich and I'm £9m in debt!

Incidentally, the actress I chose for the part of the gypsy girl was called Marina Sirtis. She later went on to become extremely famous in Hollywood through acting in a regular role in *Star Trek*. She was able to use the credit of playing opposite Faye Dunaway in *The Wicked Lady* and also another of my films, as I cast her in *Death Wish II*. I'm sure those movies helped her. We became quite close friends. I'm delighted that she's doing so well although I haven't seen Marina for many years.

PART II
WINNER'S DINNERS
REVIEWS

THERE'S A SOUL HERE

Situated at the base of a high-rise block in Monte Carlo is the fashionable **Avenue 31**. It's the most ghastly place; the restaurant and the principality. An hour there equals five weeks in Balham. Overbuilt, with tunnels under endless construction so more tax-evader apartment blocks can go up. Nothing like the villa-filled nineteenth-century delight I used to visit. My main course, blackened cod with sauce, was horrific. The fish was stale tasting, overcooked, not enough sauce. The blackened cod in e & o in Notting Hill is first-rate for a tenth of the price. A local British billionaire told me, "I like Avenue 31. Mind you, last time I went my fish was overcooked." Figure that out. The only place in Monaco that retains any charm is the grand **Hôtel de Paris** with a lovely back garden restaurant, the **Côté Jardin**, where I lunched with local Willy de Bruyn, the only amusing Belgian in the world. The top floor **Grill Room** has great views of the bay and the royal palace. The general manager, Luca Allegri, hasn't mirrored the back wall of the terrace so guests facing that could be in the YMCA. Last year he assured me he would. How long can it take to stick mirrors to a wall so guests facing it can see the view and other diners? Alain Ducasse's superb **Le Louis XV**, with a dining terrace at raised ground level, overlooks the square. Down the coast at **La Réserve de Beaulieu** the new chef, Olivier Samson, is excellent; the prices stratospheric. A small starter of spiny lobster is €105 (£94). The place was full of gross, guttural Russians with screaming children. It cost me £64,000 for twenty nights including grotesque pool service. Gerard, pool man par non-excellence, watched inactive as Geraldine lugged heavy umbrellas to shade our seats. One morning she got so exasperated she said, "I'm going." The manager, Estelle Wicky, assured us Gerard was under control and then left. Things continued as bad as ever; he even grossly insulted Geraldine's nine-year-old granddaughter. "What a different atmosphere," commented Geraldine on his day off when an efficient, charming Moroccan, Youssef Belghiti, took over. Pity the pool's so disastrous, because the owner, Jean Claude Delion, is a great hotelier. A few kilometres east of La Reserve in Eze-sur-Mer is **Cap Estel**, the most beautiful hotel imaginable. Never seen anything like it. Only eighteen rooms or suites. The two-bedroom suite with terraces, a kitchen and the most enormous living-dining room is mind-blowing. At around £6,100 a night it should be. "I presume that includes continental breakfast?" I asked the charming manager. "No," Bernard Apthorp replied, "but we could discuss it." **Tétou** in Golfe-Juan offers the best bouillabaisse ever – but so expensive. They only take cash. When I go I have to bring money I couldn't pay them the time before. In the hills above Eze the **Hostellerie Jérôme**, run by Bruno and Marion Cirino, remains one of the best restaurants in the world. In Biot, one of many beautifully preserved medieval hilltop villages, is **Les Terraillers**. The brochure says: "Chantal, Pierre and Michael Fulci are pleased to receive you in the suggestive surroundings of a genuine sixteenth-century pottery workshop to let you enjoy a very special moment." The three-course set lunch is a cheap €39 (£19). Geraldine had risotto, me a vegetable tart. Then duck, followed by almond and chocolate mousse. Service was slow. "Go in the kitchen and ask about my tart," I said to Geraldine. "No, I won't," she responded, "we're supposed to be sitting here and waxing lyrical. Loving the place we're in. There's a soul here. You can feel it." "You've had a very long time to feel it," I suggested "we came in at 12.45. It's now 1.35 and I haven't even got my starter." Later I said, "They could find me here in fifty years time. I'll just be a skeleton in the corner waiting for my main course." All this was a bit naughty, because the food was terrific. I recommend it. Take a lot of conversation with you to fill the time. This area is lovely. A lot of the rest is overbuilt and degraded since I first went to the Côte d'Azur in 1947. But the South of France is still magical. Sell the house, the children and the dog. Go there.

ACTIVELY HORRIBLE SHRIMPS

I seldom have a truly awful meal in horrific surroundings. But my visit to the pretentiously named **Time & Space** in the magnificent porticoed building housing the Royal Institution of Great Britain was a nightmare. It's part of "digby trout Restaurants". Their website claims they "create bespoke environments that integrate on every level with the style and character of your venue". So inside a beautiful period exterior they've plonked garish purple lampshades that look like a 1950s pub gone wrong, the room further cheapened by tacky black chairs, black tables and dark brown carpet. Only two period fireplaces provide distinction. The staff, led by restaurant manager Cleris Cruz, were all charming. The bread was unspeakable, like chewing gum. My first course of duck's egg on what they called *boudin noir* was bland to the point of oblivion. My main course of Newquay Witch sole, brown shrimps and lemon and parsley potatoes was beyond belief. The fish was dry and flaky. The potatoes deeply unpleasant. Geraldine tapped her sea bass and said, "This is overcooked too." The brown shrimps were actively horrible. Geraldine said, "It seems like it's been kept too long, or put in the fridge and then taken out and reheated." For dessert my apple tart tatin and vanilla ice cream was not the famous upside-down tarte (with an e) tatin I'm familiar with. It was half a baked apple surrounded by pastry unlike any I've ever eaten. It fell away from the apple. Tough, clumsy, ridiculous. The apple OK, the ice cream, weak rubbish. By now the fish and brown shrimps were leaving an unpleasant aftertaste in my mouth. A man, dressed like Cleris, but with a tie, came over and muttered at a speed hard to understand, "Did you enjoy your meal?" Since we'd left nearly all of our main courses this seemed a ridiculous question. "My ice cream was kind of crystalline, it was awful," I observed to Geraldine. "Then why did you eat it?" she asked. "Because I'm a pig," I replied. Geraldine turned to my Brioni jacket. "It's shiny," she said.

"It's not," I responded. "Put your glasses on," said Geraldine. "I've put my glasses on, it looks less shiny now," I stated. "It's probably raw silk" said Geraldine, "Like the dressing gown in your bathroom." "Given to me by the Oriental hotel Bangkok," I explained. "It's the same sort of silk," said Geraldine with finality. We entered Time & Space at 1 p.m. There were only five other diners. No one else arrived during our two-hour stay. Nearby places like The Wolseley and Scott's would have been full to overflowing. The locals in Mayfair seem to know when rubbish is among them. The Royal British Institution is part funded by the lottery and other grants. Some of that money goes to a waste of space like their restaurant. Disgraceful.

Since 1966 I've paid American Express promptly, for years around £300,000 annually. Yet my card was declined when offered to Nimax Theatres for £198. I called Raymond Joabar, American Express's UK managing director. "What's going on?" I asked. The card was reinstated a few hours after an email blast to Raymond. His response: "We were trying to prevent fraud. We look for patterns of fraudulent behaviour." "So someone ran through the Amex office screaming 'Winner's card is being used by a conman'?" I suggested. "We have to protect our customers," intoned Raymond. "Then why did you pass my card four hours earlier for tickets at the National Theatre?" I asked. Raymond's answers became increasingly bizarre. He mentioned using a vendor I'd not used before. "Does that mean every time I go somewhere new you decline the card?" I asked. Apparently not. He said I'd just spent £70,000 in three weeks. "You should be delighted," I responded. "You told me I had unlimited credit." "You do," said Raymond. "It was limited when I wanted to spend £198." I said. "Would you like to cancel your card?" suggested Raymond ominously. "So if a customer with an impeccable 44-year credit record, who's spent millions with Amex, dares to complain you

threaten to cancel his card?" I said. "I didn't say that," said Raymond. "Sounded like it to me," I responded. Mastercard don't behave like this. Things were never so nutty under Raymond's UK predecessors. If you're worried about fraud, Raymond, let my payments through, then phone me. If it's OK do nothing. If by any chance it's not, withhold payment. In the meantime folks, if you're thinking of joining Amex: think again.

TIMELESS

The "Intemporel club sandwich de La Réserve, pommes frites" is a lunchtime offering at **La Réserve de Beaulieu**, one of my favourite Côte D'Azur hotels. Intemporel, in case you didn't know, means timeless. The price of this dish is €58 or £50.43 at the rate I got of 1.15 euros for £1. You might think over £50 steep for a toasted sandwich and French fries. But it does include mayonnaise. Their spaghetti bolognaise is also over £50. My friend, theatrical tycoon Adam Kenwright, looked aghast at his miserable club sandwich. There was hardly any chicken, just some tired lettuce, a single piece of bacon, and tomatoes. He gamely ate half before exploding with indignation. "I thought a sandwich was bread or toast with a filling in between," he said. "In the middle of my sandwich, there's just two bits of toast together, nothing else." The restaurant manager, Roger Heyd, came over. He examined this poor excuse for a sandwich and agreed it was below par. "At any price," I said, "let alone at over fifty quid." "We'll make another," offered Roger. Adam didn't want to wait for that. So Roger deducted it from the bill. In fairness, previous club sandwiches had been good. "He can't do everything," said Roger, referring to their two-Michelin-star chef, Olivier Samson. "Surely he can check before something horrific goes to my table where disaster may be highly publicised," I said. Proof that people aren't on red alert when I come in.

They're on sleep alert. Rather than exhibit a photo of me with a club sandwich I chose Geraldine in our suite at La Réserve. If a week without my photo is intolerable, write in and I'll send you a personally signed one.

We now descend from the glamour of the South of France to the **Waltham Abbey Marriott** hotel in Essex. To descend further would be impossible. They took forever to check me in with computers, which didn't seem to do much. The room was below basic. No toothbrush or toothpaste. My assistant Dinah and hairdresser Joan ate in the vast, unfriendly lobby and said it was absolutely ghastly. Cold coffee. Dinah had grilled houmous and salad, she described it as twenty olives with hardly any houmous. By contrast the **Moat House** at Acton Trussell in Staffordshire, off the M6, was rather good. View of a tree-lined canal, a large suite, a first-rate breakfast. I'm not booking for New Year's Eve, but you can. I was with – but not sharing the same room, as seems so popular among Tory politicians – my favourite Rolls-Royce dealer Steve Gallimore. He found my lovely black with beige upholstery, convertible 1975 Rolls Corniche with 20,000 miles on the clock. A snip at £37,000. A recent Internet trawl uncovered the same 1975 car with 80,000 miles on the clock for £75,000. I can also tell you of the **Lion Hotel**, Shrewsbury. A place you were dying to hear about. A genuine old building – very uneven floors, marvellously aged beams. I slept but didn't eat. Dinah had a cup of tea downstairs. It came stone cold and was replaced. I spent the night at the **Old Vicarage** hotel, Bridgnorth, Shrophire, a lovely Victorian building with enormous windows and great views over gardens and the countryside. Pleasant single bedroom with chairs, called a junior suite in the trade. I couldn't work out how to get water through the shower instead of the bath taps. I meant to ask when I got downstairs but forgot. If you go there, investigate and tell me. They offer a five per cent discount to members of the armed forces who display the appropriate warrant card. I considered signing up for Afghanistan to avail myself of this, but decided against it.

Lunched at **La Brasserie** in Brompton road. It's very buzzy in a demimonde way. Cheerful customers, superb, courteous staff. Just had a makeover. Usually restaurant and hotel "improvements" are a disaster. The Connaught being the most grotesque example. The Brasserie has a large new bar, added banquettes, and still retains the genuine French bistro atmosphere. Peter Goodwin, who's owned it for thirty-eight years, was eating there. Shows faith in his product.

Watching Judy Garland in *The Wizard of Oz* on Turner Network Television I was disgusted to see my favourite song – "Ding Dong the Witch is Dead" sung by the Munchkins – had been cut out. The Munchkins themselves, a highlight of the movie, credited "The singing midgets as the Munchkins", were denuded. Apparently it's now politically incorrect to show midgets singing and dancing. This is an outrageous slur on little people. A fascistic attack on those smaller than most. Get your placards ready – "Bring back the Munchkins", "Fair deal for small folk" – and we'll gather at the MGM offices. Er, no, can't do that, Warner Brothers bought the rights. Okay. To Warner Brothers UK headquarters in Theobalds Road. 10 a.m. next Wednesday, in time to get us on TV's lunchtime news. Little people wanting to join the protest are particularly welcome. They can stand in front so taller folk don't block them.

TWICE-BAKED SMOKED HADDOCK SOUFFLÉ
The omnipotent Richard Caring was seated in what seemed to be the bar area of his **Dean Street Townhouse**, a restaurant and hotel. I thought, "We'll have a drink there and then go into the restaurant for lunch." The restaurant faced us

behind a low divide. We never moved. Apparently these few tables by the window are the best. So I had a twice-baked smoked haddock soufflé, which was among the greatest dishes ever. Followed by mince and potatoes and creamed spinach. Richard regarded it disdainfully and said, "It looks like school dinners." "Not my school," I responded, "it was vegetarian and they served us grass from the cricket pitch. Don't try that Richard. You'll get sued for a fortune. Grass is totally inedible for humans. Does nasty things. Look what happened to me." The appeal of the Dean Street Townhouse is that it serves excellent comfort food. Nick Jones of the Soho House group, now bought by Richard (what isn't?), runs this particular operation. He passed by our table looking like a student who'd been selling the *Big Issue*. That's what multimillionaires look like today. Richard Caring long ago exceeded mere millions. He's into billions. Good luck to him. He looks the part. Elegant, beautifully turned out. The opposite of me. For dessert I ordered fig tart with honey ice cream. "It's very nice," said the waiter. "As if he'd say it's a load of crap," I dictated into my recorder. Sebastian Fogg is the restaurant manager. Used to be at The Ivy (another Caring acquisition) then he jumped ship to the Monkey Club in New York, now he's here. "He's more than a restaurant manager, he's been with us a while," explained Richard. "He's exactly our image." "This man doesn't shave, he's got an open necked shirt, a jacket that doesn't fit, he hasn't combed his hair for seven years and his boss says, 'That's our image,'" I said with incredulity. "It's the Soho House image," explained Richard. Sebastian is good at the job. It was nice to see someone worse dressed than me. Richard said, "Would you like to meet the chef?" "Why not?" I replied. He was called for. "Has he got a white hat?" I asked Richard. "Yes," was the reply. "Do you think he'll wear the white hat when he comes out?" I asked. "Absolutely," said Richard. The chef, Steve Tonkin, did not wear a white hat. He didn't even have his name embroidered on his tunic. I congratulated him on the grub. Then we went to have our photo taken. On the way out we passed my literary agent, the doyen of them all, Ed Victor. "Ed can you take a photo?" I asked. "My father owned a photo shop," replied Ed indignantly. "My father owned a tailor shop. I can't make suits. I asked if you could take a photo," I said. "Will I get a credit?" asked Ed. "If the photo comes out, yes," I replied, "if not you'll get a bollocking." The photo came out. Thanks Ed. As for the rest of you, stand by and see how many iconic restaurants Richard Caring buys in the next twelve months. He gave me a clue. Even I was impressed.

The first person to write about my judging food was columnist Roderick Mann. In the 1970s I used to rate people's meals at their homes. Lost a few friends doing that. Roddy, an ex-Battle of Britain pilot, came from a long gone breed of showbusiness writers who knew their subjects. He was engaged to Kim Novak. His best friend was Cary Grant. I lunched with Roddy at **The Wolseley** when he visited from Los Angeles. Cary Grant left Roddy all his clothes. Since he nicked everything he wore in any film, it was a valuable collection. Imagine the auction price for the Cary Grant suit worn in Alfred Hitchcock's *North by North West* with the crop-spraying plane behind Cary as he ran along a country road. I asked Roddy why he didn't flog them. He seemed frightened of Grant's widow, Barbara, who Cary met when she was PR at London's Royal Lancaster hotel. Roddy interviewed me many times. As with far bigger stars, each article was witty and informative without being unkind. None left like that.

HAPPY BIRTHDAY MR WINNER
The oracle spoke: "Get thee to The Ritz for thy seventy-fifth birthday party." O was right. Why was I bothering with all those funny places? **The Ritz** is the greatest hotel in

London, maybe in the world. Elegant, historic, unspoiled by human error, a glowing tribute to its owners Sir David and Sir Frederick Barclay who cohabit on some strange island in never-never land. My first mistake was printing invitations; dark blue, copperplate embossed on card. Price £439.45 to be sent to eleven couples. £39.95 per couple. They all lost them. Phone calls poured in: "What time is it? What's the dress code?" "But I sent you an invitation," I'd reply. A couple came late saying they'd never got an invitation. We had to hold up dinner for them. "They're very courageous being late for Michael Winner," guests remarked. The final blow was from Simon Girling, Head of Private Dining at The Ritz. He said, "We'd have printed your invitations free, Mr Winner." "Not copperplate embossed," I responded. "Yes," he said. The William Kent room at The Ritz is the finest dining room in London. Only seats twenty-four people, often used by the Queen. Incredibly painted and engraved ceiling, rich textures, amazing doors and table. It looked marvellous. Fantastic flowers arranged by Paul Thomas who does Buckingham Palace. Michael Caine said in his speech, "Here we are in this incredible room, where we all feel very happy but we really know we don't belong. This belongs to someone who, when I was a young boy, I used to be a beater for when he went shooting. It was he who saw the room. I never got to see it. To be here is extraordinary." John Williams, the Ritz chef, is far and away the best hotel cook in the land. The meal was beyond belief. Everyone gawped, gaped and enthused. His canapés were all incredible. We drank Laurent-Perrier Vintage Brut 2000 and Laurent-Perrier Cuvée Rosé plus Domaine de Chevalier Blanc Grand Cru 1999 and Chateau Pichon-Longueville Comtesse de Lalande Grand Cru 1998. We scoffed terrine of foie gras with spiced pears and port wine, butter poached lobster with spiced carrot purée and ginger sauce, cutlet and fillet of lamb with artichoke mousseline and autumn vegetables, chocolate or raisin and Marsala soufflé, and more. Staff and service were great, such as you seldom see. Speeches were like a roast. I said, "David Frost promised if he was invited he'd tell his friends at al Qaeda not to blow up my house." Shakira Caine phoned me from Leatherhead, she said, "This place is full of shops for old people, wheelchairs, charity shops, basket weaving, rest homes, you should retire here Michael. My husband's written a book *Elephant to Hollywood* I'm writing a book *Hollywood to Leatherhead*." A guest I'd known since we were together at Cambridge, Academy Award winning songwriter Leslie Bricusse said, "Having known Michael longer than anyone else I've suffered more than the rest of you. The durability of his and Geraldine's engagement is an object lesson for those of us whose marriages haven't even lasted that long." Michael Parkinson said, "When we go with Michael to a restaurant it's like a snow plough scattering waiters everywhere to the accompaniment of Hildon water bottles being thrown out of windows. On our way home we say, 'How does Geraldine cope with him?' Mary and I decided Geraldine deserves some kind of recognition. So here's a Victorian Long Service and Good Conduct medal for Geraldine for service beyond the call of duty." Geraldine said, "When Michael's invited to dinner he has to know who he's sitting next to, how many people are there. Then you get the bollockings: number 21c, 34d, all the w*****s, the morons..." "We're all here," interposed Michael Caine. Geraldine's speech was funny and moving. "Lost your marbles?" you ask, "couldn't all have been wonderful. Think of something wrong." The only lack of total perfection was when they forgot to serve a brioche with my foie gras. Madeleine Lloyd Webber said, "Oh shut up," when I mentioned it and gave me some of hers.

NAUGHTY PAUL

Then Commissioner of Police of the Metropolis, Sir Paul Stephenson, was speaking at my Police Memorial Trust ceremony to pay tribute to the slain officer PC Gary Toms in Newham, east London. He ended with, "I introduce to you the Prime Minister, David Cameron." Mr Cameron was about to start speaking when I stuck my head near the microphone and announced to 400 police officers and 200 civilians, "Far be it from me to stop the Prime Minister before he's started, but Sir Paul should not have introduced the PM as I have things to say." David Cameron looked a bit confused, as well he might, and sat down. I said, "Sir Paul, you were not meant to introduce the PM. Naughty Paul, naughty Paul." I carried on with various information I always give out at this point in our police ceremonies and read a card sent with flowers from Ed Miliband. Then I introduced the Prime Minister, who gave an exceptionally good speech. When we got to the reception afterwards, police came up to me saying, "Anyone who tells the commissioner off, we like." In all fairness (why should I suddenly be fair?), Sir Paul is a particularly decent person and, as far as I know, a good commissioner. David Cameron impressed me greatly. I had just persuaded myself to vote Tory at the last election. When I turned up at the polling booth they said, "Your house is not on the electoral register." "It's the biggest house in the area. I've lived there since 1946 – wha'd'ya mean 'not on the register'?" I protested. Mr Cameron did a great job working the reception room, talking to the police. I thought he had charisma and charm and seemed very together. If he stands firm he could be a very great Prime Minister. I'll ensure I'm on the register so I can vote for him next time, if he doesn't blot his copybook. At these ceremonies I place memorials to officers where they were killed. The catering at this one was superb. I chose Philip Crowther, who's cooked for me at home. He's a lovely person and always does well. On this occasion his sausage rolls, made the previous night, were flaky and fresh. The best ever. His strudel of salmon with basil was most elegant, his caramelized red onion and herb tartlets, superb. I can, hand on heart (if I've got one – a heart, not a hand), totally recommend **Crowthers Catering**. Also present was Boris Johnson. His first words to me were, "I read you're going to vote for Ken Livingstone. Ridiculous. You can't do that." I like Boris. He's so Borissy. Adds a marvellous touch of eccentricity to any event. I said, "Boris, if you change the traffic lights at the bottom of the Mall so I can get into Trafalgar Square without a half-hour delay, I'm yours." Boris complained to David Cameron that property developers should pay a rent for taking over lanes of public roads. Apparently, it needs a law passed by Parliament. Boris is right. The Candy brothers made a fortune building their ghastly monstrosity, One Hyde Park. We sit in traffic jams.

TASTEFUL IN BRUSSELS

Clive Conway, who organised some of my one-man shows around the country, said he had a nice Jaguar car and driver. I replied, "I don't do Jaguars." "There's a very good motorway to Wales," he said. "I don't do motorways." I responded. "The train service is excellent," offered Clive. "I don't do trains," I told him. So why was I on the **Eurostar** to Brussels? My beloved fiancée Geraldine adores Eurostar. She uses it to visit her family in Paris. Her future daughter-in-law, Ayako Euno, was in *Voyageur Immobile* in a Brussels theatre. A marvellous mime, magic, dance and music event. Amazing staging. Ayako led a terrific Spanish dance where the cast had brown paper stuck to their feet so they rustled. Eurostar is amazing. In two hours five minutes you're in Brussels. The staff are charming, cheerful and efficient. Their elegant St Pancras first class lounge offered free drink, snacks, biscuits, coffee, teas, fruit, and what have you. The train has comfy seats with leather headrests and a table. Eurostar's PR, Lesley Retallack, explained they weren't allowed a naked flame (health and safety) so food was airline style. Meaning reheated. Guaranteed death for good meals. The menu offered organic couscous salad (I hate couscous); I had award-winning Lingfield pork sausages with Kent apple chutney, winter vegetables pavé and steamed winter greens. Less said the better. The dessert Bramley apple tart was ... oh, forget it. The bread, prepared by Sally Clarke's bakery, may have been OK when fresh but had become hardened and tasteless. Why not heat before serving? I enjoyed the trip both ways. Coming back, the security at Brussels was absurd. I had to put my coat, jacket and gold Patek Philippe watch through the X-ray machine. Even airport security never asked for jacket and watch. You showed passports once, then again at the UK border control – the Home Office booth where there was a long queue. Why inconvenience me while six million bizarre people come to the UK daily who are up to no good. That's a crass, non PC remark. Too bad. I will do trains in future. But only Eurostar.

The French make bad taste jokes about the Belgians just as we did (do?) about the Irish and the Americans about the Poles. I found the Belgians delightfully courteous. Geraldine chose a restaurant she'd been to when working at a theatre in Brussels. When we got to **La Manufacture** Geraldine protested, "This is not the restaurant I meant." "We only came because of you," I responded. It looked very Victorian. We settled at a shiny-topped table. I asked for champagne and orange juice, only got orange juice, became overexcited, and set the menu on fire with a low-burning candle. The first courses took forever. I asked the waitress "Where is the food?" She replied, "Nothing is prepared before, it's prepared at the time; it's better for you," and she smiled a nice smile. Geraldine had tuna carpaccio, Ayako, gazpacho and I had paté. It was all cold, only had to be carried from kitchen to table. But it was good. I followed with sole meunière with crisply fried parsley, veggies and magnificent chips. We all liked our main course. For dessert: mandarin, lychee and strawberry sorbet and something called violet ice cream. It was a no-effort place. You didn't have to work at it, as you do

in many restaurants. The next day we lunched at the **Belga Queen**. Another very old room with a lovely stained glass ceiling, comfortable chairs and tables. I had oven-roasted cuckoo from Maliens (Belgian poultry) on gingerbread with pear syrup on top, home-made chips and a mixed salad with a side of vinaigrette. Never eaten cuckoo before. And it wasn't, it was a light chicken. Splendid. They peeled my starter of langoustine and shrimps. The dessert menu included "Biscuit miserable" translated underneath as "Miserable biscuit". I didn't dare try that. I was not put on earth to console biscuits. I had Brussels waffles, whipped cream, home-made vanilla ice cream and chocolate sauce. "Very typical," said the waiter. Great waffle, possibly even better than Gary served at the Beverly Hills Hotel coffee shop in the 1970s. You won't hear bad taste jokes about the Belgians from me. I'll reserve my tasteless remarks for everything else.

Readers ask: "Why a photo of you and Boris when you've written about the Eurostar and Brussels? Are you showing off that you meet famous people?" Possible. Actually, the photos on Eurostar didn't come out well. None were taken at the restaurants. £300 to the first reader to say precisely why Boris and I are pointing and at what. Funny entries accepted. Currently I'm sending out the place cards used at my seventieth and seventy-fifth birthdays signed by Geraldine and me. They feature an unbelievably handsome photo of me in 1957. I look so good I could turn gay just to have me. Geraldine looked lovely then. She still does. And/ or a signed photo of MW. What more could anyone want?

SENSATIONAL BURGERS
I arrived at the **Mandarin Oriental** hotel Knightsbridge at 12.50 p.m. "Good morning," I said to the doorman. "It's not morning, it's afternoon," he responded. That's how not to greet a customer. I went through to the new "in" place, **Bar**

Boulud. I'd heard their receptionists were rude. The wife of a famous movie star rang to book for 8 p.m. A snooty French voice intoned, "You can only come at 6 p.m." You may ask: "Why should a big star be treated differently?" Because restaurants can always jiggle bookings. Example: Hymie goes to the theatre, says, "I want two tickets." The manager responds, "We're sold out." Hymie says, "So if the Queen came, you wouldn't let her in?" The manager says, "If Her Majesty arrives we'll find a place for her." Hymie says, "I got news for you, the Queen's not coming. I'll have her tickets." When I rang Bar Boulud seeking the restaurant manager the haughty French voice asked, "What do you want to talk to him about?" As if I was unworthy to speak to someone that important. I should have said, "I want to talk to him about going to Siberia on a yak." She had no idea who I was. She hadn't known the movie star. Receptionists nowadays come from countries where the population only recognise their mothers. Eventually I got the maître d', Paul de Tarso, who'd served me before. He's professional and charming. I lunched with Terry O'Neill, now super rich from selling prints of his great photos. The place is a swish café, no tablecloths – "Saves a fortune on laundry," said Michael Caine later – comfy chairs, two rooms; one with a bar, one with a kitchen view. The pictures on the wall looked like ink smudges. Terry was seated. "I don't do small tables," I announced to a now attentive staff. They moved us. The general manager, protected by this bevy of horrific foreigners, was Stephen Macintosh. He's good. "Your jacket looks great," observed Terry as we studied the menu. "Made for me twenty-three years ago," I explained. "Looks like you bought it yester-day," said Terry. I could see why he was so successful with the ladies. Managers came in droves, offering their mobile numbers on printed cards. "With all these people coming over I'm exhausted already," said Terry, "don't they know what they're doing giving you those cards? They're signing their own death warrant." The bread was first-rate, so was my bouillabaisse. Not up to Tétou in Golfe-Juan, but very good. We'd heard Boulud's burgers were sensational. My "today's special", a DB burger made of sirloin paté, short rib and foie gras was too fancy. I nicked a bit of Terry's New York burger with cheese. That was excellent. We rated hamburgers. Terry put Le Caprice first, Bar Boulud a shade under, then The Ivy and The Wolseley. I put The Ivy first, then Bar Boulud then Le Caprice then The Wolseley. They'd do better if they cooked their hamburgers as ordered. My dessert was a superb flourless chocolate sponge with hot chocolate sauce, mint ice cream and chocolate sorbet. The macaroons were fantastic. Bar Boulud deserves its newfound London fame. I returned with Michael and Shakira Caine and the Lloyd Webbers. The owner, chef Daniel Boulud, was there from New York. Michael Caine said, "If I opened another restaurant it would be like this." I even discovered Bar Boulud has its own street entrance. Specially put there so I can avoid the rude hotel doorman.

Reader Laurence Prince, who wrote last week about his miserable experience in the River Room restaurant of the poshed up **Savoy** hotel, adds: "They didn't even give us petits-fours with the coffee." Unbelievable, to quote my last book title. Having spent billions and taken years to restore and redecorate The Savoy they can't even afford to give guests petits fours in their most famous dining room. What is the world coming to?

GUERNSEY GACHE
In June 2001 me and my friend Tone (Blair to you) were staying – but not sharing a room – at the **Lowry** hotel in Manchester. No sign of an important fax. With people of such stupendous significance there, me and the PM, they had no paper in the fax machine. The Lowry was a mess. In 2005 I was at a literary lunch there with Earl Spencer. The

food was so horrific it's a miracle we had the energy to make our speeches. The fax fiasco was under the non-control of a manager, Chris Sharp. He later wrote from Guernsey inviting me to the hotel **La Fregate** where he was working. Two weeks ago, on my birthday, my friend Andrew Davis gave me one of his PremiAir luxury helicopters for the hour-and-a-quarter flight from Battersea Heliport. I wanted to check out Guernsey in case I needed a tax haven and a change from over-populated London, now full of strange people in funny clothes. I loved it. Peaceful, orderly, everyone pleasant. The first house I looked at was fantastic, right on the sea, uninterrupted view of a vast bay; it was owned by a Jewish man who told me this joke: "Hymie says, 'I'm going to be buried at sea.' His friend Abe asks, 'Why?' 'Because my wife said she'd dance on my grave,' replies Hymie." Open market house prices are very high in Guernsey. Buy one of those and you can become resident. We stopped at a small beach café advertising crab rolls, scones, jam, cream and Guernsey gache; that's sticky bread with currants. They added a generous spread of rich Guernsey butter. Sensational. Showing me round were David Shiel, a charming local accountant who's raising money for the only good film script I've been offered in years; his very bright Ukrainian friend Natalie; and Antony Matheson, an elegant, thoroughly professional, old-school estate agent. Lunch was at La Fregate. With no need to worry about fax paper, Chris Sharp was jolly and ran the place well. The restaurant looked onto St Peter Port, a car park, a yacht marina, some ugly buildings and a sliver of sea. The food was better than the view. The home-made bread was warm and exemplary. My starter, crab meat with shrimps was historic; caught that morning. Then an enormous portion of local salt water fish – sea bass, skate, monkfish, lemon sole and scallops. Well cooked, no stupid plate decoration. Excellent veggies. Dessert was warm apple Guernsey cake with vanilla ice cream and almonds. The warm apples were little squares round the edge. The cake was an incredibly fine sponge with a crisp top all made with Guernsey cream and butter. Then they gave me yet another birthday cake. Service was good. Cost £327 for five people. No tip on the bill, so I left £50 cash. Our photo shows, left to right Natalie, David, hotel manager, me and estate agent. Good cast for an Agatha Christie thriller. Who gets murdered first, I wonder?

Raymond Joabar, the UK chief of American Express, should watch more television. He'd see his company's commercial announcing, "If we find something unusual in your spending we'll alert you straight away." Er ... no Raymond, you don't. My Amex card was rejected at a West End theatre two hours after it was accepted at the National Theatre. Nobody alerted me, straight away or any other time. Nor was there anything unusual in my buying theatre tickets. Finger out Raymond. You're not in step with the Amex ethos. Your predecessor operated in much the same way. After a brief run he's no longer in the job.

Last year readers were offered my Christmas card. I distributed 1,800. A man in Dubai, after I'd paid expensive postage, complained he didn't like it. This year, being £9m in debt, I decline to pay the postage. If you want my lovely card, I've arranged with the Sparkle Direct fairies via Fairy Queen Kelly Barnaby who, with her pixies and elves, runs the Sunday Times Bookshop (0845 2712135) that for the knockdown price of £13.59 inc. p&p (£16.99 in shops) you'll not only get my book *Unbelievable – My life in restaurants and other places,* you'll also get my Christmas card. And – wait for it – if you've already bought the book, write in again and Kelly will send the card separately. If you want a signed MW sticker with a personal message and a cartoon, she'll provide that. Or I will, if you write to me. This is a good spiel isn't it? I should have been a barrow boy. Could I move fruit and veg.

Returned last Sunday to London's second best hotel (best is The Ritz) **The Goring** in Belgravia. Great lunch from the chef Derek Quelch: glazed Scottish lobster omelette (historic), roast beef with trimmings and coffee arctic roll with pistachio cream. The Edwardian splendour is beautifully maintained except for Lord Linley's tacky chandeliers in the dining room. His silly little lights on wires are like cheapo Christmas tree decorations gone wrong. When I said that before, I was told people flocked to the hotel just to see the chandeliers. Unbelievable.

"I JUST TASTE THINGS, I'M A TASTER"

In the 1950s I had a tiny one-bedroom flat above an Indian restaurant in Thurloe Place, South Kensington. On the right was a superb Polish restaurant, the Silver Spur, owned by an old, monocled colonel. On the corner of Exhibition Road, a fat Italian momma with a great personality ran **Dino's**. Her husband, Dino, lurked about, but she was the star. She passed on and the restaurant moved round the corner by the tube station. Other Dino's appeared in London, all similar to the 1950s version, untouched by tarting up. I took my assistant Dinah to lunch at the South Ken Dino's. Next to us sat a young man in a wool beanie hat, reading. He had a pizza, but wasn't eating. Dino's décor is horrific: crude relief pictures of Italy, chipped wooden tables. The wool hat man's pizza margherita looked terrible. I ordered one plus fried calamari and then roast veal. "Is my Coca-Cola glass clean?" I asked Dinah. "It's scratched from the dishwasher," she replied. Mr wool hat (aka Yohan) ate some of his pizza. "How is it?" I asked. He pulled a face. It was his first time in Dino's. "Will you be coming back?" I asked. "I don't know," he said. "You didn't like your pizza why should you come back?" I remarked. My calamari was like rubber, I couldn't eat it. The pizza was cloying, no taste, it hung about in the mouth. "This is going to be a very slimming lunch," I observed as my plate was removed little changed from when it arrived.

Yohan was drinking tea. "Any good?" I asked. He pulled another face. Service was slow. "I think they've gone out to buy your veal and not use frozen," said Dinah. When it arrived it was fatty, the potato was revolting, the broccoli like water, the carrots strange – all dreadful beyond belief. Dinah left most of her food, I left more.

Desserts were pictured on a card. I chose profiteroles, not easy at the best of times. This was the worst of times. Yohan used to be pastry chef at a well-known restaurant chain. He said the desserts came in bulk, frozen, and the chocolate on the profiteroles invariably got burnt in the microwave. "I never order profiteroles now," he stated. Mine were revolting. I took only a tiny bite. The waiter asked, "Did you enjoy it?" "I just taste things, I'm a taster." I explained.

Opposite, was a group of good looking girls. "Steam in there, Yohan," I advised. "I've got a girlfriend," he said, "Never stopped me," I replied. I went over to the girls, some men had now joined them. They worked for a Christian charity. Nice, cheerful people. One lovely girl, Louisa, said, "Would you come and dine with us?" "Believe me you've got enough trouble, you don't need me dining with you," I replied. We took our photo. I paid for Yohan's lunch. Opposite used to be Mascall Records where Jacqueline Bisset, with her staggering breasts, fascinated me as she worked behind the counter. She later fascinated Frank Sinatra, had quite a career in Hollywood. Coming out of the sea in *The Deep* she was a sight to see. Those were the days. Never go back.

When I asked Jeremy King if he'd be at **The Wolseley** for the lunch service he responded, "I was going to be, but if you're coming in I'll make a run for it." He was there. We discussed water. Schweppes are closing down Malvern water. It's the best, equalled only by Evian. I asked Richard Caring to buy the Malvern plant. He checked it out and said

they were building over the Malvern spring. I suggested Jeremy replace Malvern with Evian at The Wolseley. He said he had to consider his carbon footprint and not bring in water from abroad. This from a man who imported horrific mineral water from Portugal for his restaurant St Alban, who belches fumes from his 1973 Bristol with a V8 engine. "You use electricity in your kitchens?" I said. "Only from wind farms," Jeremy replied. Six hundred and thirty-eight bulbs glow nightly outside my house. To balance my carbon footprint I reuse envelopes. All the paper in my printers, photocopier and fax have something on the back. Trees only exist because of me.

I had an incredible quality breakfast last week at the new **Verta** hotel which has risen by the Thames next to Battersea Heliport. Scrambled eggs and smoked salmon on toasted muffin were historic; coffee, toast, jams, service topnotch. The private dining rooms on the 13th floor have spectacular views. If you're not superstitious, they'd make great locations for a Christmas party.

THAT'S THE METROPOLE

I don't like modern hotels. Why go to Brussels, a city steeped in history, and stay in a dump that could be anywhere? The hotel **Metropole**, built in 1895 is still run by the founding family. Its splendid grandeur remains. They sent their fey housekeeping manager, Richard Clay, originally from Derby, to meet us at the Eurostar. He resembled the hotel. Flaky, eccentric, at times incompetent – but delightful. No wonder Richard preferred it to the Hilton where he once worked. "The posh area is the Avenue Louise," he explained, "but we're in the lively part, the Place de Brouckere." My suite had cracks in the walls, ghastly reproduction oil paintings and the hot towel rail in the bathroom leaked, but there was an elegant Marie-Therese chandelier, pleasing furniture and a nice view of nineteenth-century buildings opposite. They'd left us very tasty strawberries with whipped cream and sugar and some marvellous smoked salmon. Richard told me it was smoked on the premises. I wanted dinner at 10.30 p.m. because we were going to see Geraldine's future daughter-in-law, Ayako Ueno, in a show, but by then the restaurant was closed as it is for lunch Saturday and Sunday. It's a fantastic looking room. "Not available much your restaurant," I commented to Richard. "The chef is French," he replied. "That says it all," I responded. I settled for breakfast. Bread and croissants poor, smoked salmon omelette excellent, coffee OK.

There's a fantastic, ornate bar, **Le 19ieme**, with people sitting outside under a canopy. Very times-gone-by. So was the lift. The general manager, Wouter Liekens, explained it was the oldest in Belgium. "Made by the French company Edoux who did lifts for the Eiffel tower," said Liekens, adding, "It's a bit like the Titanic." "You've obviously got another job to go to," I suggested. Outside when we took our photo (not used, I thought you'd prefer the ladies) I said, "You sit here general manager." Mr Leikens protested, "I'm not a German manager, I'm Belgian." Brownie points for Wouter. These diminished when he got ratty after not sending back some trousers I'd left. Emails from the hotel assured us they were dealing with it. They weren't. After seventeen days we got onto them again. Mr Liekens considered that pushy; dared to say my lovely PA Sarah was being difficult. Also, Richard booked a limo for the evening, but didn't tell the driver where we were going. That produced confusion. I don't mind a few rough edges in a hotel with incredible stained glass windows and ceilings, amazing ironwork and gilt bronzes. That's The Metropole. Looks good. Odd. Loved it.

Talking of books, here's my Christmas choice. Number one through 4,806 is my own, which I guess you're reading

– *Tales I Never Told!* I know impresario Michael Codron. He can be waspishly amusing but his ghastly autobiography is a self-aggrandising dirge. The most historic book ever – *Walter the Farting Dog* – was No 1 on the *Sunday Times* Bestseller list. Geraldine gave it to me. Was she trying to tell me something? It's an intriguing, illustrated yarn. Apparently hard to find, but if you ask for it, maybe Frog Ltd of Berkeley, California will reprint. Screen rights have been sold, a big movie announced. It really was No 1 on the *Sunday Times* bestseller list – the children's list. If Christmas ain't a time to be childish, when is?

The most pathetic thing I ever saw on TV was Nigel Havers in *I'm A Celebrity, Get Me Out of Here*. What a moaning, arrogant, petulant person he revealed himself to be. If you decide to do that show – I turned it down for years – then be gracious. Join in the stupidity. I'm told Havers did a TV series called *The Charmer*. In *I'm a Celebrity* he was charmless. He's a bore and a quitter.

LOOKING AIN'T ENOUGH

It's rare a hotel redesign improves what was there before so all credit to **The Savoy** hotel in the Strand. Their £200m refit is a triumph. The entrance, the lobby, the American bar, the Beaufort Bar, the Thames Foyer are all hugely elegant, well lit; as near perfect as anything can be if it isn't me. So when Sir Michael Parkinson his wife Mary, Geraldine and I entered the **River Room restaurant** we hoped for the best. Got the worst. Mary Parkinson said, "It looks like a Japanese restaurant." The view has been decimated. Two silly, black shiny annexes face the river, the windows are minimal, the main restaurant an off-white monstrosity. The food and service matched the venue. No one asked if we wanted more champagne even though our glasses, brought in from the Thames Foyer, faced us empty. It took forever to get a menu.

Only Geraldine's gluten-free bread came speedily. Then we waited. Eventually we got menus, no prices visible. A waiter explained the numbers after each dish, minus a pound sign, were the price. Mary Parkinson said, "In Chinese restaurants they have numbers for each dish, that's what it's like. I nearly ordered two 17s, a 26 and a 42." I had bottled water. A quarter of an hour after asking I got ice and lemon slices. When I complained the ice would melt in a shallow bowl the waiter said, "I wanted to bring it quickly." "Fifteen minutes to produce ice is not quick," I said with frigidity. No one got bread, butter – anything. After twenty minutes I got up, found someone, and made my feelings known. The restaurant manager, Eike Bosche, who'd greeted us briefly, had vanished. The staff and service lacked precision, rhythm and energy. It was the worst-run restaurant ever. Only after I complained did things move fast. Michael Parkinson and I had tasteless brown crab cakes, mysteriously on a bed of mashed potato. Mary liked her smoked salmon, Geraldine her scallops. After that no one liked anything. My pan-fried sea bass fillet in parsley crust looked like a sausage and was dry; the whole plate, including vegetables, bland beyond belief. For dessert I was tempted by (although fearful of) the steamed gingerbread pudding. The waiter recommended dark chocolate sorbet and espresso granita. I had both. The gingerbread pudding was sticky, heavy and inedible. The chocolate sorbet was good. Man cannot live on sorbet alone. Friday night is a ropy night for guests (none ropier than me) but this crowd was beyond belief. At the adjacent table two men were in shirtsleeves, one had a pullover. The Savoy used to be elegant. Many guests looked like vagrants who slept in nearby doorways. Why not insist on jackets for the men? The next day on Twitter Serlthegirl tweeted, "Just back from the River Room restaurant at The Savoy. Michael Winner in a strop at next table. Awful restaurant." As Michael Parkinson summed it up: "It was not a distinguished meal." General manager, Kiaran MacDonald, says in their brochure, "The Savoy looks for perfection in every detail." Looking ain't enough. Fairmont hotels should redesign the River Room restaurant and fire everyone in it. Including the guests. It's now up to Gordon Ramsay's Grill Room to save The Savoy's food reputation. That's assuming Gordon can save himself.

PS: When I rang The Savoy to make a reservation the phone rang for four minutes, thirty seconds. I rang off, tried again. After six minutes, fifteen seconds it was answered. Over ten minutes to get through. The hotel brochure boasts Fairmont's restoration of The Savoy would have the hotel "bestride the 21st century". Enough staff to answer the phone might help.

As for Nigel Havers's miserable showing on *I'm A Celebrity...* Fancy having a near breakdown, blathering that his wife would leave him if she saw him in a prison costume in a jungle toy jail? Must be a pretty dysfunctional marriage. Not as dysfunctional as Nigel. He took the money, behaved abominably and let the other actors down. My hairdresser said Nigel quit because the rain was washing out his hair dye and his roots were showing. The other junglees were great fun. Except for Dom Joly.

A SIGNATURE DISH

I've been to restaurants which are difficult to find. Never to a restaurant in a street which doesn't exist in any atlas. After much flumming and dumming I discovered Nicholas Road is new. It's off Evesham Street, W11. The area looks like the world after nuclear war. Bereft of people and activity. A sliver of light, like an oasis in a desert of nothingness, turned out to be **Nottingdale**, a restaurant owned by Charles Dunstone, one of our great entrepreneurs. Mr D started with a few quid in a flat in Marylebone, which he was soon chucked out of because it wasn't zoned for office use. He now flogs mobile phones under the name Carphone Warehouse. He's got Talk-Talk and heaven knows what else. Employs 19,000 people in the UK. We entered a brightly lit diner; long counter, chefs at work, wooden tables without tablecloths, wooden chairs minus padding. My type of place. We were joined by Charles's lovely wife Celia and Mr and Mrs Charlie Brooks. He's a famous novelist and horse racing expert; she, a super-executive in the newspaper world. I met her years ago when she was a foot soldier. One of the brightest people ever. It was a good group. Stephen Hester, chief executive of the Royal Bank of Scotland, which owns my bank Coutts, came over. I thought: "I'll ask for another £9 million loan," then decided it might be poor form in a social environment. The chef is Harry Hensman. "The restaurant manager has a very complicated name," said Charles. "It ends in garlic so I just call her garlic." For the finickity among you her name is Michele Cruz-Garlic. I asked twice for the home-made focaccia and was told to shut up because they were warming it. It was superb. We got a whole lot of sausages, ham and titbits on a wooden platter. All fresh and excellent. I ordered pizza with guan-ciale rosemary and buffalo mozzarella and some fried zucchini. The pizza was historic. "I think it should be our signature dish," suggested Charles. The fried zucchini a bit blobby. Then pappardelle with autumn truffle; brilliant. They refilled my ice regularly which is more than most restaurants manage to do. Geraldine thought her artichoke soup amazing. To demonstrate my genius as a food critic I've forgotten what my main course was. It's not on my tape or in my notes. I remember liking it. If you put a gun to my head (which many of you would find amusing) I'd say it was fish. I've often eaten Amalfi lemon tart in Amalfi. At Nottingdale it was just as good. This place is a find. If you can find it. My advice is (1) when you go, leave early, and (2) take a picnic basket just in case.

I saw an ad in *Country Life* magazine for a converted trawler. The crew takes eleven people round Scotland's wild west coast. The food looked terrific: freshly caught fish, lobster, scallops, shrimps. Marie Thoms, the **Majestic Line** sales manager, told me it was run by "two wild men" – her father Andy and Dr Kenneth Grant. She sent a photo of dad in full Scottish regalia playing the bagpipes on one of their two boats. I said I wanted the trip just for me and Geraldine. Marie responded, "You'll miss the group experience of being with other people." "I don't do groups," I explained. Next April I shall come among the Scots in full Winner regalia – shirt not tucked in, pyjama bottoms, suede loafers. Make a change from the South of France, Caribbean, Italy, Streatham High Road. You'll get a meticulous report.

After I wrote how horrible her rolls were on Eurostar – maybe they'd hung around too long – Adrian Macceleri from the **Sally Clarke Bakery** delivered fresh ones assuring me, "They're much better than you experienced." Sorry Sally but they weren't. Still heavy and chewy. My staff thought the same. Sally should go to Michael Parkinson's fantastic **Royal Oak** pub near Bray. They've started baking their own bread. Great quality.

A HOODIE CHICKEN

Marrakech has changed massively since I first visited in April 1996 and dined at **Le Tobsil**. That's, let me work it out: 2 and 2 is 4, 3 and 3 is 7, 6 times 10 is 63 ... so 1996 is ... 15 years ago next April. Regardless of "progress" around it, Tobsil remains the same – one of the world's best restaurants. It's in a 1925 riad. The inner courtyard, surrounded by balconies, now has an electronically operated roof. Candles, rugs, rose petals on white tablecloths, exquisitely decorated plates, two musicians playing somewhat stoned music: a beautiful room. The souk's old riads are being turned into boutique hotels. Major hotel chains are being constructed. The road to the airport, which was through fields, now winds among housing estates. At Le Tobsil you go through a small door and enter the world of Arabian nights. The ongoing quality is because the French owner, Christine Rio, maintains firm control. She walks purposefully through her domain, greeting and seating customers. The food is historic. My notes are full of superlatives. We started with Arab salads in little bowls, sweet tomatoes and cinnamon, courgettes, sweet carrot, cauliflower with broccoli and garlic, aubergine, celery with lemon, green peppers, pigeon pastilla in flaky pastry with almonds and cinnamon. Then chicken tagine with parsley, coriander and lemon sauce came in a big bowl with a cloche on it, like a hood. "A hoodie chicken," I said pathetically. Geraldine explained, "The lemon sauce has been cooked for ages, it makes the chicken moist." Then an enormous shoulder of lamb with apricot plus couscous with vegetables and a sensational tangy sauce. "Couscous is just the wheat rolled on their thighs like cigars," explained Geraldine. "Whose thighs?" I wondered. "Why don't they have vegetables like this anywhere else? They're so tasty," observed Geraldine. Everything complemented everything else. Except me. I was, as usual, the outsider. The dessert of cooked pears with cinnamon was superior to pears anywhere. I thought all was over when in came an enormous millefeuille cake with milk, almonds and cinnamon. "Absolutely incredible," I dictated. If Tobsil was in London I'd go endlessly.

Beware: in Marrakech if they say something's antique it probably isn't. There was a dealer (now dead) at the Mamounia hotel who swore his Chinese vases were seventeenth-century. A friend of mine lived next door to him. He saw deliveries from Hong Kong factories of new "distressed" vases. I was offered a shell and rare stone-encrusted mirror. The shop said, "Made in 1920." My guide whispered, "Made last week," He took me to the whole-saler who provided them. Their price was 80 per cent less. I bought one and turned it into a coffee table. Anything offered in the souk can be reduced by at least 60 per cent. Just hold out the cash you want to pay, if refused, start to walk out. You'll get it for what you wanted. In Britain I'd say at least 70 per cent of "antiques" in shops are wrong. They're either total fakes or messed about with, with new additions, which make them not real antiques. Same applies to paintings. Ditto the salesrooms. Many times I've caught out our major auctioneers. They dress beautifully but their morals are below those of a used car dealer in Peckham.

Drama at **The Wolseley**. Sir David Tang, the Chinese owner of the excellent **China Tang** in the Dorchester, and other great restaurants, told me he was thrown out by manager Fergal Lee, who later wrote apologising profusely. All this caused great merriment among Fergal's Wolseley colleagues. A fellow restaurant manager bought him the China Tang Cookbook for Christmas. I made a special card with three photos of Sir David with "Happy Christmas Fergal from Dave" on the front. Inside I included a remark of such gross political incorrectness I dare not repeat it in a nice paper like the ST.

GOOD: **The Ivy**'s treacle sponge pudding, organic jelly crystals from Luscious Organic Kensington High Street, Stasha's lavish cookbook *How to Feed A Man*, the higher quality seating with improved leg room in Screen One at the Kensington Odeon. BAD: the watery Cosmopolitan cocktail at **Le Caprice**, my Mistral internet/email provider, the incompetence of the QVC shopping channel, people who don't buy my book.

SIMPLIFY!

They say an Englishman's home is his castle. If so, then
Andrew Davis, owner of von Essen hotels, must be all of
a-dither. At last count (and he buys hotels like you and I buy
bags of crisps) he had Dalhousie Castle in Scotland, Amberley
Castle in West Sussex and **Thornbury Castle** in South
Gloucestershire. 'Twas there I went a-wassailing (whatever
that means). The place was around in 925 but came to promi-
nence in 1533 when Henry VIII and Anne Boleyn stayed and
again in 2010 with my visit. It's stunning. We started with
one of the best teas ever. Only let down by Tufa water. The
scones, cakes, sandwiches et al. made up for it. The charming
general manager, Brian Jarvis, informed me Kenneth Bell
put Thornbury on the map. Mr Bell was apparently awarded
an MBE for bringing French cooking to the UK. "Should've
been shot for that," I suggested ungraciously. Dinner, in
a lovely, candlelit, tapestry bedecked room, started with a
weak Cosmopolitan cocktail for £11 compared to a very good
£8.50 one at The Wolseley. Who says it's cheaper out of town?
Food was superbly served by Peppe, an aged Spanish waiter
who looked exactly like Manuel in *Fawlty Towers* forty years
down the line. In thirty-six years, he proudly proclaimed,
he'd only had one week off for illness. Stupendously good
were the pumpkin soup, seared scallops with champagne
risotto, cinnamon doughnut with spiced apple soup. OK
was Geraldine's rather overcooked turbot. My roast crown
of English partridge, croquette potato, bacon and partridge
ravioli, beetroot fondant, braised chicory, parsnip purée and
juniper juice was a confused disappointment. The bit of bird
was dry, not enough gravy. Far too many disconnected items
on the plate. Partridge is best served with game chips, bread
sauce and lots of gravy. You can also have foie gras en croute.
Red cabbage is nice, too. The chef, Mark Veale is very good, but
as I headed for the helicopter I advised him to stop trying to
be over-clever. "Simplify," I instructed as if I knew what I was
talking about. The croissants and bread at breakfast were the

best ever. They were bought in as frozen dough from the Fine Food Company in Wincanton, Somerset. The hotel baked them to perfection. All in all a place we greatly enjoyed, even though I asked for every Sunday paper including the *News of the World* and only got three posh ones. When I phoned down to seek more, no one answered the phone for twenty minutes. They obviously thought I was joking when I asked for the red tops. Titter ye not. I was dead serious. Always am.

Nigel Havers behaved disgustingly on *I'm A Celebrity...* "You're not on about it again," I hear you say. At the end when everyone stayed to see Stacey Solomon crowned Queen, Havers wasn't there. Too grand to hang around. You have to be grand to play King Rat in a Birmingham pantomime. Perfect casting. That's bitchy of me. So what? I'm a slut.

Geraldine and I had an incredible Christmas lunch at **The Ritz.** It's the most beautiful dining room in London, best service; John Williams is a brilliant chef. Our second Christmas lunch was with Michael Caine, also a brilliant chef. We'll spend New Year in Gstaad's elegant **Palace** hotel with the best restaurant manager ever, Gildo Bocchini. Nearby is the hotel **Olden**, owned by Bernie Ecclestone. I heard it was for sale and mentioned this. "It's not," Bernie said. "Everybody should have one business that's losing money to keep them on their toes." I wish you a terrific 2011. If I can provide a smile, drive you to fury or hinder your future happiness, it'll be a pleasure. Follow me on Twitter @MrMichaelWinner. If you think I'm ridiculous here, you should read my tweets.

"MATOS, MATOW, MATTER... CAN'T SEE YOU IN THE BOOK"

The best meals I've ever eaten were at **Wiltons** in St James's under Jimmy Marks. I first went in 1940 when I was five.

It continued to serve staggeringly good fresh food, simply cooked. Diners ranged from Winston Churchill to Mrs Thatcher to Albert Finney to me. Jimmy, in his grey double-breasted suit, would sway as if the place was rolling at sea when he led people to their tables. "This way my lord," he'd intone. In those days you couldn't eat in the bar area. I did. Jimmy's wife Lucille said, "Michael shouldn't be eating in the bar." Marks replied, "Michael can eat where he likes." As he approached ninety and a party that would have included Danny Kaye as well every major person around, Jimmy wilted. He sat at a table by the entrance unable to recognise his customers.

When he died Lucille took over. She hated Americans. When I said to the actor Walter Matthau, "We'll go to Wiltons," he replied, "We won't. I went with Oona Chaplin (Charlie's daughter) and this woman asked my name and if I had a reservation. I said, 'Yes the name's Walter Matthau.' 'Matos, Matow, Matter... Can't see you in the book.' She took forever. Finally I said, 'You're keeping Lady Chaplin waiting.' Then the lady said obsequiously, 'Come this way your ladyship.'"

In 2004 Wiltons went over the cliff. Lucille retired. A new chef came in who tried to be clever. A snooty restaurant manager took over. My plaice was cooked in stale oil, the veggies were like water. I stopped going. Recently my friend Henry Wyndham, chairman of Sotheby's said, "Let's go to Wiltons with Nicholas Soames, I'll get Amanda, Duchess of Devonshire to join us." Wiltons is one of the few places you have to wear a tie. I chose a 1966 thin black one, like the Beatles, dressed as bar mitzvah boys managed by Brian Epstein, used to wear. The general manager, James Grant said, "Good morning." No smile. The dining area seemed bigger. "We opened a special wing just for you," said Nicholas Soames. The bread was very good. The new chef, Andrew Turner, did well. I ordered fried plaice. Henry Wyndham observed, "I never understood plaice. Do you like plaice?"

"I've just ordered it," I replied. "Why would I do that if I didn't like it?" Henry said, "The last time you wrote about the Duchess of Devonshire you called her the Duchess of Westminster." "The Duchess of Westminster's got more money," I replied. My smoked eel was terrific. Nicholas Soames explained, "They catch the eels in Somerset, then take them to Holland to be smoked, then they're brought back." "Why don't they smoke them in Somerset, it would be cheaper," said Henry. My plaice was excellent but half the size it used to be under Marks. Amanda, Duchess of Devonshire (one of my favourite people) observed, "My paté is in the shape of a heart." "Doesn't make my plaice any larger," I commented. Amanda's grouse was served. "Do you know which moor it came from?" she asked. I almost suggested, Sainsbury's. "I came to see you in the London Clinic but you'd gone," said Amanda who's one of their Trustees. "I'd been in the clinic for ten weeks," I said, "I couldn't hang on just because you were visiting." For dessert I had treacle tart with extra treacle and cream. "I've never seen anyone eating cream with a fork," the Duchess observed. I hate spoons. Frightened by one as a child perhaps? Terrific, meal superb company. Good to see Wiltons back on form.

I've gone tweet crazy. @MrMichaelWinner I write things more vulgar, politically incorrect and downright stupid than I dare offer a newspaper as sophisticated as the *Sunday Times*. Lady Caine put me onto it. She said Michael was tweeting to help sell his book. Everyone tweets. Russell Crowe, Tom Hanks, Jane Fonda. It's a new world. I've only got a few thousand followers (please join) but their responses to my remarks are very bright. Michael Caine and I tweeted news as he filmed in Hawaii. He's a great wit.

One of London's best buys is the £20 three-course lunch or early dinner at the "in" place **Bar Boulud**. I had it: great squash soup, lovely British banger with bubble and squeak,

amazing flourless sponge chocolate cake with chocolate sauce and ice cream. Grander food is also on the cheapo menu. Divorce lawyer Lady Shackleton was there with her mum. She too thought it was great value.

GENERAL OPPROBRIUM

Gstaad is lovely, more or less unspoilt. They're building some monstrously large whatever overlooking the pedestrianised main street. How the local canton let it go ahead I'll never understand. Also, zillions of Swiss francs, deutschmarks, yen, French francs, Israeli shekels and boiled sweets were spent upping the look and standard of Gstaad's **Grand Hotel Park**. A total waste of money. I went for lunch with Geraldine and Alan Cluer, a witty man who presented Sinatra concerts and produced movies and plays. Then he hopped it to Geneva. The lobby had what seemed to be four black cow skins on a wooden floor. Easy to trip up on. Otherwise it was bleak, as was the single man at reception who cheerlessly directed us to the first-floor restaurant. Another design abortion. Chairs with stripes, lampshades that looked like the 1950s gone wrong. I ordered carrot soup and then fillet of solettes, grilled. Alan explained that meant small soles. The waiter returned to check what I'd ordered. I'd asked for it only two minutes earlier. The staff took forever to give us bread. When I went to peek-a-boo the buffet I saw a large bread selection, far more than I was finally offered. It was all heavy and poor. I took tasteless smoked salmon from the buffet. The mozzarella seemed to have been hanging around. Only two of us ordered a main course; Geraldine was served mine and I got hers. "How difficult can it be to remember two main courses in an empty restaurant?" I dictated. The solettes were very dry; everything tasted of zilch. I should have got a hotdog from the village stand and brought it with me. I asked Geraldine about her main course – fish – she pulled a face and moved her head left to right. Then said it was horrid. Alan observed, "I don't want to join in the general opprobrium but my salad is chewy. If you wanted to commit a murder this would be the perfect place because there'd be no witnesses." He also queried the inequity between the number of waiters and the number of diners. The waiters were all fluffing about doing nothing. After our abysmal main courses no one cleared the plates. When someone eventually did, no one produced a dessert menu. We just sat there. "I'd like to stay and count the time until they ask us about dessert, but if I do a week will go by," I remarked. So I called over the waiter. "Why do you not give us a dessert menu?" I asked. "And why do you not crumb down the table?" Whereupon the waiter produced a silver scoop and removed crumbs from some, but certainly not all, of the table. My millefeuille was useless – I left most of it. Alan had apple crumble, then said again, "I don't want to join in the general opprobrium but I wouldn't enthuse about my crumble. When I came in the door and took one look at those polyester-type rugs, I knew the game was up." Thus we finished one of the worst meals of all time with service to match. While waiting for a taxi downstairs in the horror-lobby we checked out a bar serving better-looking food. "We should have sat here," said Geraldine. "We should have sat in another hotel," I responded.

By contrast the **Palace** hotel, Gstaad is exemplary. A huge lounge with log fire and mountain view. The sheer volume of people was cosmic. I saw Roman Polanski handing out his latest DVD, *The Ghost*, Sir David Barclay and his beautiful wife, and a parade of interesting visitors plus a great gypsy band, led by Youri Farkas. Lightning service everywhere. I checked out the newly designed restaurant. Shock-horror. Dividing the room was a ridiculous high-backed banquette with two heavy lamps on top. The superb restaurant manager, Gildo Bocchini, was unhappy. "I can't sell those seats," he complained. "We've told Andrea Scherz [the owner] how

awful this is, customers have told him, what else can we do?" "Your saviour has arrived, Gildo," I said. "Leave it to me." Scherz's wife's decorator had done the deed. We sat down to another historic dinner from the hotel's marvellous chef, Peter Wyss. Scherz came over. I said, "You must get rid of that monstrosity dividing up the room. The theatre of the restaurant is destroyed. I know it was done by your wife's decorator, so what? Throw it away." "It's easier to throw away my wife," replied Scherz. "She's lovely. If there's a choice, keep your wife and lose the banquette. If not, drop the wife and the banquette," I said. "It is on wheels," explained Scherz. "Wheel it out," I said. The next day the banquette had gone. Scherz asked, "Did you see the fire blazing when we burnt the banquette? It lit up Gstaad." I said, "I got more congratulations for getting rid of that than on my bar mitzvah." What a hotel this is. For New Year's Eve, usually a disaster, they had 730 diners. Beyond belief – efficiently dealt with, service impeccable, great food, more caviar than I've ever seen, lovely entertainment, no drunks. The Park hotel is the worst. The Palace is the best. But be warned: I've already booked for next Christmas-New Year.

A RARE MOMENT

From the sparkling snow of Switzerland to the **Warwick Arms** pub in Kensington. I'd passed it on my nightly exercise. People rushed out and said, "This has the best Indian food in London." For Saturday lunch I proceeded from my house through Edwardes Square, where Frankie Howerd and Piers Morgan lived, past Pembroke Studios where David Hockney does strange things, to the Apostolic Church with its banner "A hearty welcome to all". Through an alley at the side to a Homebase, once decorated with a marvellously kitsch ancient Egyptian exterior, which its owners sadly removed. The Warwick Arms opposite was built in 1832 and retains the quaint Englishness of pubs determined to halt the spread of modernity. It's all twee and pleasant. The overweight landlord, Michael Reynolds, was charming. The chef Ram Singh and waiter Neil Sacharma, both from Nepal, offered Exmoor beef from Stillman's farm, Exmoor loin of pork from Lillycombe farm, chilli con carne (love that), home-made pie, home cooked salt beef. No thanks. I was after an Indian. We ordered King Prawns with white garlic and a white marinade of yoghurt, double cream, salt, pepper, ginger garlic paste and lemon juice. More information than I needed. I chucked in an onion bhaji. Prawns were OK, no more. For main course: chicken tikka marsala marinated with yoghurt, onion and Delhi spices; oh, enough already. Would it beat the historic taste of the same dish I consumed each week at a dump in Bridge Street, Cambridge when I was an undergraduate? My naan bread with lamb was too complicated. The chicken tikka, good, though massively aided by an excellent raita. Would have helped if the plates were hot. Thin green paper napkins were horrible. Geraldine described her chicken Xacuti as "scrumpelicious". I think that meant she liked it. Mine was a bit too spicy. Pleasant Indian food but not a patch on London's best as cooked by Manoj Vasaika at India Zing in King Street, Hammersmith or Rasoi Vineet Bhatia in Chelsea. For dessert I had gulab jamun, a sticky, sweet thing, with kulfi, an Indian milkshake, and Haagen-Dazs, a much praised ice cream but nowhere near as good as Marine Ices in Chalk Farm. I dictated, "This glubby thing I'm eating is really fantastic because it's light. I've had them at supposedly very good restaurants and they've been heavy." Geraldine, who rarely eats desserts, but was trying this one, said, "Exactly." Thus agreeing with my food assessment. A rare moment.

\# A terrific restaurant overlooking Gstaad is the **Sonnenhof**. We sat outside with Roger Moore's son Geoffrey and his wife Loulou, facing the snow clad mountains. Got a bit nippy by dessert, so we moved inside. This has the best rosti, a sort of hash brown potatoes, ever. The veal with sauce was memorable. At the hotel **Olden** we had another superb meal. Supposedly they were full so we were put at a small table for two. Throughout the meal I faced three larger, empty tables. The manager, Ermes Elsner told me they were reserved. For the invisible man perhaps? Ermes explained the Olden was due for a massive makeover. It'll be full of suites with saunas, swimming pools, tame tigers, tea-makers, butlers, budgerigars – the usual twaddle. It's a beautiful old place. Hope they don't mess it up.

Spending thousands on private jets is not a guarantee of an easy life. I often use 247jet. Charming people. But oh dear. For my trip to Gstaad I booked a 10 a.m. take off from City airport. On my way there I noticed the paperwork showed us leaving at 11 a.m. Their head office said, "Don't worry, your plane will be ready to leave at 10 a.m." City airport had us down to take off at 10 a.m. but at that time we were waiting for the pilot to pay his landing and fuel charges. He returned to announce that City airport wouldn't take the company's credit card. No surprise to me. In Florence with Michael and Shakira Caine we were hauled off the plane for the same reason. So Shakira and I had a whip round and paid cash for the fuel to get us into the air. The chairman of 247Jet, Paul Mulligan, always had an "answer". A mistake. The card was held up because the card company feared fraud. The wind was blowing in the wrong direction. We finally took off at 10.50 a.m. That made me an hour late for lunch in Gstaad. When I got the invoice it wasn't for the agreed amount. Easyjet here I come!

2011 started badly. My swimming pool maintenance man, Nigel Whittaker of London Leisure, installed equipment so water poured out where it shouldn't. Then the Bentley's power steering collapsed. It needed the strength of Arnold Schwarzenegger to turn a corner. Worst of all, my fantastic

PA, Sarah Shawcross, fell ill and was hospitalised in Sardinia, and will still be when she comes back to London. She said her returning to work was unlikely. Fortunately, my ex-PA Natalie, who left after having been conned by a crook she met on sugardaddie.com, came back. Who said life was easy?

SHACKED UP WITH DANIEL CRAIG

My spell as a TV star was killed by kindness. ITV execs were so thrilled with *Michael Winner's Dining Stars* they moved it from afternoon to 9 p.m. on a Tuesday and then to Friday night. "You're in trouble," said Piers Morgan, after I did his *Life Stories* show. "Nine o'clock Friday is the graveyard slot." The BBC came out with big guns against us – *Eurovision, Sports Aid*, shows that mopped up some two million viewers who would have been floating. Enough may have settled on me to make up the numbers. As it was we were below the required audience figure. Nothing did much better in the graveyard slot until Paul O'Grady came along months later. ITV put me with a marvellous producer, Nell Butler, to work on other projects. She devised *Come Dine With Me* and is classy (rare on television), bright and the daughter of Lord Butler, distinguished ex-Cabinet secretary. Nell suggested lunch near her home. "Which restaurant do you like in Haverstock Hill?" she asked. "I didn't know they had restaurants in Haverstock Hill," I replied. "Where is it?" Nell went into overdrive telling me the history of the area. The highlight was that Daniel Craig lived at the end of her road. She chose **L'Absinthe** in nearby Primrose Hill, owned by Jean-Christopher Slowick, ex-restaurant manager of The Belvedere. I sat in a nice little room. Then sat for longer. Finally I asked, "Are you selling food, Jean-Christophe? Because you could have fooled me." I started with French onion soup. Not very liquid. It was like solid onion and cheese. Nell got very excited when, while knocking back her snails, a dark-haired man walked passed the window. "That's David Miliband," she said. "How do you know?" I asked. "Because he lives up the road," replied Nell. "Goodness me," I thought, "David Miliband shacked up with Daniel Craig. Great story for the *News of the World.*" I stayed silent and ate my duck confit, braised savoy cabbage and jus gras. "Jus" is a word I hate. It's on every menu like measles. The duck was pleasant; so were the accompanying veggies. Jean-Christophe reported that the rum baba was off. "It's on the menu: rum baba pineapple," I said petulantly. "You should have it." "Nobody ever wanted it," said J-C. "Shows the class of client you have," I responded. "Come to the sticks and that's what I get." I settled for apple tart tartin. Good for a local. Nell said, "Would you like to walk to the top of Primrose Hill?" "That's like asking if I want to visit the sewers in Southend," I responded. Nell said firmly, "It's a very good view." Not for me. Instead we had our photo taken. Nell observed, "Maybe I should've worn some lipstick." "Maybe you should have had a ball gown," I suggested. Everyone started on about where the sun was and where they should stand. Unbelievable. My chauffeur took the photo standing where I told him to. That's what TV needs. Discipline.

At **The Wolseley** Fergal Lee was running the room. Very well. He's the one who threw out my good friend, Chinese mogul Sir David Tang, then apologised. It caused much merriment. I noticed a Chinese restaurant manager, "How did he get in?" I asked. "Not on my watch," said Fergal with his wonderfully quiet, deadpan Irish delivery. "My parents thought your write-up about me was very funny." "Hope they like the sequel," I said. Let's be clear, Fergal is not racist, nor am I. But I find it utterly bizarre we're not allowed to joke about other people. The brilliant US Jewish comedian Jackie Mason did *An Evening with...* for ITV. Pamela Stephenson came over at the end and said to me, "No wonder the Jews hate him, he's so anti-semitic." "Pamela," I explained, "The Jews love him." The *Daily Telegraph* theatre critic wrote that Jackie's jokes were just the sort of things he'd been taught at

school not to say. Per-lease. The Americans always had Polish people as the butt of their jokes, the French had the Belgians, we had the Irish. So what? The funniest evening I ever spent was in Belfast during the Troubles. I was there on radio's *Any Questions*. The BBC people living in Northern Ireland came out with the most hilarious stories about the Irish conflict, all politically incorrect. Political correctness is a disease. Actresses are called actors. The chairman of an organisation is called the chair. It's *Alice In Wonderland* gone berserk. Loosen up folks. It's only a joke.

"BEST-EVER"

At the souk in Taroudant, Morocco, Mohamed Samih has stocked up on dead lizards. "The lizards prefer the mountains," the scarred shopkeeper explained. I don't know what that had to do with anything. Adam Stevenson, pianist supreme, who works, and I think manages, the hotel **La Gazelle D'Or**, told me Mohamed sells dead lizards to be ground up as a herbal remedy. I'm sure this didn't cure anything, but it got rid of a few lizards. Taroudant is totally enchanting. It's the other side of the Atlas Mountains to Marrakech. You take an one-and-a-half-hour flight in a propeller plane which lands in a field. The town is unspoiled by modern development and tourists. It's just magical. Jacques Chirac, the former President and Prime Minister of France goes there every Christmas. Not to buy dead lizards, although he may have sneaked in and grabbed a few, but to stay at La Gazelle D'Or, an oasis of beautiful gardens, small bungalows and a lovely swimming pool. When I recently rang Rita Bennis, the owner, she assured me clients were sunbathing on their loungers while we froze in arctic weather. It was by Rita's pool I once met the beautiful actress Valerie Hobson, a movie star I was brought up admiring. She was with her husband John Profumo. That alone was worth the trip. Rita Bennis and Adam Stevenson have a marvellously irascible relationship. He left on one occasion. She says he begged to come back. He says she pursued him to come back. Adam is Irish, used to play piano at Soho's famous Colony Club and has ended up in this "time stands still" outpost. Rita assured me not only was all her food organic but the walls were as well. I'm not brainy enough to take that in. I understood that her dog was called Timo. Sitting in the gardens by the pool we had some excellent flaky-pastry lamb and vegetable samosas – "best ever" I dictated. For main course: red mullet with their heads on – eyes staring at me – and some sardines. Geraldine ate the sardines with her fingers, assuring me, "This is the correct way to eat them." I wasn't mad about the fish. It had been brought from the kitchen, as the pool bar wasn't operating, and had dried up. A very good salad compensated. For dessert: crème brulée and almond tart, both memorable. The éclair was moderate. A lady at the next table heard me dictating and said, "Be nice." I responded "Nice, me?" She was Canadian. They're odd for a start.

Winner's Dinners at **The Belvedere** was a delight. Total sell out. Lovely to meet so many of you. Food was good; canapés, champagne and wines first class; Geraldine an incredible and beautiful hostess. I took O. J. Simpson to The Belvedere. He hasn't answered my letter to his Nevada prison. I've also filmed there in 1957, later with Robert Mitchum and Sarah Miles. Again in the adjacent Japanese garden with Chris Rea. Live nearby.

When we were filming in Richmond, Michael Caine, Roger Moore and I lunched at Crowther's. So good. Michael Caine was going to open a West End restaurant with Philip Crowther. He didn't, but Philip and his wife Shirley now run a catering company. I use them. Recently he did canapés for me. His choux pastry filled with cheese and herb pâté was

historic. If you're giving a dinner party I recommend them. Nice people to have around.

IN THE SPIRIT OF THE WOK

Here's a dining experience from hell. I was invited by Sir David Tang to join him, his lovely wife and a couple of family members at **Hakkasan** in Mayfair. An officious woman stood at the street door, "Are you having dinner with us?" she asked. I felt like saying, "No, I hear there's a leak. I'm a plumber. I've come to mend it." What a stupid greeting. Inside it was very dark and noisy. A man asked, "Would you rather go down to the table or wait in the bar?" I said, "I'll look at the bar." This was full of people eating, the noise so loud it practically swept you back out of the door. As I didn't find the bar particularly fascinating I went to go downstairs as David Tang and family entered. Downstairs it was even noisier, very dark, badly lit, all the surfaces shiny so sound reverberated off them. David said, "They've just spent £11.5m on doing up this place, the kitchens are incredible; you must see the kitchen." I had no interest whatsoever in seeing the kitchen. All I was interested in was what turned up on my plate. David had difficulty ordering because the menu was in tiny type and where he sat there wasn't even a pool of light. First to arrive was a vegetable broth with mushrooms. Not spectacular. Next: roast duck with a tiny bit of meaningless caviar on top. David said, "It's ridiculous, they showed us the duck then it takes forever while they go away and cut it." I said, "The skin is not crisp like it is in your restaurant China Tang, it's all soggy. What's this stuff at the bottom?" David explained, "It's flour. That's wrong. Duck should be served on pancakes. The only thing you put on flour in Chinese cuisine is sweet and sour pork because that has a lot of oil in it." He'd asked the restaurant manager to move us to the private room as it was difficult to hear people sitting next to you. But the private room was taken. Other food served included a rather oily salt and pepper squid. David owns two restaurants in Hong Kong (where he lives), one in Beijing, one in Singapore and two in London. He explained, "Chinese cooking has to be in what is called the spirit of the wok. Meaning you eat it off the wok when it's hot. Here everything was lukewarm." Of the waiters David said, "Service is not hands, it's eyes. Never, ever interrupt a guest if he's in conversation. Dishes when they're finished should be removed. The waiter must have anticipation." Hakkasan's waiters were walking round the room not looking at anybody. A nuclear explosion would have gone unnoticed. The desserts were the best thing: chocolate soufflé excellent, mango sorbet fine. By this time, I couldn't wait to get out because the noise level was just horrific.

PS: David Tang food tip: Take half a tin of Heinz tomato soup, add half a tin of Campbell's beef consommé. "Delicious," he assured me.

PPS: I never write about private meals without permission. David said, "Go ahead." A waiter gave me a pad to take notes. Sir Mark Weinberg, who'd been asked late, saw me writing and said, "I thought you were taking food orders." Thus promoting me to a position well above my capabilities. If he'd said, "You look like a food critic," that would have been even further beyond my ability.

My friend, the very bright Adam Kenwright, had a birthday dinner at **Les Deux Salons** in Covent Garden. It's a well-designed brasserie; nice food included an onion tart, a sensational snail and bacon pie, a splendid rum baba. Adam started up a tiny theatrical advertising agency sixteen years ago employing one man and a dog. Actually, I think there was only a dog. He now employs 173 staff in London, Manchester, New York and Australia. I contributed to his success by persuading him not to put on shows, just to

concentrate on the core business. This was not altruistic. Every time Adam put on a play, I invested a few thousand and lost. It was getting monotonous. Adam now has an enchanting New Zealand girlfriend who I call Hymie, although that may not be her correct name. Hymie-Shmymie, wha'does it matter? She's a lovely person.

THE ITALIAN CONNECTION

I'm still reeling from the most inept example of restaurant management I've come across in my 106 years of semi-life. It was occasioned by someone I'd previously praised, Charles Pullan of the River Café. His ludicrous performance, totally unnecessary, over an advance request I made for a booking, was beyond belief. So while not counting River Café out, although I haven't been back, I looked for another Italian restaurant. I'd heard well of **Tinello** in Chelsea owned by the most gracious and marvellous chef, Giorgio Locatelli. It's run by two brothers, his lovely wife Plaxy "adopted". The chef is Federico Sali and the restaurant manager Max. The premises is not helped by silly décor. A window looking onto the street is quite narrow; one side of the place is rough brick (nice), the opposite wall is panelled in dark glass with knobs on, not literally but figuratively. This glooms the room. A simple mirror covering that wall would have widened the look of the place, added reflected light from the window and jollied things up. They also had hanging low-lit bulbs which didn't help. There criticism ends. The food is fantastic. Max is a hard-working host, the staff charming and efficient. We started with Bellinis. Peaches weren't in season so the peach juice was tinned, as it is at Harry's Bar in Venice where the Bellini was invented. We were given deep fried artichoke, some amazing Tuscan ham and other stuff, which I'm too decrepit to remember. I ordered fried zucchini followed by a large portion of tagliolini with truffles. I said, "Max I will pay extra money, I can afford that you understand, for extra truffles." The truffles came from San Giovanni d'Asso, south of Siena. Because of, or in spite of that, the dish was terrific. I tried a bit of Geraldine's veal cutlet – incredibly tender. I finished with a mini tiramisu. Max called it a tiramisu beignet. I'd say tiramisu profiterole. Very good. I also had, though wouldn't swear to it, an almond tart with yoghurt ice cream. My notes were rather confused. I'm certain that as I was leaving one of the local gentry, who, with their wives/girlfriends fill the place, said, "I have a photo of you and me taken in 1958." I replied, "Not possible. Nobody photographed me in 1958." I was wrong. It was a photo taken at a debutante dance when I was talking to Lola Wigan, a stunningly beautiful girl with unbelievable breasts. The man must have been a deb escort. Now, and doubtless then, he was well-mannered and charming. In those days, so was I. Been downhill ever since.

PS: I revisited Tinello with Michael and Shakira Caine. They loved it. Number one among other Italian restaurants is **Murano** in Mayfair. Angela Hartnett is a stunning chef; the detail and taste of her stuff is amazing. It always costs me £60 extra going to her because I get a parking ticket. I still like **San Lorenzo**, diminished by the departure of the incredible Mara, but the cook is great. If you want cheaper, **Timo**, near me in Kensington High Street, is excellent. **Scalini**, once good, has gone down the plughole.

PPS: Charles Pullan and I are now back as friends. He's fine really!

The National Theatre catering has always been a disaster. To call it pathetic would be a compliment. They should find out who caters for the Barbican complex in the City of London and sign them up. I went to see the impressive play *Black Watch* there. The worst signposted venue in history. A total disgrace. Impossible to locate. When you get inside it's

a garbled mess. No meaningful signage anywhere in a highly complicated venue. Whoever is responsible couldn't run a flower stall in Becton. But the catering was beyond belief good. I grabbed a flapjack. Sensational. Not easy, flapjacks. They're either too tough, too sticky, poor texture, bad taste; this one was perfect. Then I noticed a fish and chip counter, tore off a bit of fried pollock. Perfection. Took the rest. The batter was precise, delicious; the fish moist and excellent even though pollock is not my favourite fish. The mushy peas were splendid, so were the chips. All around were varied displays of food mostly made on the premises. Nearer the theatre was a counter with pork curry and rice which looked amazing. There's generous space for eating, lots of seats and tables, lively people. At the National Theatre the few ghastly food choices are appallingly laid out. The main restaurant is a lesson in how not to do anything. At least at the National the plays are well chosen and performed. Theatrical offerings coming up at the Barbican scraped the bottom of the barrel. A friend of mine in the business said, "They get so much annual funding from the City of London they just don't care about their audiences." Don't care is mild. Totally contemptuous, I'd say.

THE WORLD'S RAREST ELEPHANT

I've been to heaven. It's called Canouan. I didn't even have to die to make the journey. My friend Dermot Desmond had a spare plane going to the Grenadines (doesn't everyone?) and said Geraldine and I could grab a lift. To keep the pilot company, I suppose. As I was due in Los Angeles for my American Cinematheque tribute in March I suggested Mr D might like to drop me off there. A return email commented my LA suggestion was "a bit Irish". A nice way of saying, "You're a liberty-taking old git, Winner. Forget it." Thus we landed at Canouan's tiny airport – two thatched doors for arrivals and departures – and waited because the one person on immigration was dealing with a departure. Then we drove through what the Caribbean used to be. Little shacks, a village with personality; not overbuilt with apartment blocks, Little Chef restaurants, traffic-jammed highways and porticoed nouveau riche residences that make Dallas look classy. We arrived at the **Canouan Resort,** a hotel which Mr D is demolishing. He also pulled down Sandy Lane in Barbados to put up something better. If *What's My Line* was still on TV, Dermot could appear as a "Hotel knocker-down". Katie Boyle would be flabbergasted. To replace the Canouan Resort – very lovely and visited by Leonardo di Caprio, Daniel Craig and Keira Knightley – Dermot will build four boutique hotels of stunning quality. The first he assured me would open by the end of 2012. He was vastly optimistic about the readiness of Sandy Lane but this time I think it'll happen because Dermot is part-nered by an Italian construction and design group. Their chief executive, Achille Pastor-Ris, a highly professional, tough boss, is on site. He's abetted by Elena Korach, a beautiful Italian architect whose work on the island is highly impressive. Achille looks like an overweight tennis player – white clothing, sweater nonchalantly on his shoulders, the arms tied loosely round his neck. It was he who opened the resort, then managed by the Raffles group, witnessed them go and sought a hotelier to run the show. "I'm the one that trapped Dermot Desmond," he proudly announced as if he'd captured the world's rarest elephant. The first new hotel looked, from plans and a model, absolutely fantastic. Elegant colonial design, twenty-eight large suites, the beach immediately outside, two penthouses. They'll knock down sixty villas and replace them with twenty-two. Redevelopment in reverse. The island is lush, rolling hills, peaks, bluest sea I've ever seen, marvellous sandy beaches, a fantastic golf course (for a few more weeks owned by Donald Trump, then to be improved). There will be new marinas, thankfully not for cruise ships, so 3,000 tourists won't regularly descend. The whole thing will be exclusive and unspoiled. Villa plots are for sale. If I wasn't £9m in debt I'd buy one. I can't think of anywhere better, or going to be better, or imaginably better. Canouan Resort stops taking guests from May this year, but two of its restaurants stay open for villa owners and other transient zillionaires. The food I ate was amazingly good. Grilled prawns from nearby Guyana – the best ever. Beef satay, sashimi of yellow fin tuna, outstanding spaghetti bolognese, I could go on. If I can afford it, I'll be back. If I can't, it's Christmas in Southend. Oh well, swing with the punches.

John Cleese gave a fortieth birthday party for Jennifer Wade. In his speech he described himself as her boyfriend. "John," I said in my words of wit and wisdom, "what planet are you on? Boyfriend? Have you looked in the mirror lately?" The event was at **Mosimann's** in Belgravia. For seventy-five people the catering was incredibly fine. Risotto ai funghi, Dorset crab, beef, lemon tart. Anton Mosimann is a chef of amazing quality. He and his two sons run the place immaculately. Cleese was so overcome he said of Jennifer "I might even take her off the shelf." That means they'll be married. Bet your life on it. Jennifer makes John happier than I've seen him in years. So here's hoping it's fourth time lucky in the Cleese wedding stakes.

THEY ALL TASTE THE SAME

Matthew Norman is a real food critic, as opposed to me. When he was writing *The Guardian* diary he slagged me off for years. Somehow or other we became friends. For lunch I suggested **Racine** in Brompton Road. The chef/owner is Henry Harris whose brother Matthew chefs at Bibendum nearby.

Mr Norman turned up growing a beard. "You look more like a rabbi every time I see you," I announced. I was eating a freebie starter of sliced Basque pig. I started to tell Matthew about it. "It'll be some acorn-fed pig; usual rubbish they talk about pigs," explained Matthew. "They only do it to upset us." The set menu until 7.30 p.m. is £17.50 for three courses. They add a "voluntary" £1 for the homeless. I'll soon be homeless. I should have collected a quid from each diner. Instead I started with a cup of parsnip soup and herring in a street mustard dressing and rye bread toast. The food was great. Matthew observed, "When I first came here I thought it was a bit like the first class waiting room at Rome airport. But actually it's very cosy." "They haven't done anything to it since," I said. "I've got old and my standards have dropped," replied Matthew. He said of his chicken, "This bird breaks every rule of English restaurants by tasting of chicken. Other than the fact that it's over-salted, it's excellent. It's crispy and delicious." So that's how a real food critic reacts, I thought. My mullet had some sort of potato and leeks with it. "Tastes of, I don't know what it is, the sauce or whatever, it's wonderful," I dictated. That's how an ignoramus reviews food. "The minute you finish a plate they come and take it away. Very good service. Don't you agree dear?" I asked Matthew. "I do," he replied, "it might be due to the fact that two national food critics are here." For dessert I chose ouefs à la niege; Matthew selected a mixture of sorbets, saying, "They all taste the same, they inject them with some kind of carcogenic chemical and be done with it." When his multi-coloured sorbets arrived Matthew described them as "spectacular". Discussing my £9m debt Matthew suggested, "You may have to end up as a rent boy; I'll start the bidding at £5." That's what friends are for.

PS: Matthew Norman took our photo. His first set showed the ceiling with three heads intruding at the bottom. Next try had the group cut on left or right. It didn't matter because the restaurant manager, who was featured, left Racine shortly thereafter. So I returned on the way to my appearance at the BFI Southbank last Wednesday for another photo. This time by a *Sunday Times* professional. I added Geraldine because Mr Harris and I lacked glamour. To put it mildly.

Sir Peter Maxwell Davies, Master of the Queen's music, is composing a symphony to mark the Queen's Diamond Jubilee and will score some music for the wedding of Prince William and Kate Middleton. All piddle-diddle to me. Sir Peter's real achievement is that he walked out of the **Olive Grove** restaurant in Canterbury because he couldn't bear dining to an accompaniment of "idiotic pop". A couple of days later he was due to meet Roger Wright, the controller of BBC Radio 3, but couldn't stand the piped music in the BBC reception area. "It was a form of torture, like being interrogated in Guantanamo Bay. If the BBC had been let loose on al Qaeda they may have had more success than the Americans," he complained. "I was on the verge of walking out and was writing a note to Roger when he arrived." Sir Peter also walked out of Waterstone's in Oxford Street because he objected to the piped music. He opposes "moronic melodies" on mobile phones and refuses to hold for call centres if music is played. There's a campaign group, Pipedown, to fight the "insidious menace" of piped music. Sir Peter says, "I urge more people to demand that piped music is turned off. This is a protest movement that wants peace to be given a chance." I'll get my friend Lord Andrew Lloyd Webber to join. He hates piped music as much as I do.

Lunch at **The Ivy**. Room splendidly run by general manager Nicolas Jarnot. Food great: fish cakes, griddled foie gras, best hamburger ever. But their treacle sponge pudding had black treacle. Ghastly beyond belief. Golden syrup is in all the recipes (Delia, BBC etc.) I could find. Geraldine was given black treacle as medicine when a child. It tastes like medicine.

TWO OLD FARTS MAKE TEN

I was brought up at the London Palladium. In the 1950s American stars headlined twice-weekly variety. I was fourteen and wrote a column in twenty-three west London newspapers. The Palladium publicist, John Carlson, who had an enormous moustache, said, "You come in on Monday and on Thursday, I've got twenty-three columns to show the star. They think you're like Earl Wilson." Wilson was America's biggest syndicated columnist. I was the UK's smallest. Two and a half readers on a good day. Thus I met Bob Hope, Johnny Ray, Gracie Fields, Nat King Cole, Eddie Fisher and many more. The boss of the London Palladium was one of my parents' best friends, a wonderfully tall, quiet man called Val Parnell. The only time I saw Val really cross was with Al Martino, a Palladium bill-topper. "That Iteye was cooking spaghetti in the star's dressing room," said Al, apoplectic at the dishonour to his lovely theatre. Val died. The lovely theatre went into decline. The walls were grubby, the whole thing looked tatty. Until Andrew Lloyd Webber turned up and did an incredible job of glamourising the place, finding old plaster work, restoring, adding twenty ladies' loos and creating the Val Parnell room which leads up to the Cinderella bar, the most beautiful in any London theatre. During the last previews for the *The Wizard of Oz* Andrew and Madeleine (his beautiful, bright wife) wanted me to see the Val Parnell room and have dinner. Behind us in our photo (tinged pink by the Cinderella bar lights) is an oil painting by Dame Laura Knight which Andrew found in the basement of the Palladium. It depicts a royal lady (they can't figure who) watching the Crazy Gang on stage. I also saw the first ten minutes of the *Wizard*, in which Danielle Hope as Dorothy, who was found on a TV show audition, sang *Over the Rainbow*. Very moving. We dined close to the theatre at **Vasco & Piero's Pavilion** so Andrew could rush back and check on things. Vasco's offered good, plain food. As Andrew, once a brilliant food critic, said, "There's nothing about this place remotely saying it wants to stand up and be a great restaurant." My guinea fowl tortellini with Umbrian black truffle butter main course was exemplary, but took forever to arrive. Andrew used my line and asked the co-owner, restaurant manager Paul Matteucci, if they were serving food. He also looked at me and observed, "You have a very celebrity life Michael, like me." To which Madeleine responded, "Two old farts make ten." I'm not quite sure where that fitted in, but it made me laugh. Starter was carpaccio of pear. Very good. Dessert came like lightning. It was panna cotta with cherries from Umbria. Fine.

PS: Last Tuesday we went to the first night. *The Wizard of Oz* is fantastic. Amazing special FX. Cast great, Danielle Hope wonderful, Michael Crawford (nearly seventy) underplays excellently. Always liked him. We did two movies together. One of my Twitter followers described the show as "magical". I agree.

I arrived late at **Scott's** in Mayfair after appearing at the National Film Theatre, which is now BFI Southbank. I was going to Sir Michael and Lady Caine's birthday dinner for Shakira. I ate soft roes on toast. I know nowhere else that does them. Absolutely fabulous. Followed by excellent rhubarb cheesecake. The old Scott's was a waste of space. Richard Caring turned it into one of the best places in London. But why are they like MI5, MI6 and the CIA rolled into one? I wanted to tell Shakira I'd be late. All numbers to Scott's produced hideous recorded messages or referred me to their website. Why can't they have a number for the restaurant desk like The Wolseley does? By the time you've listened to crap music and a recorded voice talking drivel you may as well top yourself. A call centre in Bangladesh is preferable. I can hear it now. Yahya calls Shakira Caine at Scott's and says, "This is Yahya Rahman speaking from Chittagong. The people of Bangladesh greet you. My family

salute you. Very important man Winner says he'll be seven minutes late for dinner. You don't care? Never mind, great honour talking to your ladyship. Salaam alaikum."

CHOCOLATE CAKE AND CHIPS

This broad Juliet stood on the balcony wailing, "Romeo, Romeo wherefore art thou Romeo?" Not there, for sure. Otherwise she wouldn't be asking. Why didn't she just go into Via Capello and accost passing strangers: "Have you seen that rat Romeo? He's meant to be here. Can't trust a Capulet these days." It's possible Romeo may have been a Montague. Or Juliet might have been a Capulet. I can't be bothered to check my *Shakespeare for Kiddies*. It's unlikely that the balcony at 23 Via Capello in Verona was really Juliet's balcony anyway. The Verona authorities suggest it is because they do weddings there in the house, and make a fortune from tourists clocking the spot where probably nothing happened. Round the corner at 3 Vicolo Scudo di Francia is definitely where I had lunch. That may not attract the same tourist interest, but if you're in the area, go. The restaurant was **Antica Bottega Del Vino**, a recently redecorated place with wine and plates on the wall. The family that's had it for years has just sold it to some other Veronese folk. I had a dish called risotto all'Amarone. Journalists would come in from a nearby newspaper and by the time they got there that was all they had left. I was on time, that's what I got. There was a big deal with Geraldine, tasting the wine. Geraldine is greatly expert at wine tasting. She smells, swills, smells again, goes through the whole gamut of facial expressions. She could spin it out to a week if she set her mind to it. They should have an intermission and sell ice cream in the middle of her performance. Not infrequently the finale has Geraldine declare, "Bouchonné," which means it's corked or worse. Once, four bottles were bouchonné, one after the other. I had a three-course meal with coffee and liqueurs while it all went on. Eventually the wine tasting ended, this time happily, and my piping hot risotto was put in front of me. The manager stood adjacent holding cheese and a grater. "Should I have Parmesan cheese?" I asked. "I wouldn't," he replied, "it ruins the original taste." The portion was so big I left half of it. Geraldine had sausages and beans for her main course. I got an enormous plate of braised meats accompanied by thinly sliced fried potatoes as I hate the advertised side order which was polenta. Geraldine looked at me critically, "He comes to the best restaurant in Verona and eats a plate of chips. Unbelievable," she remarked. She went on about it as I ate the potatoes. The manager observed, "You're eating like a bird." I'd eaten all the potatoes and most of the meat. "I'm eating like a pig," I told him. For dessert I was recommended coppa con crema di zabaione e amaretti. "I'll have that," I announced. I couldn't pronounce it but I ate it. They're very proud of their wine – the family makes it or someone else makes it; it was a long story. My mind wandered. "Would you like to see our wine cellar?" the manager asked. "I don't do cellars," I replied. Geraldine said, "The only thing you do is chocolate cake and chips." She's got a point there.

The Wolseley is one of the best restaurant creations ever. An enormous credit to Jeremy King and Chris Corbin, the owners. I go there more than anywhere else. The other Saturday I had, for the second time, the day's special: Vijay's Chicken Curry. My waiter said to me, "Was the curry a bit dry?" "It was diabolical," I replied. "What was wrong with it?" asked the waiter. "Everything," I said, "Texture, taste; nothing worked." Jeremy King told me they had a chef, Vijay, who did curry, so they specially put it on the menu under his name. Later I asked the waiter, "Is Vijay here today?" "He's just come in," said the waiter. "But it's 2.45 p.m. Lunch service is largely over. Why wasn't he here to make his curry? Clearly no one else can," I protested. The waiter was silent.

The only other food disaster I've had in the eight years The Wolseley has been open was near the beginning when I was with a movie star and we ordered Welsh rarebit. Beyond belief awful. I struggled through most of it. Then the star said, "I can't be seen to leave food, Michael. You eat mine." He plonked his portion in front of me. That was a horrifically memorable experience. They've got the Welsh rarebit right now. If Vijay could be persuaded to come in when his special is on the menu, I'm sure the curry would be good too. If he's not there, I'll order something else.

ON THE RAMPAGE

Sarah Taylor was firm, "Mr D does not wish you to go to his **Ickworth hotel**," she announced. "I want to go there," I said. "It's reasonably close to where I'm doing my one-man show in Saffron Walden." "Mr D says it's full of children, you'll hate it." "Tell him to get an extra 100 kiddies in for me," I suggested. "Do you really want to go?" asked Sarah, sensing defeat. "Sarah," I said, "if you look out of your window you'll see three letters each ninety feet high with lights flashing on them and the letters are Y-E-S." Thereafter Anthony Davis, the mythical "Mr D" (closely related to Dr No) capitulated. Ickworth is a grand eighteenth-century mansion set in 118 acres of beautiful parkland. The outer hall displayed two dozen pairs of tiny Wellington boots. The hotel is grand but decorated and furnished with the biggest load of tat I've ever seen. David Williams, the manager, explained, "The children can run around and rampage." We were ushered to their one elegant room with eighteenth-century Chinese wallpaper. Hidden on it is a dragonfly. Mr Williams gives half a bottle of champagne to guests who can find it. It's above the door to the lounge. There, that'll cost him a few half bottles. I had very good coriander soup, excellent bread and some fruit. "We'll serve you lunch tomorrow here in the Chinese room," suggested Mr Williams.

I responded firmly: "I want to be in the dining room with screaming kids."

The next morning we drove to Lavenham in Suffolk to see the Church of St Peter and St Paul built in 1000. There was a sizeable shop in the church. No one there. A sign read: *Please put money for shop purchases in cash slot.* Say that in London and they'd break open the money box. We purchased a lot of very good chutneys, jams and a few other bits and pieces.

Back at the ranch (Ickworth actually) we went to the conservatory for lunch. I was quite hungry because breakfast hadn't been a total success. Lumpy croissants, reasonable kippers but served on cold plates, jam so stringy you could hardly get out of the jar. The manager, David Williams, showed us to a table. They've got a special menu headed Lord Bristol Menu. "Is this what killed him?" I asked. I had tomato and pimento soup, organic salmon fishcake, coriander and lime potato salad, baby cress and lemon oil. Plus chips. The food was surprisingly good. The chef, Nick Claxton-Webb, deserves credit. Geraldine thought her lobster thermidor benedict the best she'd ever had. My fishcakes were exemplary, but why sit them on cold salad? The panettone bread and butter pudding was a bit heavy. The room had been peopled with children, but by the time we finished lunch there was only one family left. Except for a kid on a highchair with muck all over its face. "Let's forget him," I advised. Instead I grabbed Helen Upton, the lady seated next to us. She had two kids: Freya in a pink T-shirt with a bear on it, and Evie in a striped sweater. Stuck 'em in the photo. Left for London. If I regress to childhood I'll go to Ickworth. For kids it's great. Adults must grin and bear it with nobility.

Back last Tuesday from Los Angeles. The American Cinematheque/British Academy of Film and Television Arts tribute to me and my movies went well. Six movies screened

over three nights. I did my one-man show to start things off, then spoke between movies on the other two nights. Superbly organised for the Cinematheque by Grant Monninger and his brother Ed. Good to see John Landis in the audience and my cameraman Richard Kline who recently got the Lifetime Achievement Award from the US Cinematographers. Also Jay Kanter, who put three of the six films into a "go" position when he was the UK head of Universal. Jay, a messenger boy for a big agency, was once sent to greet Marlon Brando at the airport and became his best friend and agent. I travelled on Virgin. Superb lounge at Heathrow with genuinely good food: bread, rolls made on the premises, a variety of smoked salmon, great choice. Even the scrambled eggs were perfect. Virgin personnel were cheerful and professional. At Los Angeles airport they use the less amusing Air New Zealand lounge. London's Heathrow airport is horrific, LA even worse. I remained calm, charming, witty and obliging. Killed two airline employees and three passengers. When I went to LA, I used to be taken out by Brando, Mitchum, Bronson, Orson Welles, Burt Lancaster. All dead. The only way to have a good dinner was to organise a séance. Still, I ate out a lot. Most of the food was grossly disappointing. I'll tell you about it over the coming weeks, months, years, decades, centuries. Hang around.

FIRST-CLASS HOTEL MINUTIAE

I resided for twenty-four years at the **Beverly Hills Hotel** intermittently between 1967 and 1991 when I wasn't renting apartments or houses in Los Angeles. I returned recently for the tribute to me by the American Cinematheque. The Beverly Hills hotel is old Hollywood at its best. It's set in 12 acres of lush tropical gardens and walkways. Banana trees are rampant, even on the corridor wallpaper. Not the same banana leaves I was used to. There was a copyright problem, so slightly different ones went up. Other hotels – like the

Peninsula, where they embroider your name on the pillow-cases – have arrived. The Beverly Wilshire has had a major facelift. But the Beverly Hills hotel still reigns supreme. You feel any minute you could bump into Marilyn Monroe or Humphrey Bogart. The staff at the Beverly Hills hotel is the best I've seen ever, anywhere. Polite, charming, friendly, highly efficient. I can't say the same of the general manager Alberto del Hoyo because I never saw him. Probably the first time in fifteen years a general manager has been that hidden. If Mr Hoyo ever came down from his ivory tower he may notice strange things. Why was there no full-length mirror in my suite? Easy to put one on a door. Ladies like to see what they're wearing in case they want to take it off and start again. Why, in the men's swimming pool toilets and changing room, are there no towels? Soap. Hot water. But to dry your hands only flimsy tissues which fall apart. And no bin in which to put them. The place was littered with used tissues. This is not first-class hotel minutiae. Get your finger out Mr Hoyo or, if you can manage it, your whole body.

What a difference from the Winner's Dinners hotel manager of the year 2010, Hans Meier, from another resort hotel, the **Setai** in Miama. He was everywhere. Greeting, meeting, checking. The Beverly Hills hotel pool is the stuff of legend. Who did what to whom in the tented cabanas boggles the imagination. I was told *West Side Story* was written there. Other less creative (or more creative?) acts also took place. The pool attendant, Michael Ormsby, was the only staff member to irritate me. There are fourteen cabanas each with three sun loungers. Geraldine and I were the only people using any of them. Suddenly a noisy couple was placed next to us. "Why," I asked Mr Ormsby, "Is it necessary to destroy my tranquility?" I got some guff about a regular guest who'd asked for that cabana. "Then why not warn me and see if I wanted to move one or or two away?" I said. The food at the hotel is good. Not fancy, not pretentious. Not great. But definitely good. Executive chef Alex

Chen runs a number of restaurants, the main one being the famous **Polo Lounge**. I used to see studio executives and agents devour four breakfasts, meeting different people for each one. Now the guests looked like tourists. I saw no movie stars. Not even the hot and cold running call girls that used to trip merrily up and down the corridors. The Polo Lounge is a lounge bar, leading to a fairly posh restaurant, leading to a paved garden full of greenery with even more tables. A terrific setting. I had a great pina colada, yellow squash purée soup, delightful pasta with historic meatballs and marvellous prawns. Unfortunately the cobb salad, for which they were famous, had been discontinued. They did something similar which was so large if I'd had a vegetarian dog he could have lived for a month on the leftovers. At the pool restaurant, I kept repeating my order for a hot dog. Perfect sausage, marvellous bun. I'm a sophisticated diner. If you go to Los Angeles, stay at the Beverly Hills hotel. It's unique in a changing world. That's rare.

"IS A LANGOUSTINE THE SAME AS A PRAWN?"

I don't know which of my two favourite lunch companions, Henry Wyndham, chairman of Sotheby's Europe or Nicholas Soames, the most ebullient and excellent Member of Parliament, chose **Ristorante Semplice**. It's in a Mayfair cul-de-sac which no one in their right mind goes to. Facing me, a place labelled Semplice. This was **Trattoria Semplice**, poor relation of the real thing a few doors away. They told me it was the "cheap end" offering classic dishes – lasagna, fried calamari, spaghetti bolognese, braised beef with mashed potatoes. All stuff I like. Instead of eating it I exited for Ristorante Semplice. One of my hosts had chosen it because the *Financial Times* described it as a perfect romantic spot for Valentine's Day. What romance had to do with our lunch I know not. The place was about as romantic as a DHSS office in Becton. Tacky gold wallpaper, lurid lighting; functional to the point of tedium. The charming manager and co-owner, Giovanni Baldino, showed me a table close to another for seven people. They'll arrive and be noisy, I thought. I chose one facing the cash desk and the door. Space was limited. Life is not always easy. I sat at my chosen spot and heard everything said by four people next to me. So I switched back to the first table. Henry came in followed by Nicholas who'd also gone in error to Trattoria Semplice. Henry described the menu as "very posh". We all had artichoke soup with langoustine in it. I thought there were four prawns floating in the soup. I asked Nicholas, "Is a langoustine the same as a prawn." He said, "No." "What's the difference," I queried. He said, "I don't know." The soup was pleasant whether with langoustine, prawns, cuttlefish, sharks or human remains. To follow I had barley and semolina spaghetti with barrata (a soft, creamy cheese from Tulia), salmon roe and red onion. It was tepid and uninteresting. My dessert was three apple fritters. Nicholas took one of them. I'd said he could, but they were so good I wish I hadn't.

I've no more to tell you about Ristorante Semplice so here's a true story about Sotheby's. In 1949 Sotheby's auctioned two watercolours of street scenes by Adolf Hitler. My friend Henry Thynne, then Marquess of Bath, father of the present louche one, collected Hitler and Churchill memorabilia. The auctioneer announced: "Two paintings by Adolf Hitler. The bidding starts at 300 guineas." A Jewish dealer stood up and shouted, "It is a disgrace that Sotheby's deals in Hitler paintings. How dare you publicise Hitler and his work. I bid 300 guineas. I will burn the pictures right here on the floor of the sale room." A shocked silence was broken by the Marquess of Bath saying in quiet English tones, "320 guineas." He got the pictures.

Onto my Twitter site @MrMichaelWinner comes Saif Gaddafi. I asked, "Are you a relation of Mr Gaddafi of Libya?"

Reply: "He's my father and make me say bad things on TV. I good man and like to move to UK. Can you make flight for me on your jet? I have much money." I tweeted I couldn't take money and asked him to prove he was Colonel Gaddafi's son. He tweeted: "I have very large zibbi, favourite colour blue, mother name Safia, favourite trouser brown jumbo cords. OK?" I responded, "This is not conclusive proof. Could you get a sworn statement from dad?" Twitter is for nutters. Perfect for me.

JUST A MOUSSE

They say it's an ill wind that blows no good. The ill wind was, unsurprisingly, me. It started when my Twitter page recommended I follow Victoria Coren. I had no idea who she was. On checking her entry I saw she had many more followers than me. I informed my Twitter group and asked, "Who is she?" Answers poured in, many referring to her, apparently, ample bosoms. A ribald, but in my view not over the top, Twitter exchange followed. Miss Coren was appalled. She phoned my house at 10.25 p.m. and asked Geraldine if a fourteen-year-old derelict had hacked into my Twitter site. Fact was a fourteen-year-old derelict ran it. Me. I was not amused by this late night call as it woke both me and Geraldine, trying to recover from jet lag after a flight from the Caribbean. This went into my Twitter mix. I also mentioned Victoria's father, the brilliant Alan, was strange and that her brother Giles, noted restaurant critic of *The Times*, had stabbed me in the back. The temperature rose dramatically. Even though Giles conceded, when I wrote explaining to him, both remarks were not without foundation. Then Victoria devoted her *Observer* column to a fearsome attack on me. The politest thing she said was that I was a dirty old man. Even a mental derelict could see things were getting out of hand. Peace is always better than war. So I invited Victoria and Giles to lunch, which they

graciously accepted. We all reported, on our best behaviour
(an effort for me), to **Bibendum**, a Chelsea restaurant I've
always liked. The event was a delight. Victoria Coren is
beautiful, intelligent and witty. Her brother marvellously
energised and charming. Geraldine thought they were
great too. I suppose I should mention food, even though
Giles, speaking on my *Piers Morgan Life Story*, remarked I
was the only food critic who knew nothing about food. As
I've said that many times it hurts me not at all. Victoria
ordered chicken liver and quail eggs to start, then kidneys.
Giles explained that middle white brawn with egg is pig's
head meat, adding, "It's very gloopy and cartiledgey." I
didn't know what it was, let alone the rest. We both ordered
it as a starter. Much as I admire the chef, Matthew Harris,
I thought it tasteless and the eggs on top too hard-boiled.
"We've got a very sophisticated meal," assured Giles. "But
mine is nicer," said Victoria. "I always choose a daring
thing," said Giles. "There's a difference between daring and
reckless," I observed. Victoria tried her kidneys, then
swapped them with her brother's fish. "They look too like
kidneys," she said, "I wanted them to trick me into thinking
it didn't come from an animal." Bit nuts this girl. I approve
of that. Geraldine was in overdrive. She passed me her
empty plate and took the remainder of my kidneys. Giles
loved them, described the kidneys as bouncy and praised
the mustard sauce and the bacon. "What's that lumpy thing
over there?" he asked, pointing to my veggie plate. "It's a
potato dear," I explained. "It's his first time in a restaurant,"
said Victoria. Then, reading the dessert menu, she asked me
what a bavarois was. "Have you got a wrong number," I said,
"Your brother opposite is a food genius. Ask him." "It's a sort
of meringuey nougat," said Giles. When it arrived it wasn't
that at all. Just a mousse. Giles had ordered spotted dick.
"At least I know what that is," he said. The menu promised
chocolate sauce with the bavarois. There was only a decorative smear. "I'll get you chocolate sauce," I said gallantly to

Victoria. A quick wave here, a barked order there and the first-rate restaurant manager Karim Miftah brought a jug of chocolate sauce. Giles said he'd intended to have his hair cut for our photo but his barber was over-running. Victoria produced a mirror and lipstick. I remained au naturel. Giles said, "Let's do this again." Victoria wisely cautioned, "Wait until we see Michael's column."

PS: Victoria hosts a BBC4 TV quiz show with difficult questions. That counts me out. She's also a top class professional poker player. She made $2m on that (no tax paid on gambling winnings) and bought two flats in Belsize Park. Lives in one, rents the other. "She's a slum landlord," commented Giles. Nice girl too. I'll ask them both to my house for dinner. Will they accept?

TOP OF THE LEAGUE WAFFLES

There is a little part of the Beverly Hills hotel that is forever historic. It's a small, narrow room at the bottom of stairs that lead to a corridor and the pool. There's a long bar curved at both ends. Stools are screwed to the floor. You can just squeeze by between diners and the wall. Unassuming, reminiscent of the bars in ice cream parlours I frequented when I first visited the USA in 1953. It's called the **Fountain Coffee Bar**. When I was making movies in LA for twenty-five years, I'd go there for breakfast. Soberly and quietly filling the seats were movie folk, all reading the "trades", *Daily Variety* and the *Hollywood Reporter*, before they went to work. A friend told me she was there a couple of months ago and saw Leonardo di Caprio in the Fountain Bar every breakfast time. I doubt it. I only saw tourists and a commander from the City of London Police I met when I was guest of honour at one of their dinners. But the excellence of the Fountain food and service remain. The main man there used to be Gary. He handed out the best waffles in the world. He was quietly and superbly efficient. The great thing about the Fountain Bar is that everything is totally fresh. Order orange juice and they put oranges into a juicer and hand it over within seconds. If you want a waffle it's with you as soon as it's out of the machine. Bacon, eggs, hash brown potatoes, pancakes; all come from the griddle directly to your plate. That's how food should be eaten. The bar is now run by a pink-dressed waitress, Ruth Cortez. The chef is Benito Juarez who's been there eight years. Julio, the chef who was with Gary in the old days, is still working but had done something to his foot so was on medical leave. The chef on the day of our photo was Jose Manilo. The first thing I ordered was a waffle. To my surprise my taste buds realised it was not the same as on my last visit twenty years earlier. A thorough investigation took place. Ruth checked and assured me they still used Carbon's waffle mix, an original recipe from 1937. "It seemed to have less vanilla flavour than before," I explained. "We add the vanilla here," said Ruth. "I don't think you're adding enough," I said. So they put in more vanilla and the waffle returned to top of the league. Geraldine had corned beef hash, poached eggs and hash brown potatoes, all "done" in front of her. This is a great little corner of the hotel. I know of no other coffee shop remotely like it. Every movie star in the firmament has eaten there. It's open early morning until early evening. A true gem.

PS: You can get Carbon's Golden Malted Waffle Flour in the UK. If you make waffles this is far and away the best mix to use.

It was strange returning to Los Angeles and not working on a movie. The first film I made there was *The Mechanic* in 1971. In England a standby painter laid out forty cans of paint and brushes, and stood waiting to be asked to paint something. First day in LA we had to paint the end of the

wooden camera track the same colour as the pavement. I called out, "Standby painter." A prop man said, "We don't have a standby painter sir, you want something painted, do it yourself." He threw me an aerosol spray. I said, "Fine" and started spraying the track. The prop man took over. Back in England I said, "We're not having a standby painter. The props can spray paint." My production manager asked, "What will the unions say when they don't see a standby painter on the unit list." Unions were very stroppy then. I said, "At the top of the unit list it will say Producer, Director and Standby Painter, Michael Winner." It did. Thus we saved £10,000 on unit costs on *The Big Sleep*.

ROAMIN' IN THE GLOAMIN'

"The mist of May is in the gloamin' and all the clouds are holdin' still," wrote the lyricist Alan Jay Lerner for the musical *Brigadoon,* set in Scotland. For my trip on a converted trawler up the west coast of the Scottish Highlands, the mist of April wasn't confined to the gloamin'; it was everywhere. Clouds weren't still, they raced across the sky, depositing almost endless rain. When I told people I was cruising the west coast from 2–8 April they said in amazement, "Why?" I replied, "It seemed like a good idea at the time." It started with my favourite magazine, *Country Life*, where I saw a photo of a trawler in calm waters, with blue skies and the Scottish coast behind. The ad was for the **Majestic Line**, which runs trawlers that carry eleven passengers. I spoke to Marie Thomas, daughter of the co-founder Andy Thoms, explaining, "I don't want anyone on the boat except me and my fiancée." Marie said, "You'll miss the group experience." "I don't do groups," I replied. So Geraldine and I went to Oban one sunny day and boarded the trawler *Glen Tarsan*. Cabins small, the big bed so close to the wall you needed to be a contortionist to get by. The communal lounge measured approximately 15ft 6in by 5ft 4in. Imagining eleven people fighting for space there left me in shock-horror. First day: intermittent sun, very cold. I was surprised when I got up at 7 a.m. to find no crew. They appeared at 7.45 a.m. "Where have you been?" I asked. "I thought jolly matelots rose at crack of dawn and spliced the mainbrace. Isn't it embarrassing that a landlubber's up before you?" This made no impression. Food on the boat was good. The chef, Stephen Boswell, produced marvellous biscuits, vegetables and the best venison ever from the Duke of Argyll's estate. The brochure and Marie had indicated freshly caught lobster, crab, mussels, scallops. They were all bought in local shops. I did no fishing. Instead, ate fantastic soups from cock-a-leekie to cullen skink. Great kippers. Risotto with mushrooms, pear and fruit crumble with almond and home-made custard. No complaints about the food except the dirty plates sat for ages before being cleared. There was a crew of four but Stephen told them to stay out of his kitchen. The weather was so bad we couldn't do the full trip but the lochs and views we saw were spectacular. Mist with clouds often covering mountaintops, mostly calm water – I never felt seasick. Every night we parked (OK, moored or anchored) in still coves. I'm sure you're familiar with the west coast of Scotland so you'll know the locations when I tell you where we cruised: Lochs Creran, Linnhe, Leven, Aline, Sunart, Na Droma Buidhe, and past Lismore, the Sound of Mull and Ben Nevis. I could go on. We saw some miserable-looking seals. Not as happy as the ones who balance balls on their noses. Geraldine encountered stags when she went ashore. Later we disembarked on Mull, walked in a deserted world of peace and trees, the sea a few yards away, when suddenly we came upon a big house called **Torosay Castle** with two posh people and labradoodle dogs – one white, the other black. The lot (possibly minus the dogs) is on the market for £2.8m. Only disadvantage is that winter in Scotland lasts forever. I wore a thermal vest, a shirt, leather zip-up jacket, thermal pull-over, waterproof jacket and waterproof trousers. Looked a real idiot.

Twice we went ashore and stayed in hotels. We had six nights (less two in hotels) and five days on the boat. There were times when a mutiny to take the vessel and head full-speed for civilisation seemed highly desirable. Glad we didn't. The views, the atmosphere, the whole experience was magically memorable. Returning to Oban, Andy Thomas met us with Angus the bagpiper wearing an informal black shirt that surely came from Oxfam on a bad day. I said to Marie jovially, "No wonder the boat doesn't normally oper-ate until a week later. I think it was a plot to kill me with cold and rain." She just smiled. I don't know why the Scots never took me seriously. Everyone else does. Don't they?'

PS: Take the price of the boat, add private jet to and from Glasgow and other "extras" and it cost me more than my nine days in Los Angeles, flight included. If you're one of eleven people, it's £1,695 for a six-night trip. I recommend it. Try June, July or August. Safer.

FRIED WHATEVER

I'm the world expert on Kensington High Street having lived close by since 1946. It's gone from genteel old school to rowdy, brassy and common. Like me. Premises regularly open, fail and close. I saw a big empty space in a new building on the Eastern end of the High Street and thought, "They'll never let that." Within days it was a restaurant called **Aubaine**, always full. Geraldine and I passed a counter on the way in from which I nicked a croissant. They come from a central bakery every morning. Pretty good, so was all the bread. Geraldine advised that the imitation French eighteenth-century chairs were covered in toile de jute. "Would you care to tell me what my trousers are?" I asked.

"Crap," said Geraldine. "They're meant to be Egyptian cotton but they're crap." It's nice to dine with an expert. The floor was a tiled with wood laid in the middle, stainless steel pipes, globe lights, shelves with drink bottles displayed, flowers on the tables. Attractive room, light and airy. "The only thing is, it's noisy," observed Geraldine. What restaurant isn't these days? Aubaine is for ladies who lunch. Some looked quite classy, as if they'd fallen on hard times but were making the best of it. Like me. Geraldine ordered Ugly Oak smoked salmon; probably came from a tree. Then sea bass. My monster portion of salt and chilli squid, lime aioli was sensational. Fried whatever, good batter, great taste. I'd ordered tagliatelli with cep and truffles. The waiter returned to say, "We don't have truffles." So I plummeted downmarket (an easy journey) and switched to corn fed chicken pot au feu. I bet no one actually checked if this chicken was fed on corn, human remains, dead cats or foie gras. It took a long time to come. Perhaps they were stuffing corn down it. I got two large slices, veggies underneath and a broth. Broth tasty, vegetables good, chicken dry; I left most of it. Geraldine was impressed with her sea bass. They had horrible wispy float-away paper napkins. I hate paper napkins, these were the worst. The waiter came round with a platter of cakes. I chose many in order to perform my function as taster for the world. Coffee arrived long before the dessert. Geraldine, who doesn't eat gluten, got a gluten-free chocolate cake. She pulled a face, pouted her lips and rolled her head from side to side. I took that as meaning she didn't like it. The carrot cake was awful – didn't taste like cake – the millefeuille was good, the choux pastry on the chocolate éclair was heavy, the whole thing too lumpy. Geraldine said "Excellent coffee." I liked the people running the room, general manager Christian Emereau and supervisor Jean Baptiste. Lots of French spoken. Geraldine liked that. She worked in Paris for thirty years. It's not an expensive place, very much for shoppers and doppers. My bill came to £104.06 including service charge. That's because I ate all those extras just to keep you informed. Or possibly because I'm a greedy pig. Either way I decided to give you a break. I grabbed the Olympus camera and stayed out of the photo. Just took it. Loverly, innit? Terry O'Neill, eat your heart out.

Michael Winner impressions are legion. Brando did a particularly good one, so did Bob Mitchum. Professionals from Rory Bremner up down and sideways get close to my voice. On a scale of one to ten David Cameron is a five. But he is Prime Minister and "Calm Down Dear" played a distinguished venue: the House of Commons. Totally absurd was the response from an over-excited Labour front bench conducted by its deputy leader, Harriet Harman. To hear their contrived outrage you'd think our Dave had put down every woman in the land. "Calm Down Dear" has been part of our national language since I wrote and performed it on a TV ad ten years ago. It makes people smile. With all the important political issues, which they should be spending time on, for the Labour party glums to over exercise themselves about Dave's remark is just silly.

IT QUACKS LIKE A DUCK

There's another **Ivy** restaurant which is nothing to do with the London version. It's in Los Angeles on North Robertson Boulevard, a nothing street that divides Beverly Hills from West Hollywood. I booked and did a number so the restaurant manager Jaime Burajas knew how unbelievably important I was. "I'll keep a table for you on the patio," he promised. When I got there with Geraldine and my Hollywood cinematographer Richard Kline, there was no table free on the patio. We were shown into a pleasant, farmhouse-like interior – blue plates on the walls, very twee – and told to wait. "I don't do waiting," I said. "It's going to take ten to fifteen minutes to get rid of those people on the patio," Jamie explained. "Get six waiters to stand by the table and shame them into leaving," I instructed. "I'll be one of them," said Jamie. "Take a machine gun," I advised. I'd just ordered a mint julep when Jamie returned. "They've gone," he announced, "I told them they had thirty seconds before the restaurant caught fire." It was very crowded and very buzzy. Definitely an "in" place. Fantastic menu ranging from three scones with jam and butter through, oh everything. "It's very nice sitting in the sun here on the terrace," I observed, "But I think they've forgotten the fact that we came here to eat." "I don't think they want to serve you," said a pleasant lady next to me. "I've been to places where no one will serve me. I'm used to that," I replied. At last, a waiter. I ordered crab cakes (as recommended by Shakira Caine) with white rice over steamed spinach and some chips. For a starter I got Ricky's spicy chilli. This was sensational. Why they don't do chilli con carne more in England I will never know. A great, great dish. My mint julep was full of vodka. "Would you like a mint julep with vodka," I asked the lady next to me. She said, "It's meant to be Bourbon," adding, for no reason I could work out, "It quacks like a duck." It was Bourbon, but why should I know? The main course came like lightning. I've never seen so much on a plate. Five large crab cakes, salad and chips. Enough for six people. The waiter asked, "Would you like to take any of it away?" Los Angeles is full of people leaving restaurants with doggy bags. Must have more fat dogs than anywhere else. I'd ordered home-made pumpkin pie à la mode, which was a mistake because I forgot that I hate pumpkin pie. Silly me. So I just had the ice cream.

On the whole, Los Angeles restaurants were appalling. Worst was **Cecconi's**, so good here in London. We were placed under an electric heater. "I'll be well done in half an hour," I protested. "Nobody ordered well done, dear, turn the heat off, it's like being under the grill." We waited forever for our order to be taken. Chris Kim was acting restaurant

manager. Dreadful service. I'd requested ice on the table and lemon slices. The ice melted in seconds even when I'd asked them to keep an eye on it. No lemon slices came at all. I had a black truffle and pregiat pizza. OK, nothing more. Dessert was the most terrible apple crumble and almond gelato. It was underdone apples with great tough lumps of heavy pastry. Geraldine's salmon was very dry. Horrid place. **The Grill on the Alley** on Dayton Way, Beverly Hills was gloomy; high booths, dark wood, like a gentlemen's club gone wrong. Only men seemed to be there in the evening. My fillet steak was large but totally tasteless. **Bouchon** in North Canon Drive was more or less empty but for me and writers Dick Clement and Ian La Frenais. Food: moderate. I said to the man at the desk on leaving, "It's not very busy, is it?" He replied, "This is the week people do their tax returns. They're all with their accountants." Oddest reason I ever heard for no customers. Dreadful beyond belief was **e.baldi** on Canon Drive in Beverly Hills. Full of major executives and stars. Food horrific. Dreary meatballs, the driest sole ever. A famous agent seated next to me kept pointing out far better Italian restaurants including one on the opposite corner. Academy Award winning songwriter Leslie Bricusse, who I was at Cambridge with, took us to **il Piccolino** back on North Robertson Boulevard. Pretty good. Every table had a B list celebrity at it. Leslie also took us to **Shutters on the Beach** a charming hotel in Santa Monica. Lovely old-style place looking out onto beach and sea. Wonderful menu. Marvellous breads: nut bread, pistachio, cranberry and wheat, one with red currants. Crab cake starter was brilliant. Then steak, frites, arugula and Parmesan, fried marinated tomatoes. This was a very good lunch indeed. That made a change.

CONTROLLING THE ROOM

I had a horrible evening at **Dinner**, Heston Blumenthal's restaurant in the **Mandarin Oriental** hotel, Knightsbridge, which harbours his chef, the grandly named Ashley Palmer-Watts. We were given a table by the window which didn't mean much as it was dark outside and Hyde Park wasn't lit. They brought the best virgin Mohito ever. Then total collapse. Opposite was a table of seven men in shirtsleeves and jeans; sweating, yelling, laughing loudly. The din was horrific. Impossible to enjoy food with that row going on. Our first course was mandarin jelly round foie gras. Described on the menu as "Meat Fruit" – mandarin, chicken liver parfait and grilled bread circa 1500. Superb. But soured by the increasing din from the baying twits opposite. Protected from this noise by glass, Palmer-Watts and his merry men worked away in the kitchen. I said to the charming restaurant manager, Josephine Stead, "This noise is impossible." She offered us a "better" table in the main dining area. Beyond belief catastrophic. We now faced two tables, some eight men at each, obviously part of the same group, making enough noise to drown out a pub full of drunken rowdies. I said to Geraldine, "The noise here is a problem." She responded, "The noise is what?" She was inches away and couldn't hear me. One of the stupid group started imitating a chicken, waving his elbows up and down and making loud clucking sounds. His fellow dimwits bayed with laughter. When I complained, Josephine Stead said it was a corporate booking. "You shouldn't accept corporate bookings," I said. "You think I should throw them out?" asked Josephine. "I can't if you're here." "If you did you'd be my hero," I assured her. But Josephine just wandered around looking elegant, as if everything was in order. It wasn't. Restaurant management is not just grinning and greeting. You have to control the room. Leadership is essential. It's no good being a seven furlong horse in an eight furlong race. Why didn't Josephine, if necessary accompanied by her male managers, say to these louts, "If you can't keep the noise down we won't be able to serve you." To let a raucous group dominate the restaurant and spoil the ambience for other diners, is unacceptable. Geraldine said, "I bet if this restaurant wasn't in a hotel it would be full of very smart people." It's not a charabanc stop. There's a long waiting list. They don't need to take block bookings. The general manager of the Mandarin Oriental, Anthony McHale, can't evade responsibility for what happens in his restaurants. I congratulate him on getting two first class places, Dinner and Bar Boulud, into what had been a culinary desert. But getting them in and running them properly are different things entirely. Forgetting (which I can't) the horror of the evening, I can commend the food. It is absolutely superb. Ashley-Smashley is one of the best chefs in the country. Rice and flesh circa 1390 was followed by spiced pigeon circa 1870 and artichokes, Geraldine got roast pork chop, Robert sauce circa 1860 based on Carême's residency in London. The descriptions were twee, the chips best ever. I finished with Tipsy Cake circa 1859 with a roast pineapple on the side. The roast pineapple unnecessary, the cake brilliant. This should have been a great evening. It was a nightmare. I've been going to sophisticated restaurants for decades. This experience was, as my friend the actor Bruce Dern would say, "Bottom five world."

KNAIDLACH AND KREPLACH

Chasen's has gone. They did great chilli con carne. Elizabeth Taylor had it flown to Rome when she was making Cleopatra. It was at Chasen's where Ross Hunter, who produced many Doris Day movies, managed the extraordinary feat of smiling warmly at Jay and Kit Kanter (he an important Hollywood agent) and freezing me out even though I sat between them. This because I'd turned down a Steve McQueen movie he'd offered me. Dominick's as it used to be, has also gone. That had no sign it was a restaurant. Dominic, if he liked you, let you in. They were two key places when I first spent time in Los Angeles in the 1960s and 1970s. One restaurant

that has lasted is **Nate 'n Al** which remains in the heart
of Beverly Hills on North Beverly Drive. Established in
1945 by Al Mendelson, it's the archetypal Jewish deli, now
run by his grandsons Mark and David, who were absent on
the Saturday I went for lunch. I phoned and convinced the
manager I was unbelievably important, otherwise you can't
book and have to queue. It looked much as it did when I went
regularly with Peter Falk. Then, every star in the firmament
was there. Now Larry King can be seen having breakfast on
most days. Otherwise it's tourists, tourists, tourists. The
sales counter still on the left, booths all over. Our table
was chipped, the place looked run-down. What used to be
Jewish staff were now Eastern Europeans, not Jewish. I had
a Dr Brown soda. Forgot how much I liked those. Our waitress, Raisa from Russia, served me the most ghastly chicken
soup with lockshen (vermicelli), matzo balls (aka knaidlach,
a Jewish dumpling) and kreplach (squares or triangles of
pasta dough filled with meat). "The soup looks very watery,"
said Geraldine. She was right. The matzo ball, which should
have been fairly firm and brown, was a gargantuan, albino
matzo ball – white, flaccid, tasteless. The kreplach a whop-
ping ravioli of poor quality. None of it as good as it used
to be at Nate 'n Al in the old days, or at the Stage Deli in
New York or the Little Carnegie, Woody Allen's hangout
before he switched continents. Not, by a long way, as good
as Reuben's in London's Baker Street. I couldn't finish the
soup. Raisa refused to take it away even though I asked her.
"How can you not finish soup?" she chastised and went to
get my pastrami sandwich on rye bread. That was almost
perfect. Raisa told me she was from Belarus. "When did you
come over?" I asked. She refused to reveal this. "Are you in
the secret service?" I asked. "Yes, I'm in the secret service,"
confirmed Raisa. "What do I have to pay to get you to take
the soup away?" I asked. Raisa said, "Five dollars. Leave five
dollars on the table and I'll take the soup." "I'm asking you
again," I said, "this time for another five dollars, when did

you come from Belarus?" "1989," said Raisa. My dessert, apple strudel, was spectacularly good. After scoffing it I said, "Come on Raisa, let's go into the street and take your photo." "I'm so ugly in a photo," protested Raisa. "You're beautiful and ten dollars richer than when I came in," I responded. Raisa went a bit bonkers when Geraldine stood in the busy street to take our picture. Nate'n Al is not what it used to be, but still has quality. That sums me up too.

When I abandoned the **Bombay Brasserie** – hated the redecoration, the new manager, the food declined – readers directed me to **Indian Zing** in King Street Hammersmith. Brilliant. I recommended the chef, Manoj Vasaika, to Shakira Caine to cater a Sunday lunch, which he did marvellously. Manoj has now opened **Indian Zilla** in Barnes. From outside it looks more elegant than the Hammersmith one. I'll be there soon.

RUSTY NAIL PARFAIT

The Inner Hebrides island of Mull lies off the West coast of the Scottish highlands. The sea front of Tobermory, the main town, has little houses painted in various bright colours. Pretty it may be, but what a surly lot serve in the shops. We went to Mull Pottery; no one else there. The lady behind the counter didn't say "Hello," didn't greet us or offer to help. If she was the main attraction Mull wouldn't get a single visitor. We progressed to the Isle of Mull Soap Co. Again, the girl behind the counter said nothing. In the Tobermory Pharmacy a man behind the counter never uttered a word. Geraldine said thank you (for what?) and goodbye. The man stayed silent. "There must be a surly school nearby," I observed. "These people graduated with honours."

Everyone else on Mull was very pleasant. We were met by David Currie who, with his wife Josephine, owns and runs the **Highland Cottage** hotel, where everything bears the mark of absolute care and good taste. In an unattended bar there were no bills, "We trust them to pay," said David, adding that he lost a pint of beer occasionally. Lovely bedroom with a four-poster bed, charming cottage-like decoration. I got very overexcited because the TV didn't work. It wasn't plugged into the wall socket or the wire plugged in to the TV itself. David fixed it. I lived. Mum cooked dinner, daughter Catriona helped out. The menu advised: Jo's cooking is honest and down to earth. We got a green apple sorbet. I ordered cauliflower velouté, scallop bruins. "What does that mean, David?" I asked. He replied, "It's a poncy way of saying 'bits of'." Then he changed it to "small bits of". He can go on about this a long time if we let him, I thought. For main course I chose twice-baked goat's cheese soufflé, toasted pine nuts and basil dressing. It was fine. The menu offered Parfait Rusty Nail. David said it was, "Drambuie and whisky, a semi-frozen parfait, the other stuff gives it flavour." A major triumph. Very good raspberries around it. For breakfast there was just-squeezed orange juice, exceptionally good home-made bread, marmalade and a bowl of lemon curd. The scrambled eggs and smoked salmon, nice.

David took us on a tour of Mull. Mostly unspoiled, but a few ghastly new houses going up here and there. Rugged, great beaches, moss on old walls. We lunched at the **Bellachroy Inn** in Dervaig: The oldest inn on Mull, established 1608. Owner Nick Hanson used to work at the Michelin-starred Vineyard at Stock Cross Berkshire. I had lentil soup and langoustines which had just come in from the sea, presumably to do some shopping, and died of boredom dealing with the storekeepers. Geraldine had liver from a farm 500 yards way. All extremely pleasant. I liked Mull. If I had a spaceship that got me there in five minutes I'd go regularly. As I don't, I'll probably never see Mull again.

Far be it for me to criticise **The Wolesley**. It's my favourite restaurant; I go there more than anywhere else. So I'm familiar with the dishes. The other Sunday, after chatting with Albert Finney, I ordered choucroute. Theirs consists of a frankfurter, slices of three other sausages, sauerkraut and boiled potatoes. When it arrived I noticed one sausage was missing. I ate up quietly, then pointed this out to restaurant manager Daniel (not related to James Bond) Craig. He went to the kitchen and explained, "The chef said one sausage didn't come in today." "Then why not tell the customer he isn't getting the normal choucroute?" I asked. Later I phoned their superb restaurant chief, Robert Holland, to ask for a whole cheesecake for a dinner party I was giving. "I've got some good news and some bad news," I announced. "I know the bad news," said Robert. "The choucroute; I've already created hell in the kitchen." Quite right too Robert, The Wolseley shouldn't deplete dishes without telling diners who order them. Especially me.

A ROOM WITH A VIEW
Never trust a restaurant with a view. It thinks that's enough. The top floor of the **Royal Garden Hotel**, Kensington, overlooks Hyde Park and Kensington Palace – where Princesses Diana and Margaret used to live (not together unless there's more scandal to come out) – and the distant spire of the Hilton hotel on Park Lane. If you want the "legendary Beijing duck" at its **Min Jiang** restaurant you have to order in advance. What's that about? Go to Chinatown, or any Chinese restaurant, say "duck" and you get it. No need to forewarn anybody. My guest on this minuscule adventure was Nicholas Capstick-Dale. A "nice young man", as mothers might say. When Nick was married to Lord Rayne's daughter he frequented the Sandy Lane hotel. I was selling a portfolio of property. A "mixed bag", they called it in the trade. Meaning some

great, some rubbish. I'd been offered £18m, a lot of money in 1988. Now, not worth getting out of bed for. Nick and I were walking on the beach. He was 25 and working his way up (or down) as a property dealer. "I'll get you more than that," he said. "Good," I responded. He got me £21m. The deal boosted Nick into the big time. Today he's doing a lot of the King's Cross development and much more. We turned up at a fairly empty restaurant. He looked smart; I looked strange. I ordered prawn crackers. The restaurant didn't do prawn crackers. "Too posh," I observed.

Then we got dumplings. "We're two people and the waiter's brought sets of three dumplings," I said. "What are we supposed to do – cut one dumpling in half?" They were not great. Up came prawn rolls with asparagus, baked barbecued pork in puff pastry, sweet radish; spicy ... the usual clobber. The Beijing duck may have been legendary, but it was small. After being exhibited, it was removed, and we got a minute amount of crisp skin served in a tiny bowl. "I just had that in Bangkok," said Nick. "This is as good." Normally the duck is cut up into reasonable pieces. You put them in a pancake, adding a plum or hoisin sauce and some spring onion and other raw veggies. Not at Min-Minnie. It had depleted and extremely tough, stringy pancakes in little bowls. It added some non-succulent, dry duck. Totally awful. Ridiculous – the worst duck of any kind I've ever experienced. "The duck should look like it was going to fall off the bone – this one didn't," commented Nick. Then the staff brought some rice, assuring us the rest of the duck was mixed in. Could have fooled me. The bill showed £36.18 for half a duck, including VAT and service. Worst money ever spent. We got sweet and sour chicken when I'd ask for sweet and sour pork – not very good. The excellent desserts didn't save the day: cinnamon cheesecake, snowflake jasmine tiramisu, chocolate-coated lychee with ginger parfait. Man cannot live on dessert alone. Overall: pathetic. What's the point of phoning in advance to book a disaster?

\# On 8 and 17 November at 7.30 p.m. in the beautifully restored Wilton's Music Hall, Graces Alley, London E1, I perform my one-man show, presented by *Times+*. The show started in 1967 at the National Film Theatre and has grown and immatured with movie star and other stories, plus audience participation. I've played at the American Film Institute in Washington and Los Angeles, and earlier this year at the American Cinematheque in Los Angeles. I've performed it at Oxford, Cambridge and many other universities, at the King's Head theatre in Islington, London, and other venues up and down the land. In *The Guardian*, John Patterson said, "Michael Winner shows us how a real raconteur grabs his audience. He had us in the palm of his hand." In the *Sunday Express*, Sandro Monetti wrote, "Being in Winner's company is a great pleasure. He has few rivals as a storyteller." Tickets are £7.50 for *Times+* members, £10 for non-members. Why tell you so early? Because booking opens today. Phone 0871 620 4027. The theatre seats only 280 people. Burt Lancaster came to see it; so did Michael Crawford, Oliver Reed, Francis Ford Coppola, Ava Gardner, Hymie Pockle and Joseph Schlemiel. Get with the group.

A GREAT CABARET

Ad agency owner Adam Kenwright, his marvellous New Zealand girlfriend Hymie (aka Sarah), Geraldine et moi travelled far from the hotel Chateau Bagnols so I could revisit **Auberge du Cep**, a restaurant in Fleurie. Chantal Chagny, the owner, has owned it and cooked there for forty-two years. When I first went, her daughter Helene ran front of house. "She stupidly married a chef," explained Chantal. "Never marry a chef because they're all of bad temperament." Pleasant room, flowered curtains, tapestries, plants everywhere but we waited fifteen minutes and no one even offered us a drink. Geraldine was translating the menu item by item. Adam said, "It's like the *Antiques*

Roadshow." He got up, exasperated, to try and order a drink, going through praying motions with Chantal. When he came back, I said, "Did you achieve anything, Adam?" He said, "She's coming. She's very happy." In fact she nearly threw him out. Chantal, passing by, said, "I have one table before you for the order, they have been here half an hour." I asked, "You got any wine?" but Chantal had gone. Geraldine had brought her own gluten-free biscuits. "Are they in your pocket?" I asked. Geraldine said, "Yes." "Then share the biscuits out," I requested. "At least we'll get something to eat." Geraldine declined and continued her translating. "Thank God it's a big menu," I remarked. "It'll fill in the time. We should have brought sandwiches; at least we could have eaten something while we're waiting." Chantal said, "Ice and lemon is ordered and I come back to you." Then she sailed off. After thirty-five minutes ice and lemon appeared on the table, plus some Vittel. I'd ordered Evian. The waiter went to get it. Chantal said, "I'm here, you've got the water," then she went away. When she returned I said, "Darling, I thought we'd never see you again." Chantal said, "In this village life is like that." Chantal suggested, "Try the frogs' legs, a pigeon, a little one." "How little?" I asked. "As it should be," said Chantal. Adam ordered spring vegetables with crayfish followed by spring lamb. Geraldine switched to the lamb. Then we got some freebies. "Fantastic," I said reaching out for toasted, home-made sausage sandwiches. They were historic. We got a carafe of the local Beaujolais. I asked Chantal, "Where's your husband?" "I don't have a husband," she replied. "Was your daughter a virgin birth?" I asked. "No, I was married to a Welshman fifty years ago, I didn't survive," said Chantal, then she left. I said, "We'll go and see the church because Adam's meal will take an hour. In fact we could go to two or three churches." "And a Mass," added Sarah/Hymie. I noticed we were the only table without a bread basket. Eventually I got roasted frogs' legs with parsley, garlic and spring salad. "You see that white-haired lady in the corner," I observed, "she came here when she was sixteen." Chantal, who's immensely amusing and a real Tartar, gave us a dessert menu. Adam chose a flambé dish which Chantal recommended. She said, "No one else must have that dish," and walked off. The rest of us hadn't even ordered. Chantal went to the table next to us, then across the room to another table while we waited to finish our dessert order. When she returned I said, "I thought you'd left me forever." "Be careful," warned Chantal. I had oeuf à la neige; enormous portion, very good. Le Cep has one Michelin star. On the internet a customer is quoted: "Un service lamentable." True, but great cabaret.

\# It drives me nuts when people say one thing, do another. I don't go to restaurants. I go to tables. I asked Richard Irmiger, assistant manager of **Bibendum** in Fulham for my usual corner table. He assured me I'd have it. Then, shock-horror. I was shown somewhere else. Irmiger said Michael Hamlyn always had that table. Michael, an old friend, is co-owner of Bibendum. "Did you tell him you'd promised the table to me?" I asked. "Yes," replied Irmiger. "And he refused to go elsewhere?" I said. "Yes," replied Irminger. When Michael Hamlyn appeared he said: "I'd no idea you were coming. Of course you can have this table." Karim Miftah, the restaurant manager, was off that day. He's good. Mr Irmiger, er, say no more.

\# At the first night of *Shrek*, a jolly new musical, was Judi Dench. On another theatre visit, I'd bought Judi a Spam sandwich. This time Judi came at the end of the intermission with a plastic cup of champagne for me. Went well with my ice cream. She's a delight as actress and person. As long as you don't expect *Hamlet*, see *Shrek*. Great dancing, first-rate performances, colourful, funny.

PEERLESS

The House of Lords is peopled by those who failed upwards. Typified by Michael Grade whose oily charm far outweighs his talent. I know I should love my neighbour. I do. He's Jimmy Page, Led Zeppelin superstar. Michael Grade is not my neighbour. The host for our Upper House lunch was Lord Evans of Temple Guiting, a witty and intelligent man who was boss of the publishers Faber and Faber, for five years a junior Labour Minister, now chairman of EFG which I thought made fairy cakes but he assured me was the second largest Swiss private bank. He lassoed a marvellously talkative Welshman, Lord Brookman of Ebbw Vale, to take our photo. The **Peers' Dining Room** in the House of Lords is gloomy, as are the corridors and all the rooms I spotted. Victoriana at its dullest. The table d'hote menu was £21 for three courses. For parties of six and over (we were three) they add a discretionary ten per cent service charge. Lord Evans – Matthew – went to a Quaker school in Saffron Walden. They played cricket with my Quaker School, St Christopher in Letchworth. "We looked forward to that," said Matthew, "because your boys were so useless. Once we bowled St Christopher out for six runs." Having spent eleven years there I'm surprised we got as many as six. The restaurant manager, the efficient Biagio Lammoglia, used to work at the Dorchester, Inn on the Park and Aspinall's Casino. "What's the difference between those places and this?" I asked. "This is the House of Lords, you can't get higher than that," replied Biagio. "This man lives in cloud cuckoo land," I thought. My set menu starter of oven-roasted fresh peaches with Somerset brie, mixed leaves and sun-blushed tomatoes was revolting. One shrivelled bit of peach, cold but burnt at the edges was the lowlight of a stupid dish. The main course, chicken pie, was mush served in a soup bowl. The crust sitting on top was rather good. The interior tasted like it had come from a works' canteen tureen. After two dreadful bits of gristle I stopped eating. Dessert was apple and strawberry crumble with cinnamon custard.

The waiter said, "Very good. Excellent." As he put it down he pronounced, "Look at that," as if he was presenting a culinary masterpiece. It looked a mess to me. It was terrible. Poor pastry, indifferent apples and strawberries; just mush. If their lordships had any brains when they entered the house, a few weeks of this food and every fibre of body and soul would be severely diminished. For dessert, Matthew ordered from the à la carte menu: crunchy toffee ice cream. The waiter said, "I'm going to check that one because I was told earlier they might not have it." "It's on the menu, now he's got to check if they've got it," I said. The waiter returned to say it was very popular but it's all gone. "So it's not available," he explained, adding, "the rhubarb fool ice cream is fantastic." Matthew said, "It's on the menu." I said, "So was the other one, doesn't mean they've got it." It was that sort of lunch. Beyond belief.

I've had curried goat three times: Once on the beach at Frenchman's Cove, Jamaica, then at The Metropole, Monte Carlo. Third time it was ghastly, cooked by Dean Lewis, a Jamaican contestant on my *Dining Stars* TV show. To impress me he'd not done it his usual way. It was dry and tough. Undaunted by non success on my show, Dean gave up his job as a house basher-down and opened a restaurant in Manchester. He was an awkward cuss, but I wish him luck. Recently at **Locanda Locatelli**, one of the best restaurants in London, I had roast kid goat. Utterly exceptional. Goats should be everywhere. It was cooked by the sous chef as Giorgio Locatelli was filming a BBC2 TV programme in Sicily from whence he phoned to check I had my usual table. There is no nicer person on the culinary scene. I hope TV stardom doesn't turn him into the Italian Gordon Ramsay. Although, I'm enjoying Gordon's salacious, personal soap opera.

At **The Wolseley**. Mitchell Everard, the restaurant director, excitedly said to me, "We've got two Daniel Craigs here."

One was their restaurant manager, the other the more famous DC who plays Bond. I was making a teenage musical, *Play It Cool*, at Pinewood studios in early 1962 when Sean Connery was filming the first Bond movie. Columbia pictures turned it down. Everyone thought it would be a disaster. Proof that "everyone" can be wrong.

WEARING MY PYJAMA BOTTOMS

Years ago I was greatly impressed by **Inverlochy Castle**, a hotel outside Fort William. Fate recently led me to return. I'd been told it was sold to a Malaysian and gone downhill. In fact it was a Malaysian businessman living in Glasgow and it was still lavish, beautiful and well run. Jane Watson, the general manager, was a waitress when I came before. The chef is now Philip Carnegie who has a Michelin star. Not always a good sign. A castle was first built there in 1270; the current pile was finished in 1866 which makes it Victorian. Luminaries who stayed include Queen Victoria, US President Jefferson Davis and, surprisingly not mentioned in the literature, Hymie Pockle, Abe Schwarz and Moishe Pippick. There are only seventeen rooms. For dinner they offered three menus: gluten-free, vegetarian and normal. You have to wear a tie and jacket. I know of only two places in London that require such formality. Jane explained that when they relaxed the dress code people came wearing sneakers and no socks. I wasn't wearing socks but she didn't notice. I was also wearing my pyjama bottoms. I did sport a tie, long-sleeved shirt and proper jacket. Geraldine said, "You look gorgeous. I'd so like you to dress like this." "When?" I asked. "Every day," said Geraldine. "You seduced me because you were so well dressed." "Just shows how things can go wrong in a relationship," I observed. Geraldine, as always, looked totally beautiful, elegant, good-natured, charming, witty and gluten-free. I suppose I'd better deal with the food. Other than a lady at the next table who ignored her friend/husband/plumber and attended relentlessly to her mobile phone, nothing much was going on. Although I could hear the piano from the grand hall where a white-evening-dressed pianist was playing the Vangelis theme from *Chariots of Fire*. We ordered my new favourite drink, a virgin Mohito. It seemed we'd get it until Jane came to announce they had no mint. Posh restaurant like that should have mint. My Loch Linnhe prawns with pearl barley risotto and ham hock beignet were superb; then I had sweetbreads "with something" I dictated (please don't ask what) and truffle. Also terrific. The dessert of mango panna cotta with orange and passion fruit was a let-down – too solid, seemed to have far too much gelatin in it. Good meal though, pleasant staff.

PS: On the coffee tray brought up to the bedroom was a sign: *To have your tray uplifted please dial 204.* I suppose if I'd done that, to see the tray was properly uplifted, a crane would have arrived accompanied by a JCB digger, six burly Scotsmen and a passing seagull.

I put two pieces of jade into a Sotheby's auction recently. They were in my TV lounge at home. I never looked at them. To my surprise one was estimated to sell for £50,000–£70,000 the other £70,000–£90,000. The first one went for £360,000, the second for £70,000. So I received well over £400,000 from Sotheby's. The pieces had been left in London by my father when he went to live in France, taking with him about fifty immensely superior jade carvings. Many were so important they were illustrated in the *Encyclopedia Britannica* under "Jade". My mother sold them, even though they were only left to her for life and then to me, to pay her gambling debts at the Cannes Casino, along with highly valuable paintings, furniture and, finally, the penthouse she lived in. All left to me. I used to say at today's prices she nicked £50m. In view of the jade prices I now raise this, conservatively, to £100m. Doesn't

matter. Mumsy was a gambling addict and a marvellously mercurial person. God bless her. But boy, could I use the dosh.

I'm an avid tweeter. My tweets are hilarious. My followers grow in number each day. Many have phoned 08716204027 to book for my *Times+* one-man shows on November 8 and 17 at 7.30 p.m. at Wilton's Music Hall, east London. The second show was scheduled after the first one sold out in two weeks. A lovely lady tweet-follower, Julie, brought me an original US poster for my movie *The Jokers*, then posters for *Death Wish* and *Death Wish II*. Another tweeter, claiming to be a memorabilia seller, offered me £15,000 for the two *Death Wish* posters if I signed them. They're not for sale. Nor can I get Julie to accept anything: money, goods, whatever. She's a rare.

BEST-BUYS IN VENICE

In Venice someone's always suing. Arrigo Cipriani, whose **Harry's Bar** is my favourite place, was sued by Orient Express who own the **Cipriani** hotel because he used the name Cipriani for his London restaurant. I was a witness for Arrigo. I made the judge laugh three times. Arrigo lost; it cost around £10m including damages. Before that Arrigo wrote a book insulting James Sherwood, the Orient Express founder and the manager of the Cipriani hotel, Dr Rusconi. He made up with Rusconi but is suing the hotel for using the name Cips for one of its restaurants. He also sued his sister who was running the fantastic **Locanda Cipriani** on Torcello. It's a miracle I got out without being handed a writ. Food in Venice is difficult. My best-buys are a small restaurant, **Alle Testiere**, the Locanda Cipriani, Harry's Bar and a long boat ride away, **Ristorante Da Nani** in San Pietro in Volta where locals go. I now add **Ristorante Antica Dogana** in an 1893 Customs House in Treporti. You sit facing a wide, peaceful expanse of water and a stunning sunset. It's owned by Giuseppe Trevisan. His chef, Andrea Simato, is the best. It started badly with awful bread. Then everything went stratospheric. Very good anchovies on toast, excellent scallops with shrimp and a marvellous sauce, six cooked mussels with cuttlefish. It's like peasant food out of mama's kitchen. Geraldine said, "Some of the best I've ever eaten." I finished with millefeuille a crème de lemone. The whole thing was sensational. I reminded the co-owner of Alle Testiere, Luca di Vito, how important I was. By comparison the Pope was a street cleaner, the Chief Rabbi a toilet roll salesman, the Queen of England ... mustn't say anything about her. Like her. I have a signed photo she sent me in one of my nine toilets. The result: I couldn't get one of Luca's thirty seats.

He recommended **Il Ridotto Castello** in Campa San Filippo e Giacomo owned by Gianni Bonacorsi. I asked Gianni what we should have. He said, "A lot." The bread was good and warm. My light asparagus pureé with almond and langoustine had an incredible taste. Gianni said, "I mix, it's the idea that's important." Ravioli with water of tomato and green basil was perfect. I sat waiting for the fish. Geraldine asked, "What is it you want?" I said, "A waiter." Geraldine replied, "You need a clip round the ear. I was going to have semifreddo with chocolate and basil ice mousse but Gianni said I should try the apple tart with vanilla ice cream and balsamic vinegar. A mistake. It was an apple cake and not very good. Everything else was amazing. We also tried the strange **Bauer Palladio Hotel** a few doors from the Cipriani. We sat in a very bleak courtyard facing a dreary garden. The food was good but it was a gloomy place. The Cipriani hotel has always been one of my favourites. It has three restaurants. One by the swimming pool on the lagoon, another facing St Mark's Square called Cips and the rather grand Fortuny, which no longer requires jacket and tie. The new Fortuny restaurant manager, Fabrizio Zarattini, replaced an absolute dud who had replaced another dud. All the food is good. To sit by the lagoon at the pool restaurant is sensational. I was bemused by a reader's letter which said I was shouting at waiters. I remember no ruck with any Cipriani waiter. They were all pleasant and excellent. I've known most of them for years. I checked with Geraldine who said, "No, you were as usual rather quiet." I did raise my voice on the mobile phone because the reception was bad. I was surrounded by guests on mobile phones. I could hear all their conversations. The Cipriani is a splendid hotel with an enormous garden around an Olympic size pool and an amazing suite personally owned by James Sherwood, which I always get. The hotel is run by Maurizio Saccani, skilled boss of the Orient Express Italian hotels, and his young manager who had improved since my previous visit. On arrival we found in our suite a tray of canapés. Five chocolates, five biscuits, five strawberry and raspberry tarts. Four days later the strawberries and raspberries were going rotten. I mentioned this to the manager, Giampaolo Ottazi. Then they were changed. Not major. One swallow doesn't ruin a summer, or some ridiculous remark like that.

A TRIP WORTH TAKING

If it's as difficult to get out of HM Prison High Down as it is to get in, then it must be the most secure place on the planet. All I wanted was to nip over for lunch. I was invited by the ex-convict, ex-cabinet minister Jonathan Aitken and his lovely wife Elizabeth. She was my neighbour when married to the actor Richard Harris. You might expect my old friend Jonathan would ask me to The Ivy or Scotts, but he's a prison groupie. He explained that **The Clink**, a special restaurant in High Down jail, is run by the inmates. What a palaver. The Home Office said, "You can't bring a camera." I said, "BBC TV did a programme on The Clink. They used cameras. Why should mine be banned?" After more poncing around than I care to recount, me, Geraldine, the camera, my Rolls Phantom and chauffeur appeared at the prison, situated, if you want to make a booking, in Sutton, Surrey. Jonathan pointed to a sign at the prison entrance which read "Heightened state of alert." "That's because they know I'm coming," I suggested. We waited forever. Jonathan explained, "The important factor of prison life is to be trained in queuing." I don't do queuing. I was further disappointed not to be sitting with prison inmates. They were just cooking and serving, under the supervision of the professional prison chef, Alberto Crisci. An elegant prisoner restaurant manager, Kane Sterling (in for drug offences), showed us to a corner table where we could gaze on other punters: Japanese tourists and various hoi polloi. A representative of HM Prison Service asked me, "Is there anything you need?" "A cloth napkin please," I said, declining the paper one. Elizabeth explained, "It's all made by the prisoners; tables, chairs everything." It was very posh. Abdul Vutt was one of our waiters. Efficient. Cheerful. He was in for fraud. I asked, "Did you get much out of it?" He replied, "No, it was intentional." Didn't get that, but so what. Our main waiter was Wayne Anthony White from Barbados. Jonathan had told me, "In prison you learn not to ask anything because you always get an untruthful answer." I said to Wayne, "Why are you in here?" He said, "Because I did something regrettable." I asked, "Did you murder six people?" He said, "No, illegal substances." Let this be very clear: all the staff was fantastic. Polite, on the ball, far better than the dodgy lot you get in most West End restaurants. Before I left I said to a group of them, "When you come out if you want a reference get in touch with me. You were all terrific." I started with deep fried Stilton quenelles followed by saddle of rabbit en croute. I also asked for a cocktail of passion fruit juice, papaya, blackcurrant, pineapple, mango and a dash of essence. "Wayne," I said, "I don't want to wait for those seven people you've just taken orders from. You must get your priorities right. My order comes first." All the food was beautifully presented, well cooked; absolutely excellent. It was a superbly run restaurant. Abdul explained they were a bit short of waiters that day because on Friday a lot of prisoners go to the Mosque. They'd run out of vanilla and coconut ice cream so I had strawberry and raspberry. I wanted to photograph Abdul and Wayne but was told I couldn't because they hadn't been cleared. So we did Alberto the chef and Jason James, a prisoner from Saint Martin, who made the starters. He'd already been cleared for the BBC. This is a marvellous restaurant. The prisoners beat normal waiting staff by a million miles. A trip worth taking. I won't return in case next time they don't let me out.

We were early for the prison. So we stopped in Station Road, Belton (part of Sutton) and nipped in to the **Arty Café** for a coffee. They bought in their cakes. Next door was **F.M. & L.J. Stenning**, family bakers. They baked almost everything themselves. I took a sausage roll and a pink icing-topped fairy cake back to the Arty Café to accompany my excellent deluxe cappuccino and a packet of lightly salted "nothing artificial" Kettle crisps. The fairy cake was sensational; the sausage roll historic. A girl, eating breakfast in the café, looked at my Rolls-Royce Phantom and asked, "Did someone die?" "No, I'm just about alive," I advised her. The café owner, Diane Wilkinson, told me the girl was a special needs person who came in regularly. So I paid Diane for her breakfast and also for the next day. Members of the public came and took photos with me, I signed a few autographs. Very pleasant. If you're in Belton, visit those places. It's life like it used to be.

SERVED IN A COFFIN

Billy Connolly once said, "The great thing about Glasgow is that if there's a nuclear attack it would look exactly the same afterwards." My new best friend, 33-year-old self-made multi-millionaire Shazad Baksh, who was brought up in a Glasgow council hostel, drove me round the city he was proud of. A few lovely old houses, the central George Square good, but they've put some stupid additions on top of one of the old buildings. Glasgow is a great place for the Glaswegians. I like them. Not crazy about the town. Shazad had arranged for a friend, who owned four of Glasgow's Indian restaurants, to open the best one, **Balbir's**, for Geraldine and me to eat Saturday lunch. It's in a faceless, ghastly street, with interior decor to match. Mostly black with some tacky chandeliers. Balbir Singh Sumal, the owner, greeted us pleasantly. Nice man. No idea of how to decorate restaurants. Food started well with a Bombay dish called bhel – puffed rice, roasted pulses, tamarind, apple and mint. Cold. Good. They took the poppadoms away. "Bring them back," I said. "I can't believe this place, they've got no customers but us to give them to and they remove the bloody poppadoms." Geraldine said they were the best she ever tasted because they weren't heavy. "Shall I bring the next course?" asked Balbir. "Yes, I've got to keep moving, just throw them in," I requested. Balbir responded, "People usually say we rush them." "Nobody could rush me in a restaurant," I replied, "the speedier everything is, the better." Along came scallops with an exquisite butter and masala sauce. "Local?" I asked. "Very local," said Balbir, adding, "for you now, the most successful dish talked about in Oban." It was a piece of salmon roasted in the tandoor, with three blobs of colour. "The red one's my wife's carrot and tomato chutney, the green is apple and mint chutney." I never learned what the third one was. Altogether OK, not great. I won't be talking about it in Holland Park. Balbir announced he once took cod liver oil and it came back to him all day from his stomach. "Just what I want to hear when I'm eating lunch," I said. "If you've got any other medical problems keep them to yourself." I asked him to turn the piped music off. Some local mussels arrived in a very spicy sauce, the whole thing rather like a soup. Pretty good. I'd asked for chicken biriani but got lamb biriani. So-so. As often happens, restauranteurs try and give me everything including the kitchen sink. So up came some buttered chicken tikka chasney, central Indian style. Balbir told me this was the most popular dish in the west of Scotland. I thought it was sickly-sweet. The west of Scotland is indeed beautiful, but foodies can forget it. The bread arrived late. Balbir said, "It goes very well with the biriani." But we didn't get it with the biriani. There was nice yoghurt with mint which had a cooling effect. Balbir offered, "We can make a chicken biriani but it'll take a few hours." "I'm getting on a private jet, can't wait," I explained. Dessert was gulab jamun, like a little rum baba. That was excellent. The "best Italian ice cream" with it was the worst vanilla ice I've ever eaten in my life. A patchy meal. Would have tasted better if it wasn't served in a coffin.

PS: Two days after I left Glasgow, Shazad was on Loch Lomond in a friend's speedboat. His friend drove recklessly into the wash of a bigger boat. Shazad reckoned the boat rose 30ft in the air. When it crashed down he was seriously injured. Dislocated back. So bad, Shazad will never be more than 90 per cent mobile again. I'd sue. He's too nice.

I recently had the non-pleasure of returning to hospital. First was a major emergency (won't tell you what) when I ended up on the National Health Service at the Chelsea and Westminster. I was saved. In for four nights. As usual, if the illness doesn't kill you, hospital food will. So the saintly Geraldine went out into Fulham Road and got from **Tray Gourmet** really good baguettes with tomato and basil, croissants aux amandes and yoghurt. Coffee from **Starbucks**. One a morning a croissant. Strangely Starbucks did raspberry, strawberry, apple and blackcurrant jam, but not marmalade. Also, superb soups from **Carluccio's.** A week later they had to give me another full anaesthetic

operation to check what had been done. That was one day in the London Clinic. Food from the greatest deli ever, nearby **Ruebens** of Baker Street. Amazing fried fish, chicken soup with trimmings. Funny way to review restaurants, really.

A FAMILY AFFAIR

Our photo shows Geraldine holding the best menu in the world. Its cover painted by Paul Roux who created the famous hotel **La Colombe d'Or** in St Paul de Vence in 1920. The impressionist artists came to his rustic farmhouse on the Côte d'Azur, couldn't pay for their meals, so left artwork now worth millions. Encouraged by Matisse, Paul started his beautiful flower compositions in 1946. Not only is the cover of the menu a work of art, the text is bold, beautifully inscribed and clear. The food is exemplary. Not over-fussed French pretentious. Just good. The chef, Hervé Roy, has been there for twenty years. His loup de mer is the best ever; the sixteen bowls of hors d'oeuvres are world famous. I even like the cassata ice cream. The rooms are not chain hotel. They're individual, a bit distressed, marvellous. This is one of the great hotels of the world. A haven of peace. It's been run by the same family forever. Now by Paul's grandson, Francois and wife Danielle. Someone wheeled a clattering suitcase by. Danielle commented, "I'm going to insist on rubber wheels for all suitcases here. I'm going to make that a special thing." Every major star in the firmament has eaten on the terrace of La Colombe. Many have stayed there. I remember when it looked onto a valley of vineyards. Now there are villas. That one owned by Richard and Judy; over there Bill Wyman's. But the place is still magical. It's on the edge of a well-preserved medieval village which sits on top of a hill. Steep cobbled streets run up and down. When I first went the houses were all homes. Now at street level they have art galleries, clothes shops, trinket places. The little restaurants tucked away in the village look good. My only previous experience of one was ghastly. I murdered it. The owner then wrote to me, not complaining, but thanking me, because he'd been inundated with British visitors asking for exactly for what I'd eaten and hated. So I was not over-optimistic when we dropped in to **Le Tilleul**. A picturesque, small restaurant with exterior tables that spilled onto the other side of the pathway. Inside was blandly modern. Piped music. The single waiter didn't rush to take our dinner order. Luckily only six people were there. "If there were more we'd be waiting 'til one in the morning," I observed. Geraldine ordered sashimi. The waiter said, "I'll bring your sashimi, he [that's me] can wait for his risotto." "No, no," advised Geraldine, "give him his risotto, he can have his dessert while I have my main course." Clever girl. The risotto, not much good anyway, had lots of glumpy vegetables on top which had to be cut up. As they were tough this was difficult. "That's because you hold your knife like a pen," said Geraldine. She got an enormous entrecôte steak. It was pretty good. My millefeuille tasted as if it came from a supermarket although they assured me it was made on the premises. Either way, it was gooey and stringy. Inedible. A brave, but senseless foray. Written on the menu of **La Petite Maison**, in Nice, is: "Tous les celebres ici," meaning everyone's a celebrity here. Regular customers Elton John, Michael Caine et al. have more celebrity than most. All celebrities are not equal. Then it says, "Mind your bag." Thieves are obviously not celebrities. The place specialises in truffles with everything, when in season. It's been superbly and eccentrically run for twenty years by a marvellous character, Nicol Rubi. Forget the second-rate London spin-off. This is the real thing. Don't miss it.

\# The death of Lucian Freud, who I first met in 1960, saddened me greatly. When I worked in Wardour Street we'd sit next to each other at the bar of Wheeler's restaurant in Old Compton Street. Me, Lucian and Francis

Bacon. In the decades that followed I often saw Lucian at The Wolseley, where he dined almost every night and for lunch as well. Only a few weeks ago I asked, "Lucian do you ever exercise?" He replied, "No but I bathe. Often three times in one day." A marvellous, witty, outgoing, warm person. The Wolseley covered his regular table with a black cloth and wouldn't serve anyone there out of respect to a great man.

PIKE AND LEEK PIE

Leicester Street runs behind the Empire cinema, Leicester Square. It's an impossible place to park. This worries me not because Westminster Council doesn't tow cars away. I just leave mine and embrace a £60 ticket. Outside the **St John Hotel**, owned by Fergus Henderson and his partner Trevor Gulliver, the general manager, Matthew Rivett, was waiting for me. He's the ex-banqueting manager at The Ritz. St John recently opened. Matthew explained, "I've been here a year building the hotel." "Very good with bricks and mortar are you, Matthew?" I suggested. Matthew said, "I've lost a lot of weight." Could have fooled me. This is a small boutique hotel. I asked, "Who on earth comes here?" "Americans," said Matthew. "Fergus has a very big following there." In England Fergus has two restaurants somewhere in or beyond the city. Areas I do not choose to be familiar with. At one of them the food was excellent but it had the rudest restaurant manager I've ever come across. The chef at the hotel is Tom Harris who came from St John in Smithfield. The menu is intelligent. Not too large. There are eight starters, six main courses, a few side orders, nine desserts. The cooking goes on at one end of a minimalist room. Luckily there weren't many people for lunch. If there been, the noise could have been deafening. A child screamed a few tables away. I said to Amanda, the restaurant manager, "If there's any nonsense with that screaming child throw it out. Preferably take it to the third floor and throw it from there." The baby kept screaming. Geraldine said, "He's talking." I said, "No he's not, he's screaming." I was the only person in the room wearing a jacket, which is rare. Everyone else was in shirtsleeves. Thankfully, the baby was taken out. Matthew said, "Have a bowl of peas in the pod at the table and pick on those." They were tender and tasty. The brown and white sourdough bread was clammy. Geraldine assured me that was its normal texture. Still tasted ridiculous. My first course, cured sea trout, cucumber and dill tasted like gravadlax, but was excellent. Geraldine had crab, fennel and chervil; she was happy. For the main course I ordered pike and leek pie, only offered for two people. It was historic. I left nothing. The pastry was perfect, the filling very delicate. It was as good a course as you could wish for. Geraldine went nutty ordering a main course for two people, an enormous bowl of bacon and beans. She ate it all. I was somewhat full. So what? I was on a run. The waiter recommended custard tart. The pastry chef, Therese Gustafsson, agreed. So I had that and a poached peach with toasted brioche. The tart was warm, light and as memorable a custard tart as you could wish for. The warm brioche outstanding, the poached pear with lovely syrup, excellent. You won't get better food than this anywhere in London. Later I took Michael and Shakira Caine and John Gold, ex-owner of Tramp. I can't remember what they ate but they loved it. When we'd all ordered, I said, "You've got to try the pike and leek pie." That went down like a lump of lead. Nevertheless, the pike and leek pie was put on the table and by the time we'd finished there wasn't a morsel left. Fergus Henderson is supreme beyond belief. He's not one of those stupid chefs who yatters away on television or sells beef cubes, or ponces around the posh magazines. There is no better restaurant in London than his one at the St John Hotel. Arrive by parachute because you certainly won't be able to park.

\# Parking is no problem at the **Sofitel** hotel near the corner of Pall Mall. But shock-horror. They serve teabags. Their Earl Grey was tasteless. Then where to put that soggy thing on the end of a string? I made my views known to Denis Dupart, grandly titled Area General Manager, Sofitel, UK, Ireland and the Netherlands. Scones and sandwiches were good. At least they spared me wrapped butter. Nothing more depressing than when teabags and butter-wraps litter the table.

\# **Le Caprice** closes tomorrow for redecoration and general tarting up. Reopens (in theory) on 1 September. They've already got an awning outside and tables for smokers. It's one of my favourite places. I remember when it was all red plush benches and chairs. After first nights we all wore evening dress. Noël Coward one side, Ivor Novello on the other, the Oliviers in poll position. Jews were stuck in an adjunct at the back on the right. I got better seating because I went with a famous theatrical agent. In its current life it's a Jeremy King–Chris Corbin creation, Richard Caring has kept up the standard totally.

GLOOMY "VICTORIAN JOIE DE VIVRE"

St Pancras Railway Station has been restored to its original Victorian splendour. Housed within is the **St Pancras Renaissance London** hotel. The brochure describes it as "a celebration of Victorian joie de vivre and sophistication". You can vote yes or no on that. It offers the **Gilbert Scott** restaurant, named after the architect who originally designed it all. My visit started dismally. I phoned, gave my name, and asked for Chantelle Nicholson, the restaurant manager. A receptionist said, "What is it regarding?" then said, "she's not available." I rang again and got an unobtainable tone. The third time, I was left holding on forever. The fourth time the receptionist said, "She'll be with you in a moment." I waited for three minutes, before giving up. Fifth time I got Chantelle and made a reservation. By then I needed rest and a Valium. Chantelle led me past the old booking office, now in the enormous Victorian lobby beset with tacky bar furniture, past a grand staircase to the restaurant. There I was greeted by Dominique Corolleur, the floor manager. He used to be restaurant manager for **Gordon Ramsay at Claridge's**. When I awarded Dominique Worst Restaurant Manager in the World he bravely came and collected it at the Winner's Dinners Award ceremony. In a lesser position he's very charming, not snooty as he was at Claridge's. I rejected a small table, pointing to another one. The restaurant is a far-flung outpost of Marcus Wareing, the two-Michelin-star chef with his own place in the **Berkeley hotel**, Belgravia. He explained this new concept was based on Jeremy King and Chris Corbin, his restaurant idols. Gilbert Scott has a way to go to reach their standard. The white bread with fennel seed and sage was fantastic. The toast Melba a disaster: too heavy, too thick. The crab was buried beneath an enormous salad. By the time I'd dug far enough to get to Australia and back I was too confused to decide whether it was any good. The room was impressive, with marble pillars, gilt cornices and large prints of highly decorative paintings by Nina Pohl. For my main course I ordered a pie called Suffolk Stew. The pastry was soggy, the interior adequate, the meatballs glumpy and solid. The only good part of my main course was colcannon, a mixture of potato, leek and beans. For dessert I chose Beeton's snow eggs, Everton toffee, peanuts, burnt honey and custard. That was sickly. I also went for a Bakewell tart with almonds, jam and Jersey cream. I consider myself a world expert on Bakewell tart. Chantelle worried me, saying, "It's our take on a Bakewell tart." It was overweight, the icing far too sinewy. At best a distant cousin of the real thing. Chantelle, seeing I'd left a lot, said, "Shall I take this to the Bakewell graveyard?" "I have a feeling it came from there," I responded. I turned my attention to a Kendal mint choc ice. This was fantastic.

At the next table, the nice looking Sheppard family was celebrating the twenty-fourth birthday of daughter Emma. Rather than just photographing me and gloomy restaurant staff, I made a major artistic decision: include the family. There wasn't enough room for dad so I asked him to step aside. Marcus looked nervous. You can see mother Penny, birthday girl Emma and sister Libby all far more attractive than the people behind, namely Marcus Wareing, me and Chantelle. The service and Chantelle were exemplary. The meal wasn't. Pity, because I like Marcus. Back on the street I had £10 ready for the doorman who stood there doing nothing. Heaven forbid he should have taken twelve paces to open the car door for Geraldine. So he didn't get his £10. That'll teach him.

HISTORIC STEAKS

Film director John Landis and his wife were taking Geraldine and me to dinner. We drove down Rodeo Drive in Los Angeles. I asked where we were going. John said, "The Grill on the Alley". I showed disappointment. Been there, got the T-shirt. John asked, "You don't like it?" "Well ... er," I started. "We're near Wolfgang Puck but we'll never get in," John said. "Try," I suggested. So John rang **Wolfgang Puck's Side Bar Cut** restaurant in the Beverly Wilshire hotel. "There's an hour's wait," reported John. I shouted out, "Tell them I'm the most famous food critic in the world." We decided to take a chance. In the bar of Wolfgang Puck's, Uzma, a snooty lady at reception (who'd probably answered the phone) said, "There's still a 45-minute wait, I'll take your drink order." She then returned to her desk. I elevated myself to my full height of 7ft 3in and said, "Excuse me, I am the most read food critic in the world. I am here because the American Cinematheque is giving me a three-day tribute for my movies but my hotel and restaurant column in the London *Sunday Times* is extremely important. I don't do waiting. Is Mr Puck here?" Uzma answered, "Yes." I said, "Then I suggest you tell him I'm here." She said, "The room is full." "There's always a way," I advised. I must have said it with authority because Uzma left her stand, disappeared into the restaurant and three minutes later came back to announce "Mr Winner, please follow me." We were taken to the best table in the room. Wolfgang Puck, who's extremely famous in America, joined us. He mixes fine restaurants, such as the Cut, with a supermarket range. I spotted one of his cheaper outlets at Los Angeles airport. Wolfgang advised his favourite steak was from Snake River Farm, Idaho, "Where Evil Knievel jumped over the river," he explained. I asked how many people he had working in the Cut. Wolfgang replied, "I don't count. It's too expensive to think about them." I said, "Do you count the bills?" Apparently he doesn't count money either. That why he's so cheerful. It's quite a noisy room. They had rock music playing which made it worse. Wolfgang turned the music down. He decided we should have a selection of steaks: the Snake River Farm, a New York steak, a Nebraska dry, aged for thirty-five days, and pure Wagoo beef from New Zealand. Vegetables came with, plus a phenomenal sauce béarnaise and Wolfgang's own steak sauce. From the large dessert selection I chose a banana cream pie, which was beyond belief great. Wolfgang's mother was a cook in Austria. He went from there to France and on to America. He's upbeat and cheerful. The meal was one of the finest I've ever eaten. All the steaks were historic. Wolfgang is coming our way. On 1 September he opens his first European restaurant at **45 Park Lane**, a new boutique hotel owned by the Dorchester Collection. If he does as well in London he'll be top of everyone's list. I'll make an early reservation on the assumption, having won the battle once, I won't be asked to wait forty-five minutes. Happy ending: when John Landis asked for the bill, nothing happened. I knew why. Wolfgang intended to give me a free meal. That, I never accept. The waiter returned and said, "Dinner is on Mr Puck." We'd had wine, champagne, the best steaks; it must have been very costly in a place famous for being expensive. John Landis was delighted. "I must go out with you more often, Michael," he said, beaming.

EARL OF SANDWICH

Being extremely conservative, I greatly admire the buccaneering spirit. Those people who go forth and take risks which I always avoid. Robert Earl doesn't look like a buccaneer. Errol Flynn he ain't. He's short, podgy and wears garish sports shirts. Having left university penniless, with no rich parents to help, Robert became an assistant banqueting manager at a Jewish reception place off Hanover Square, owned by Joe Lewis who went on to wealth beyond the dreams of man. Robert worked his way up to launch themed restaurants, the most famous being Planet Hollywood. Its fortunes rose and fell like a yo-yo. On one occasion staff were locked out of the Coventry Street premises because the rent hadn't been paid. A gambling club, Fifty, in St James's vanished in a mire of disaster. But Robert, and this makes him very special, persevered. He always managed to segue from drama to further success. Planet Hollywood, now in Lower Regent Street, thrives. I genuinely thought the food was great. In Las Vegas there's an enormous Planet Hollywood casino-hotel. Robert was boss of the Hard Rock Café. He now has, among other enterprises, Buca di Beppo, an Italian chain restaurant with eighty-eight outlets in the US, four in England and more to come. He's also a successful Hollywood film producer. With considerable flair, Robert signed up the Earl of Sandwich (yes, there really is one) to use his name on a chain of sandwich places. There's an enormous Earl of Sandwich in Disneyland Paris. Robert intends to have twenty in the US by year's end; another twenty in the UK. The first one in the UK is in Ludgate Hill, with St Paul's looming grandly nearby.

The Earl of Sandwich is exceptionally well designed. Dickensian in a restrained way. I've never seen so many people trying to get a sandwich. Robert, who speaks with gargantuan energy, started haranguing me, "If you heat a sandwich you're charged VAT, but if it's cold you're not." He'd like the British tax structure changed. If anyone can see it happens, Robert will. His handsome son, Robbie, was on hand. He's learning the business before going to Boston University to study hospitality. Two Robert Earls might be more than the world could take. When I met son Robbie years ago in Las Vegas he was a brat. He's now charming and clever. I stayed a brat. Why break the mould? The first thing thrust upon me was tomato soup. Very good indeed. The sandwiches come elegantly wrapped in a gold brick. Hot and labelled. I started with tomato and mozzarella. The bread was fantastic. The beef sandwich was good too. Then, and you can't say no to Robert, I got the All American – turkey, cranberry, lettuce and tomato. Followed by a tuna melt – tuna and Swiss cheese. The bread is made from their secret recipe in America, baked locally and finished off the in the restaurant. My only disappointment was Robert's favourite, the chocolate brownie. I found it sickly. The strawberry and white chocolate cookie was OK. "We opened on 18 April," said Robert, "You were meant to come." "I wasn't asked," I responded. "Don't forget to say the sandwiches are £4.45 or £4.75, including VAT," instructed Robert. Then he turned his attention to the next table, telling them: "We can serve your whole office." Never mind some stranger's office. What I want is the next Earl of Sandwich very close to my house. I can suggest a few rubbish restaurants near me that desperately need replacing.

THE ODD COUPLE

Groucho Marx once said, "I don't want to belong to any club that would accept people like me." Occasionally I'm asked to join prestigious clubs. Why should I pay money each year only to pay more when I go there, which I'm unlikely to do anyway? The best club in London is still **Annabel's** in Berkeley Square. It was bought, to a chorus of horror from the establishment, by Richard Caring, the man chosen by founder and boss Mark Birley to carry it on in the way he'd run the place. I don't go to Annabel's because (a) I'm not a member and (b) I don't do nightclubs. Recently I arranged to meet Richard Caring there for dinner at 8 p.m. I got there at 7.50 p.m. The place was locked. A burly door-man announced in a gruff voice to someone below, "I have some people here." I said, "You have Michael Winner who, as I told you, has come to dinner with Richard Caring. You should go back to doorman school." Inside, everyone was charming. The place looks as it always did. The walls covered with good oil paintings, the atmosphere refined, even though diners can now enter without ties. Richard took me upstairs, past oil paintings of dogs (Mark Birley loved dogs) to a new area. Annabel's Garden is where people can smoke. It's a greenhouse-like room, beautifully decorated, mirrors facing me. One was covered with cloth. "Why is that covered up?" asked Richard. "Maybe your staff forgot to take the cloth off," I suggested helpfully. Richard responded, "It's a bit obvious isn't it?" There will soon be steps down to an outside terrace. In the dining room I started with foie gras, as good as you could hope for. Then goujon of sole with rice. The restaurant manager, Marco Piras, asked, "Basmati or carnaroli rice?" Did he have a wrong number? I don't know one vegetable from another, one meat from another, one dessert from another. Why should I know about rice? "I'll leave it to you," I said.

Richard still owns an enormous clothing business. He's been in restaurants and hotels for five years. Many people in the "hospitality industry" sneered at an amateur enter-ing their sanctum. Richard showed he is the professional. Many of his detractors struggle or have gone broke. I don't know how many places Richard has. By the time you read this he'll probably have added another sixty-eight. There's the Soho House hotel group, The Ivy, Le Caprice, Sheekey's. In Mayfair, Harry's Bar, George, Annabel's and Mark's Club together with popular chains such as Côte. Why did he go into restaurants? Richard said, "I had good people managing my clothing empire, so I decided to play golf. That lasted three days." Then someone suggested he buy Wentworth Golf Club. "I overpaid," Richard admitted. He asked the Ivy Group to do the catering at Wentworth. "They were going to charge so much," Richard said, "I decided it was cheaper to buy the Group." He later bought Mark Birley's clubs for £100m. There's still a huge waiting list wanting to join the 4,000 members of Annabel's. Mark Birley hoped his legacy would remain. "I think I've done that," said Richard. He introduced live entertainment. They had Lady Gaga a few months ago. Nobody told me. I'd have gone. Richard said, "I don't understand kitchens. I employ people who understand kitchens. I understand front of house, image, consistency and quality."

My goujons of sole were very light with marvellous batter. Excellent. For dessert I tasted a banana sticky pudding, as good as you could hope for. Their special chocolate ice cream was staggering. If you didn't have to pay a fortune to join for the pleasure of turning up to eat, and there was an Annabel's near my house, I'd be there regularly. By 9.15 p.m. punters were pouring in. Few men wore ties. They looked perfectly respectable to me, which isn't saying much. Richard was, as ever, immaculate. If we set up house together we'd be the odd couple. Richard the precise one, me the slob. When I left at 9.45 p.m. people were still coming in. "It goes on until 4 a.m.," advised Richard. I can't remember when I was last up at 4 a.m. Nor do I wish to.

PART III
WINNER'S DINNERS AWARDS
2011–2012

WINNER'S DINNERS AWARDS
2011–2012

LIFETIME ACHIEVEMENT AWARD: Sir Terence Conran

BEST UK RESTAURANT: Fergus Henderson's St John Hotel, London

BEST HOTEL IN THE WORLD: The Palace Hotel, Gstaad

BEST HOTEL CHEF IN THE WORLD: Peter Wyss of the Palace Hotel, Gstaad

BEST CLUB IN LONDON: Annabel's in Berkeley Square

BEST RESTAURANT MANAGER IN THE WORLD: Simon Girling of The Ritz Hotel, Piccadilly, London

BEST DOORMEN IN THE WORLD: Those at The Ritz Hotel, Piccadilly, London

BEST HOTEL BOSS IN THE WORLD: Maurizio Saccani, Vice-President of Orient Express Hotels, Italy

BEST FISH RESTAURANT IN THE WORLD: Tétou in Golfe-Juan

MOST FUN RESTAURANT IN LONDON: The Wolseley

MOST COMFORTABLE RESTAURANT WITH THE BEST
ACOUSTICS IN LONDON: Bibendum

BEST DELICATESSEN IN THE WORLD: Reubens of Baker
Street, London

WINNER'S DINNERS AWARDS

The Winner's Dinners Awards are a bit of a giggle. Important beyond belief, but fun. They are not handed out with great pomposity after a dreadful mass dinner for hundreds of people in some hideous hotel ballroom. They're not preceded or followed by speeches from the head of the brewery company that's sponsoring the event or the head of some other ghastly organisation that is muscling in as much as it can. They are not awards chosen by a committee of people who think they know what they're talking about. They are purely and simply awards that I feel like giving out as a semi (all right illiterate) food expert.

They take place at a champagne reception at The Belvedere in Holland Park. This does not exactly tire anybody because of the length of time it takes place. Last year we handed out fourteen awards in twelve minutes, which must be a world record. What was certainly a world record is that we didn't actually have the awards to hand out because I left them at home! So the presenters simply congratulated people and later we chased the winners up and gave them their award!

These awards attract presenters who are the most talented people in the country as well as very famous and often legendary chefs, hotel managers, hotel owners, restaurant owners, and the like. Last year the awards were handed out by Sir Michael Caine, Lord Andrew Lloyd Webber and Barbara Windsor. If that isn't worth the price of admission (and admission was free) then I don't know what is. Among those who won the awards were Richard Caring for the Best

UK Restaurant, Scott's; the brilliant chef Pierre Koffman for the Best UK Chef; Christopher Corbin and Jeremy King got the Lifetime Achievement Award; Arrigo Cipriani came from Venice to receive the Best Service Award for Harry's Bar. I could go on.

This year's awards will attract a similarly excellent group of people to give out the awards as well as those who receive them. There are also many major celebrity guests in the audience. This year's awards are listed above. And here's a brief note on the people who got them and why they got them. Or if this books comes out before the award ceremony, those who will get them!

Lifetime Achievement Award

It is because Terence Conran (then not knighted) was such a pain in the arse that I started writing about food some fifteen years ago. I'd written a complaint about atrocious service and food in Le Pont de la Tour and received a scathingly sarcastic letter back from Conran. As a result, I wrote about it in a general article in the *Sunday Times* relating my misfortunes in restaurants. This later became a column at the request of the then editor, Andrew Neil. For six years Terry Conran and I insulted each other in the press. I, to him, was public enemy number one. He, to me, was restaurant enemy number one. This fairly dopey state of affairs ended some nine years ago when I was sitting by the pool of the Cipriani hotel, Venice and saw Conran with a couple of friends and his lovely wife Vicki not far away. I thought to myself, "A public argument is one thing but private is another" and I went over to say hello. A look of total fear crossed Terence Conran's face as I approached. I could see that he was thinking, "Oh my God, Winner's going to cause a scene. It's going to be too ghastly." In fact, we shook hands, spoke very politely and he was suddenly my new best friend. So much so that a couple of hours later his wife rang me in my suite and said, "Terry cannot get into the ground floor level of Harry's Bar (the only place to be) could you help?" So I called my friend Arrigo Cipriani and the Conrans got their chosen seating area at Harry's Bar.

There is no question that Sir Terence Conran is one of the great influences, not only on design and furniture and objects, but on restaurants and food in the United Kingdom and, indeed, also abroad. He is a timeless innovator of the very best kind. He's has created so many restaurants it would require another book to list them all. He still has a 51 per cent share of (among others) the Almeida, the Bluebird Café, Kensington Place, Butlers Wharf Chop House, Quaglino's, and many more. Outside London his interests include the Alcazar Paris, the Botanica Tokyo, Guastavino's New York, and others I haven't heard of. He's part owner of one of my favourite restaurants, Bibendum. He introduced and maintains a simple style of French cooking that does not bemuse, bewilder or confuse. His interior design of London's Michelin building, which houses Bibendum, is a textbook lesson in how to take old buildings and make them still look marvellous. He also owns Lutyens, a private club within the former Reuters building in Fleet Street. Since no club, quite rightly, wishes to have me as a member, I guess that's somewhere I won't be going!

I'm absolutely delighted that Sir Terence Conran should be coming on the evening of our Awards to receive a Lifetime Achievement Award. He is a man whose lifetime achievements are totally remarkable. On top of that he will eventually be moving his Design Museum into a rather strange building close to where I live, the Commonwealth Institute. That will be a far better use for it than what it housed before.

The award for the **Best UK Restaurant** goes to Fergus Henderson. Although he has a number of restaurants, the one I've recently eaten in is his St John Hotel just off Leicester Square. It's an unimposing room, not unpleasant, in a small boutique hotel. The food is absolutely outstanding. There is a review of it in this book so I will not wax on about it again. It is just the sort of food I like. Simple, direct, tastes of something and made with great precision. Fergus Henderson personifies what a chef should be. He doesn't spout a load of nonsense on television. I do not see him advertising beef cubes or anything else. He just gets on with the job of running restaurants and training up people who, while they may not be quite as good as him (although I don't know that), produce absolutely staggering meals.

The award for the **Best Hotel in the World** goes to the Palace Hotel, Gstaad, and its owner Andrea Scherz. This is a bit of a laugh, really, because at one point I had the most blazing row with Andrea Scherz and his father who owned the hotel. But then I have rows with nearly everybody. If they lasted I would have to become a hermit. The younger Andrea Scherz took over as manager a few years ago and has grown into the job superbly. The Palace is a grand hotel in the best sense of the word but at the same time it has a clear local ambience. It stands among towering mountains. One of the great pleasures is to sit in midwinter on the terrace with deep snow a few feet away and the sun sparkling on the snow covered fir trees. The main lounge, with its log fires and views over these great mountains would be a perfect setting for an Agatha Christie novel. I always expect to come downstairs in the morning and see one of the guests dead in a leather chair. Eventually they would discover who did it. Probably me. The food is absolutely superb. Their chef, who gets **Best Hotel Chef in the World**, is Peter Wyss, a totally charming man, utterly unpretentious, who produces (often in very large numbers) the most marvellous food. New Year's Eve is always a disaster. If I have to see idiots blowing whistles and getting drunk and putting on funny hats again I'll throw myself from the basement window.

Last year I spent New Year's Eve at the Palace Hotel. It was brilliantly done without too much fuss; excellent food. I believe it was a buffet but for reasons, which revealed immense common sense, every course was served to me. I've never seen so much caviar devoured. The whole atmosphere was delightful. The lounge of the Palace Hotel is full of young people; the whole place is remarkably alive. From Roman Polanski sitting in one corner to multizillionaires in another.

The award for **Best Club in London** goes to Annabel's, owned by Richard Caring. Richard Caring is a controversial figure. When he came from the rag trade into hotels and restaurants many of the so-called professionals sneered. Later, a great many of them went broke. Richard carried on keeping a remarkable standard and expanding his empire by the minute. By the time I finish writing this article he'll probably have opened eleven more hotels and another thirty-seven restaurants. Good luck to him. There are always those who sneer and say the class of people at Annabel's and Mark's Club and Harry's Bar has gone down. It hasn't gone down. It's just enlarged itself to be a more representative selection of the people of this country. I don't think I've ever seen anybody enter an industry from another industry and make such a success of it as Richard Caring. Annabel's, once owned by the marvellous Mark Birley, retains its standard and has been given added life.

The Ritz hotel is the last really grand hotel in London. All the others have been messed about, redecorated but not improved, and generally gone down the plug hole. Two or three remain good. The Ritz remains supreme. Its restaurant and banqueting manager, Simon Girling, rightly receives the award for the **Best Restaurant Manager in the World**. He is a professional to his fingertips. Charming, on the ball and utterly in charge of this extraordinary place. To enter The Ritz is to enter another world. A world that has now largely gone. The décor is as it used to be. The dining room has not been carved up and made to look like an airport lounge, the tea room is absolutely majestic and the staff, all of them, extremely friendly and pleasant.

In this respect, the doormen of The Ritz hotel stand supreme. Most doormen in London are a load of lazy louts. Heaven forbid they should walk six paces and open the car door for you. Heaven forbid they should greet you with a smile. The fact that general managers at extremely good hotels keep these idiots in situ is pathetic. The Ritz doormen, on the other hand, are on the ball, welcoming and they massively deserve to be named **Best Doormen in the World**. Each one is a character in his own right. There is Michael O'Dowdall, the tall Irishman who always tells jokes, some of which are very good indeed. The others are respectful and highly professional.

The award for **Best Hotel Boss in the World** goes to Maurizio Saccani who is the vice president of Orient Express Hotels Italy. That means he's in charge of the Cipriani in Venice, the Splendido in Portofino, the Villa San Michele in Florence, and at least three other hotels, all of considerable quality. When I first met Maurizio he was measuring the distance between sun loungers at the Splendido in Portofino. To say he is a great details man is to put it mildly! He said to me, "I can't help tinkering with everything." That is good. The hotels are beautifully decorated, they are well run and they have the stamp of someone who cares who's in control. Like nearly every hotel in the world, what used to be more spacious has become less spacious and the tables are a bit closer together to get more people in. That is inevitable. Maurizio drives or flies between hotels in Sicily, Ravello and all his other little kingdoms. We had a blazing row (who haven't I had a blazing row with?) when Maurizio sent me the most appalling letter saying that details that I had mentioned in my review of his hotel Caruso in Ravello were highly inaccurate. In fact, they were all totally accurate. For a while I blasted him in the *Sunday Times*. But these things happen among friends and family. We have long since made up. My appreciation of his work and the care he takes of these remarkable hotels is abundant. He well deserves the award of Best Hotel Boss in the World.

The **Best Fish Restaurant in the World** is Tétou in the Côte d'Azur port of Golfe-Juan, just to the east of Cannes. It's a glamorous hut right on the beach. It's been owned by the same family forever and Pierre Jacques Marquise, who will accept the award, is in the very best sense of the word a typical Frenchman. The bouillabaisse soup is unbeatable in the history of the world. Everyone says it's expensive, and indeed it is. I'm not sure if they still only take cash but they certainly used to. I never had enough cash to pay the bill. I'd brought what I thought was a generous amount yet there was always a shortfall. So rather than go to a local cash machine I simply gave them what I owed them the next time I went in. I've been going to Tétou for sixty years at least. It's the best.

If there is such a word as legendary it applies to Jeremy King and Chris Corbin who founded the current life of The Ivy, Le Caprice and Sheekey's. Then they sold out and went on to open The Wolseley which gets the award for the **Most Fun Restaurant in London**. The atmosphere is electric. There are invariably well-known people there with whom one can have a brief chat. Lucian Freud was probably the most regular customer. I've never been there without some interesting and talented star of one profession or another illuminating the room. It is superbly run with very smooth service and a consistently high standard of food. It is not plate decoration rampant food. It is pleasant food that is a delight to eat. Corbin and King are about to open, or may have opened by the time this book comes out, yet another restaurant – this time in the Aldwych. They are also planning a hotel in Mayfair. They are absolute gents, which is extremely rare in the so-called hospitality industry. They look like gents, they dress like gents, they talk like gents. Most people in the hospitality industry look like spivs, dress like spivs, and talk like spivs. For that alone Corbin and King deserve an award.

Another superb restaurant is Bibendum on Fulham Road. It receives **Most Comfortable and Best Acoustics in London**. It was opened by my friend Lord Hamlyn (although he wasn't a Lord then) together with one of the great restaurateurs of our age, Sir Terence Conran, and the chef Simon Hopkinson. Simon decided kitchen life was not for him and left after a few years. His sous chef, Matthew Harris, took over. The food is excellent. What is most remarkable is both the beauty of the room and above all the comfort. Most restaurants today have a sound problem. Not really a sound problem; a disaster. The noise is so great you can't hear the person next to you. The chairs are uncomfortable, the tables are too close together. At Bibendum the tables are nicely spaced apart, the chairs are immensely comfortable and the acoustics are perfect. You can have a conversation and hear it. You're not talking to the person at the next table because they're so close to you they have no choice but to hear what you say or you to hear what they say. The room was designed by Terence Conran and remains one of the best and most beautiful rooms in London. It is a favourite place of mine.

Among the Jewish community there is a grotesquely bad taste, but I think highly amusing, phrase that is often used: "Delicatessen food killed more Jews than Auschwitz." Delis were common in London in the 1950s and 1960s but have somewhat decreased in the United Kingdom. In New York they were absolute staple food places. And still are. Woody Allen would eat regularly at the Little Carnegie Deli on 7th Avenue; then there was the Stage Deli down the road, and a great many more. They specialised in a whole series of food that was part Eastern European, part German, part Polish, part God knows what! But it was, by and large, delicious. Healthy? Probably not. But man cannot live on health food alone. In London, I guess the most well-known chain of delis is Harry Morgan which has branches in St John's Wood, Harrods and various other places. There's also a very good deli in Selfridges. But for me, far and away the **Best Deli in the World**, even better than the New York ones and Los Angeles ones such as Nate 'n Al, is Reubens on Baker Street. It's not a pleasant looking room. The upstairs could generously be described as tacky. I've never been downstairs but I understand that ain't one of the great décor award winning places of the world either. I wish they'd redo the seating part of it. The food is unbeatable. Its run by Ann and Tam Reubens and their family who are there all the time, work very hard and are immensely charming. I've only actually eaten on the premises once. I do have takeaways from Reubens again and again. They are fantastic. The chicken soup with lockshen and knaidlach is absolutely marvellous. I've never tasted a chicken soup as good. The latkes (fried potato pancakes) are superb; the salt beef of the highest quality... I could go on but I don't even understand everything they've got. Although I know how to eat it. When I was in the London Clinic nearby, very sick, I would get takeaways from them which Geraldine would pick up and bring to my room. Again and again. They say that chicken soup is the Jewish penicillin. Even though I was dosed up with morphine, the taste of the food from Reubens came through loud and clear. Their fried fish is phenomenal. I keep thinking of things that are good there. I could fill almost an entire book if I mentioned them all. It well deserves its award as **Best Deli**.

Although he is not getting an award this year I feel like mentioning Andrew Davis who for many years owned von Essen Hotels. They went into liquidation in 2011 which seemed to produce (the hospitality industry being as bitchy as any you'll find in the world) great glee from a lot of people. This was a year when corporate hospitality was more or less wiped out because companies were afraid to take over posh country houses, castles and hotels for events in a time of financial crisis and where people choosing to have parties or weddings went down cost-wise a notch or two or three. In those circumstances it was difficult to run and make a profit from luxury hotels in the country.

I visited a number of Andrew Davis's hotels. None of them were bad; most of them very good. One thing that came through loud and clear was that I have never found in my life staff at all levels who so liked their boss. Andrew knew all their names, all their histories, all the gossip, all the dirt, all the good stuff, all the bad stuff and dealt with it with immense good cheer. He greeted all his staff by name, went round the hotels regularly in one of his fleet of helicopters (which he still has) and I do not join in this dreadful attitude of many people that if someone goes down that makes the people who are still there better. The number of restaurants that have gone broke, or as near broke as makes no difference, are numerous. That's part of the game. Andrew still has a number of hotels, including the Verta, adjacent to the Battersea helicopter pad which he owns, Llangoed Hall in Wales and the Forbury in Reading; I'm sure he will bloom again. Although owning three hotels, the largest helicopter fleet in Great Britain, the Battersea Heliport and a private jet company does not seem to me to leave him destitute! Above all, Andrew is the most jovial, witty, outrageous, politically incorrect person you could wish to meet. To me those are great qualities. I wish him well for the future. I also hope that the hotels he

ran so well will be taken over by people who keep them up to
his standard.

RESTAURANTS REVIEWED

There's a Soul Here
Avenue 31, Tel: 00 37 797 703 131
Hotel de Paris, Tel: 00 37 798 063 000
Côté Jardin, Tel: 00 37 798 063 939
Grill Room, Tel: 00 37 798 068 888
Le Louis XV, Tel: 00 37 798 068 864
La Réserve de Beaulieu, Tel: 00 33 493 010 001
Cap Estel, Tel: 00 33 493 762 929
Tétou, Tel: 00 33 493 637 116
Hostellerie Jérôme, Tel: 00 33 492 415 151
Les Terraillers, Tel: 00 33 493 650 159

Actively Horrible Shrimps
Time & Space, Tel: 0207 670 2956

Timeless
La Réserve de Beaulieu, Tel: 00 33 493 010 001
Waltham Abbey Marriott, Tel: 01992 717170
Moat House, Staffordshire, Tel: 01785 712217
The Lion Hotel, Shrewsbury, Tel: 01743 353107
Old Vicarage Hotel, Shropshire, Tel: 01746 716497
La Brasserie, Tel: 0207 581 3089

Twice-baked Smoked Haddock Soufflé
Dean Street Townhouse, Tel: 0207 434 1775
The Wolseley, Tel: 0207 499 6996

Happy Birthday Mr Winner
The Ritz, Tel: 0207 493 8181

Naughty Paul
Crowthers Catering, Tel: 07980 970485

Tasteful in Brussels
La Manufacture, Tel: 00 32 2 502 2525
Belga Queen, Tel: 00 32 2 217 2187

Sensational Burgers
Bar Boulud, Tel: 0207 201 3899
Mandarin Oriental Hotel, Tel: 0207 235 2000
The Savoy, Tel: 0207 836 4343

Guernsey Gache
The Lowry Hotel, Tel: 0161 827 4000
La Fregate, Tel: 01481 724624
The Goring Hotel, Tel: 0207 396 9000

"I Just Taste Things, I'm a Taster"
Dino's, Tel: 0207 589 3511
The Wolseley, Tel: 0207 499 6996
Verta Hotel, Tel: 0207 801 3500

That's the Metropole
Metropole Brussels, Tel: 00 32 2 217 2300
Le 19ieme (as above)

Looking Ain't Enough
The Savoy, Tel: 0207 836 4343
River Room Restaurant, Tel: 0207 836 4343

A Signature Dish
Nottingdale, Tel: 0207 221 2223
Sally Clarke Bakery, Tel: 0207 221 9225 / 0207 229 2190

Royal Oak, Tel: 01628 620541

A Hoodie Chicken
Le Tobsil, Tel: 00 212 524 444 052
The Wolseley, Tel: 0207 499 6996
China Tang, Dorchester Hotel, Tel: 0207 629 9988
The Ivy, Tel: 0207 836 4751
Le Caprice, Tel: 0207 629 2239

Simplify!
Thornbury Castle, Tel: 01454 281182
The Ritz, Tel: 0207 493 8181
Palace Hotel, Gstaad, Tel: 00 41 33 748 5000
Olden Hotel, Tel: 00 41 33 748 4950

"Matos, Matow, Matter... Can't See You in the Book"
Wiltons, Tel: 0207 629 9955
Bar Boulud, Tel: 0207 201 3899
The Wolseley, Tel: 0207 499 6996

General Opprobrium
Palace Hotel, Gstaad, Tel: 00 41 33 7 48 5000
Grand Hotel Park, Gstaad, Tel: 00 41 33 7 48 9800

A Rare Moment
Warwick Arms, Tel: 0207 603 3560
Sonnenhof, Gstaad, Tel: 00 41 33 744 1023
Olden Hotel, Tel: 00 41 33 748 4950

Shacked Up with Daniel Craig
L'Absinthe, Tel: 0207 483 4848
The Wolseley, Tel: 0207 499 6996

"Best-ever"
La Gazelle D'Or, Tel: 00 212 5 28 85 2039
The Belvedere, Tel: 0207 602 1238

In the Spirit of the Wok
Hakkasan, Tel: 0207 907 1888
Les Deux Salons, Tel: 0207 420 2050

The Italian Connection
Tinello, Tel: 0207 730 3663
Murano, Tel: 0207 495 1127
San Lorenzo, Tel: 0207 584 1074
Timo, Tel: 0207 603 3888
Scalini, Tel: 0207 225 2301

The World's Rarest Elephant
Canouan Resort, Tel: 001 784 458 8000
Mosimann's, Tel: 0207 235 9625

They All Taste the Same
Racine, Tel: 0207 584 4477
Olive Grove, Tel: 01227 764388
The Ivy, Tel: Tel: 0207 836 4751

Two Old Farts Make Ten
Vasco & Piero's Pavilion, Tel: 0207 437 8774
Scott's, Tel: 0207 495 7309

Chocolate Cake and Chips
Antica Bottega Del Vino, Tel: 00 39 045 800 4535
The Wolseley, Tel: 0207 499 6996

On the Rampage
Ickworth Hotel, Tel: 01284 735350

First-class Hotel Minutiae
Beverly Hills Hotel, Tel: 001 310 276 2251
Setai, Tel: 001 305 520 6000
Polo Lounge, Tel: 001 310 887 2777

"Is a Langoustine the Same as a Prawn?"
Ristorante Semplice, Tel: 0207 495 1509
Trattoria Semplice, Tel: 0207 491 8638

Just a Mousse Bibendum, Tel: 0207 581 5817

Top of the League Waffles
Beverly Hills Hotel Fountain Coffee Bar, Tel: 001 310 276 2251

Roamin' in the Gloamin'
Majestic Line, Tel: 0131 623 5012
Torosay Castle & Gardens, Tel: 01680 812421

Fried Whatever
Aubaine, Tel: 0207 368 0950

It Quacks Like a Duck
The Ivy, Los Angeles, Tel:
Cecconi's, Tel: 001 310 432 2000
The Grill on the Alley, Tel: 001 310 276 0615
Bouchon, Tel: 001 310 271 9910
e.baldi, Tel: 001 310 248 2633
il Piccolino, Tel: 001 310 659 2220
Shutters on the Beach, Tel: 001 310 458 0030

Controlling the Room
Dinner, Tel: 0207 201 3833
Mandarin Oriental Hotel, Tel: 0207 235 2000

Knaidlach and Kreplach
Nate 'n Al, Tel: 001 310 274 0101
Bombay Brasserie, Tel: 0207 370 4040
Indian Zing, Tel: 0208 748 5959 / 0208 748 2332
Indian Zilla, Tel: 0208 878 3989 / 0208 878 2480 / 0208 878 7766

Rusty Nail Parfait
Highland Cottage, Tel: 01688 302030
Bellachroy Inn, Tel: 01688 400314
The Wolseley, Tel: 0207 499 6996

A Room with a View
Min Jiang, Tel: 0207 361 1988
Royal Garden Hotel, Tel: 0207 937 8000

A Great Cabaret
Auberge du Cep, Tel: 00 33 474 04 10 77
Bibendum, Tel: 0207 581 5817

Peerless
Peers' Dining Room (no tel)
Locanda Locatelli, Tel: 0207 935 9088
The Wolseley, Tel: 0207 499 6996

Wearing My Pyjama Bottoms
Inverlochy Castle, Tel: 01397 702177

Best-buys in Venice
Harry's Bar, Tel: 00 390 41 528 5777
Cipriani Hotel, Tel: 00 390 41 520 7744
Locanda Cipriani, Tel: 00 390 41 73 0150
Alle Testiere, Tel: 00 390 41 522 7220
Ristorante Da Nane, Tel: 00 390 41 527 9110
Ristorante Antica Dogana, Tel: 00 390 41 530 2040
Il Ridotto Castello, Tel: 00 390 41 520 8280
Bauer Palladio Hotel, Tel: 00 390 41 520 7022

A Trip Worth Taking
The Clink, Tel: 0207 147 6524
Arty Café, Tel: 0203 581 8062
F. M. & L. J. Stenning, Tel: 0208 669 5543

Served in a Coffin
Balbir's, Tel: 0141 339 7711
Tray Gourmet, Tel: 0207 352 7676
Starbucks, Fulham Road, Tel: 0207 795 1772
Carluccio's, Tel: 0207 376 5960
Reubens, Tel: 0207 486 0035

A Family Affair
La Colombe d'Or, Tel: 00 33 4 93 328 002
Le Tilleul, Tel: 00 33 54 927 0940
La Petite Maison, Tel: 00 33 4 93 92 5959

Pike and Leek Pie
St John Hotel Restaurant, Tel: 0203 301 8069
Sofitel, Tel: 0207 747 2200
Le Caprice, Tel: 0207 629 2239

Gloomy "Victorian Joie de Vivre"
Gilbert Scott, Tel: 0207 278 3888
St Pancras Renaissance London, Tel: 0207 841 3540
Gordon Ramsay at Claridge's, Tel: 0207 499 0099
Marcus Wareing at The Berkeley, Tel: 0207 235 1200

Historic Steaks
Wolfgang Puck's Sidebar & Cut Restaurant, Tel: 001 310 276 8500
45 Park Lane, Tel: 0207 493 4554

Earl of Sandwich
The Earl of Sandwich, Ludgate Hill, Tel: 0207 236 2846

The Odd Couple
Annabel's, Tel: 0207 629 1096

ABOUT THE AUTHOR

Michael Winner is a celebrated film director, author, food critic and gourmet. His 'Winner's Dinners' column appears weekly in the *Sunday Times*, he had his own TV series, *Michael Winner's Dining Stars*, and his books include *The Fat Pig Diet* and *Winner's Dinners*.

He first wrote for the public with an article for the *Kensington Post* group of twenty-seven newspapers in September 1950. He went on to work, whilst still at Cambridge and before, on many national newspapers, including the *Sunday Mirror*, the *Daily Express* and others. He was the film critic for the *New Musical Express, Films and Filming* and other magazines. His first produced fi lm script, *Man With a Gun*, was written in 1958 when Winner was twenty-two years old. He followed with many other scripts for famous films made in England and Hollywood over the years. He has written six books and, he says, '2,483 notes to my housekeeper'.

He has become one of the most well-known characters in Great Britain and thrives on a somewhat controversial persona.